BY DESERT WAYS TO
BAGHDAD AND
DAMASCUS

by

Louisa Jebb

ISBN: 1-59048-135-6

This book was first published in 1908

Publisher's note: We have added a few
explanatory footnotes. The author's
own footnotes are in italics.

www.horsetravelbooks.com

DEDICATION

This 2004 edition of "By Desert Ways to Baghdad and Damascus"
is dedicated to Long Rider

CATHERINE WARIDEL
AND HER HORSE ZORIA

who undertook a courageous solo journey from the Crimea to
Mongolia in the late twentieth century.

"Oft have I said, I say it once more,
  I, a wanderer, do not stray from myself;
I am a kind of parrot; the mirror is holden to me;
What the Eternal says, I, stammering, say again."

CONTENTS

PROLOGUE

It was a hot midsummer's day; X and I sat on the long grass under an apple-tree; she had a map of Asia and I a Murray's Handbook.[1] We were about to travel together in the East. X was going primarily in search of health; but she had studied comparative religions and was prepared to be incidentally intelligent about it – visit mosques and tombs, identify classical spots, and take rubbings of inscriptions.

I was merely going with X. She had unearthed me from a remote agricultural district in the West of England with the idea that contact with the agricultural labourer would have fitted me for dealing with the male attendants who were incident to our proposed form of travel.

We were fully agreed on one fundamental point – that we should choose a country which could be reached otherwise than by sea; and that, having reached it, its nature should be such that we could travel indefinitely in it without reaching the sea.

Now of all the continents Asia Minor is the one best adapted for this purpose; for if you were a giant you could easily step across the bit of inland sea which separates Europe from Asia in the neighbourhood of Constantinople[2]; and once landed on the other side your field of operations is practically unlimited, extending even into the adjoining continent of Africa; for any one who could step across the Bosphorus could also step across the Suez Canal.

But having once settled on the particular continent, our ideas were somewhat vague. How indeed can they be otherwise if you propose travelling in a country which has not yet been ticketed and docketed for the tourist? This produce of a modern age can, thanks to Messrs. Cook and Lunn[3], already tell, in the corner of his own fireside, the exact hour at which he will be gazing at the dome of St. Sophia on any particular day, with the number of courses specified, in the hotel the outside appearance of which is already depicted on the itinerary. But it was not to be so with us. What we should eat and what we should gaze upon was still wrapt in the mystery of the great unknown.

---

[1] A guide book, originally written between 1859 and 1883. It contained details about day to day life in India, such as information about how to get there, advice on food, health, railways etc.
[2] Called Istanbul today.
[3] Famous travel agents of the day.

X took a pencil and marked a straight line from Constantinople across the Anatolian Plateau and the Taurus Mountains to Tarsus. "That looks a good point to make for," she said. "Alexander led an army over the Taurus." Then, having stopped within measurable distance of the sea, she drew her pencil eastwards across the Euphrates to a point on the Tigris high up in the Kurdistan mountains; from here she drew another line following the Tigris to Baghdad. At this point we were coming dangerously near the sea, so turning back she marked a line in the contrary direction across the Syrian desert to Damascus.

"That will do for a start," she said; "we can fill in the details when we get there."

Now this method of undertaking a journey might have its disadvantages in what is known as a civilised country; for here we are all such servers of time that unless we arrange everything beforehand, as everybody else does, we are apt to get pushed aside; you must, therefore, take your place in the general hustle and secure your bed and your dinner and your right to look at sights by ticket long before you are in need of them. In short, you must make a plan.

But in the untravelled parts of the East you reign supreme; there is no need to go about securely chained to a gold watch which metes out with inexorable exactitude the dictates of railway timetables, steamers, diligences and the *table d'hôte*[4] summonses.

Ignore Time, and he is at once your servant; treat him with respect, and he at once becomes your master.

In those countries where Time has become master he develops a system of locomotion to which you must conform or lose its benefits; it will not accommodate itself to you. But in the East, do you but recognise the principle of making Time your own and at once plans become unnecessary. Systems of locomotion, for instance, spring up in answer to a preliminary wish in your brain; and their existence being solely due to you, it is possible to use them when and where you will. You want to get from one point to another; your wish is passed on, and a mule or an araba[5] appears at your door; and whether it be punctual, or whether, as is more usual in the East, it be late, it is of no consequence, for Time is waiting for you and will wait for ever. Once you are started, moreover, the stopping places are not arbitrary; you have merely to wish, and at

---

[4] A communal table for all the guests at a hotel or restaurant.
[5] *A native cart.*

once the mule or the araba stops. In the same way when you wish to sleep your bed is where you make it; and when you wish to eat you need wait for no summons. And should it so happen that you have been misguided enough to make a plan, it is of no consequence should you think fit to change it. One only asks "Why have made the plan?"

Thus it was that, without any more preparation than this preliminary idea of our route, X and I were able to carry it out in detail exactly as we had sketched it in the rough.

The drawbacks of course were there. Sometimes we had nothing to eat through not having arranged for food; and sometimes we slept out in the wet. But does this never happen to those who have made elaborate plans against all possible contingencies? And have they not had the worst of it after all, for they have had the planning with no result, and have suffered the annoyance of having their best laid plans mislaid.

Is it possible, moreover, to judge this method of travel by our standards in the West? In a civilised country where beds abound and it is merely a matter of arrangement to acquire one, there is no delight in passing the night under a damp hedge with drips down your back; there is shelter round the corner, and you merely curse yourself for your own stupidity, or pretend you like it, and take care not to do it again.

But when you lie on your back on a sandy desert with nothing within measurable distance of you, and the rain beats mercilessly down or the wind howls through the crevices of your garments, you are conscious of battling against great primeval forces akin to the unknown elements of your own being; you cannot escape from the, for there is no shelter around the corner; you are brought up face to face with something fundamental; all the little accessories with which we have learnt to shield ourselves fall away, and you are just there, stripped yourself, and in the middle of naked realities. And if only you have been wet enough, or cold enough, or hungry enough, it has been worth while, for you never forget it; and the remembrance of it will come to you ever and anon when you are once more tied up in the bonds of convention and are struggling to keep a true idea of what is a reality and what is not.

So it is, perhaps, that in setting out to write any account of such a journey, one is dominated by the remembrance chiefly of facts which in this country seem trivial. All the little details of life take on an exaggerated form; for what in civilisation we are apt to ignore and take as a matter of course, occurring almost unnoticed in the ordinary routine of daily life, become out there of enormous importance. A good meal, for instance, seems of far greater moment than an attack by brigands, because of its rarer and more unexpected occurrence.

If you are travelling for no particular purpose, with people whose language you do not understand, and in a country where the manners and customs are not familiar to you and you are merely moving on slowly from day to day – all you can get is a passing impression of outside things. If you are not a scientist or an archaeologist or a politician striving to catalogue each new acquisition on your particular subject; if, in fact, you have no particular knowledge of any sort, but your pores are wide open to receive passing impressions, what you get is a vivid idea of the appearance of things. This is all that you can hope to pass on.

In the following pages I do not propose to give a connected account of the various places we visited or of the many adventures which befell us; this is not a travel book. I shall have no intelligent remarks to make on the historic spots we passed, journeying slowly through this country so rich with still undiscovered monuments of ancient times; a country which is also destined to become, as civilisation advances with the Baghdad Railway, the centre of future political interest. What justification is there then for writing a book at all?

The Danes have given us a definition of their idea of education: "It is," they say, "what is left after everything that has been learnt is forgotten." So it is with any form of travel; the value of it to the traveller himself is what is left after lapse of time has effaced all recollection of minor incidents and softened the vividness of strong impressions. In very slow travelling though desert countries, where day after day the same trivial events occur in similar yet different settings, the essential facts of that country sink into you imperceptibly, until at the end they are so woven into the fibres of your nature that, even when removed from their influence, you will never quite lose them.

There are certain notes in the East which form part of a tune sung the world over, but which give a clearer and more definite sound in the land which first gave them birth. The sketches given in the following pages are framed on them; they are what I have left, and what I would fain pass on to the reader.

If I have succeeded in striking these notes true there is no need of an apology to those who have already heard them in the country whence they spring: for any one who has ever travelled in the East welcomes anything that will once more touch that particular chord, at whatever time or place. And if I have succeeded in striking them so that here and there amongst those to whom the East is still but a name, there are some who may hear a faint echo of the real thing, I shall feel that there has been some justification for this contribution to the literature of the desert.

"It avails not, time nor place – distance avails not,
I am with you, you men and women of a generation, or ever so
    many generations hence.
Just as you feel when you look on the river and sky, so I felt;
Just as any of you is one of a living crowd, I was one of a crowd;
Just as you are refresh'd by the gladness of the river and the bright
    flow, I was refresh'd;

   Just as you stand and lean on the rail, yet hurry with the swift
current, I stood yet was hurried." . . .

PART I

BRUSA TO DIARBEKR

CHAPTER 1

DISENTANGLEMENT

It was our first night in camp; little mysterious hillocks shut us into a world of our own; we had it all to ourselves and only the stars overhead knew, and they seemed to be congratulating us on our escape; they twinkled and winked and beckoned. Constantin had lit a fire, and this at once became the centre of our world; the door of our tent looked out on it, the muleteers, the Zaptiehs[6], and our men sat round it, our supper was cooking on it, and we all thought about that; the horses and mules, tethered in a semicircle, turned that way and blinked at it; far away a jackal saw it and barked. It drew us all together, and its smoke went quietly up towards the beckoning stars.

They would be eating their dinner now in the hotel at Brusa just the same as last night; the thin young man who had asked us what we should do if it rained, the old lady who wanted to know if we were doing it for pleasure, and the middle-aged spinster who thought we had no business to expose ourselves to such dangers unless it were for missionary work. The waiters would be bustling about; good Madame Brot would be carving diligently at the side table with an anxious look; bells would be ringing; men and women would be coming and going and talking and laughing and scolding; down below in the hot kitchen the men wash one pile of dirty plates after another…

Yes, it is very quiet out here; the men speak in undertones and the fire crackles in the cool, still air. Constantin lifted the pot off the fire. "Mangez[7]," he said. He was Greek but could speak a word or two of

---

[6] Turkish policemen.
[7] "Eat!"

French. He ladled the onions and rice on to two plates and picked out the
bits of mutton; then after handing us the plates, he began to beat up eggs
for an omelette.

We had been stretched out on the ground; we drew ourselves up, and
sitting cross-legged balanced the plates on our knees. The food tasted
excellent although it had been cooked in one pot. Constantin had wanted
to bring three pots; he had been camp cook to the beset people on
hunting expeditions – three courses for dinner, with clean plates and
knives for each course. He looked the part: his clothes were European,
except for the fez. He remained on the border line of civilisation and
reminded us of what we had left. We had had a scene with him before
leaving Constantinople; he had accumulated a large assortment of
saucepans and kettles, of pans for frying and pans for stewing, of pots for
boiling and pots for washing; we had gone through them critically and
disregarded everything but a stew-pan, a frying-pan, and one pot for
boiling water. "Pas possible, mademoiselle," he kept on ejaculating,
"pas possible, comment faire cuisine?[8]" But we were adamant; we
wished to travel light and live largely on native food.

As it was we had a whole araba loaded up with our belongings; there
were the two tents for ourselves and the men, our camp beds and sacks of
clothes, and the cooking utensils. It all seemed a great deal now, and yet
we were only taking necessaries. But then it had been so very hard to
know what necessaries were; it is very hard to get disentangled from the
forces of tradition. We had escaped now and would know better. Life
was becoming extraordinarily easy, for we had left behind most things
and forgotten all the injunctions and warnings of our friends.

* * * * * *

But there was still Constantin in his European clothes and his
aristocratic ideas and his broken French.

* * * * * *

However, he does make delicious omelettes; we will forgive him for
smuggling in that omelette-pan in defiance of our orders.

---

[8] "Not possible, Miss, not possible – how can I cook?"

* * * * * *

It was getting very dark; we could no longer see the hillocks, but we knew that they were there. We could hardly see the horses tethered beyond the fire, but we could hear them munching and stamping, and now and then one would neigh suddenly.

Constantin lit a lantern and hung it on a stick; then he washed up the dishes. The other men sat on by the fire and we looked through the smoke at them. There was Calphopolos. Now Calphopolos was a Greek, and he was a mistake. We have said that Constantin was on the border-line of civilisation and reminded us of what we had left. But Calphopolos was right in it without really being of it – so that when he was about one forgot that there was anything to be said for civilisation and only remembered its drawbacks. His unbrushed black clothes contrasted painfully with the native dress, especially when seen through the smoke of a camp-fire. He always carried about a little black handbag, out of which his tooth-brush was constantly falling. But his worst offence was that he spoke a language which we understood, and jabbered French at us from morning to night. He was in the employment of well-meaning friends whom he accompanied when they made business excursions into the interior. They had sent him to start us comfortably on the way; his knowledge of the amenities of life was to pave the road leading away from civilised methods of living.

Then there was Ibrahim, a long, lean Turk with a smiling face. He put up the tents and rode in attendance upon us, and haggled with the villagers over milk and eggs. They had told me earlier in the day that Ibrahim was troubled in his mind; "never before had a woman looked him straight in the face and shown him a watch." Two Eastern precepts had been violated, and I had been the unwitting offender. It was at Brusa, which we had left with such difficulty that morning. We had arranged the night before to start at 8 o'clock. But 8 came, and 8.30 came, and 9 came, and then the Zaptiehs came who were to have come at 8 to escort us on the way; but there was no sign of our own retinue, of Constantin, of Ibrahim, of our own hired horses, of the arabas and muleteers with the baggage.

The news of our departure had got about and the people of the hotel gradually collected at the door. "Where is your dragoman?" they said; "why do you not send for him?" We confessed to having engaged no dragoman. "No dragoman! That was very rash. We could speak the language, then?" No, we had only a Turkish dictionary. They gave us up then as hopeless. Another individual pushed his way up to us. "You will never get your men to start or do anything else," he said; "you do not realise what these Turks are."

I recognised him as a professional dragoman offered to us by Cook the week before. But he was only telling us what everybody else out of the trade had been dinning into our ears ever since we planned the journey.

I repaired to the inn where the men and horses had been collected the night before. In the open yard stood the araba, unpacked and horseless. Constantin sat on a roll of baggage near by, with a resigned expression and a settled look, as if he had been sitting there for hours.

"Pas possible, mademoiselle," he said.

Ibrahim stood in the stable door, smoking complacently, and our muleteers were squabbling violently over the roping of a box.

It was at this moment that I stepped up to Ibrahim and showed him my watch. He looked at me with a startled expression, his jaw dropped, and he turned hastily on the muleteers. But it was not till later that I learnt how his inmost susceptibilities had been roused. One is at a decided disadvantage with no knowledge of a suitable language, but by dint of gesticulating with my riding-whip and pointing at everybody in turn, I managed, at the end of another half-hour, to get the araba and the men under way, and mounting my own horse rode behind them to the hotel. In another five minutes we had sallied out on our road. X and I rode ahead with Ibrahim and Calphopolos and the two Zaptiehs, then came the araba with out baggage and the muleteers, then Constantin with bulging saddle-bags suggesting the intrusion of various forbidden cooking utensils.

Our road ran unshaded and dusty through the outskirts of Brusa, with Mount Olympus towering above us. Bit by bit we left behind the staring tourists, the staring native children, the unconcerned stall-keepers displaying their wares of Brusa silk and printed cottons from England; then we passed the country people riding in on mules with their vegetables and chickens; we passed the little cultivated patches and got amongst the larger fields, stretching away on each side of the road. "Tutun," said Ibrahim, pointing at them with his riding-whip. I looked at him inquiringly. He tapped his cigarette and pointed again at the field.

"Tutun," he repeated. "Tobacco, you understand, mademoiselle, tobacco – such as he is now smoking." Calphopolos always would insist on explaining the obvious.

The day got hotter and the road got dustier. At midday we skirted a willow plantation, and a stream gurgled through the damp green patch, inviting us to come in and rest. We crawled out of the sun under the low willow bushes, and the men tied the horses to the stronger branches. This first lunching place will always remain indelible printed on my memory: the slices of brown bread thickly spread with solid cream; the watermelons and the grapes; the men grouped about amongst the willows, eating great hunches of bread and cheese; the horses breaking loose and straying about, browsing the finer herbage which sprang up through the dried and yellow tufts of older grass; the joy of being out of the sun and the dust; the cool sound of the water in the brook; the sense of rest and freedom, the sense of having really escaped at last ….. On recalling this lunch with X, after many adventures had made it seem very remote, I found that she retained equally vivid recollections of it. I heard her murmur reflectively to herself, "And we thought it was always going to be like that!"

Then we had reluctantly left it all, the unwilling horses were pulled and dragged away, snatching at last bites, and we rode off on the dusty road again, until we reached the village near which we had arranged to camp. We had ridden round and chosen this site in the middle of the mysterious hillocks, which shut us out so effectually from everything except the stars.

We were destined to spend many more such nights in camp; but perhaps none can give you exactly the same thrill as the one on which for the first time you sleep out in the open.

It is full of surprises; you expect it to be quiet, and you find the darkness and stillness is full of noise. Nothing escapes you; the breathing of men and animals, the crackling of the fire, the rustling of leaves and grass; there seems to be a continuous movement very close to you. You sit up many times expecting to see something in your tent; it all makes you very wakeful. You drop off into a disturbed sleep very late, and are awakened before sunrise by the stir in the camp. You are positive you have not slept all night and that strange people have been prowling round you in the dark.

Yet as one lay in this semi-wakeful state of excitement and mystery, one's strongest impression was that of wanting protection merely against a few primitive forces; with the wild beasts we shared the dangers of cold and hunger and attacks from man. Slowly and painfully you have crawled out of the net in which you have all this time been unconsciously enveloped, and emerging stripped and bewildered you grope about for what is actually going to serve and protect you in this primeval forces of nature; a state, moreover, where protection against the dictates of an organised society is no longer needed. To those who are confronted with this problem for the first time, it is almost impossible to walk straight out of the net and have an impartial look round. Tradition still clings to us in little bits, and we grope hopelessly about, wondering what will be an essential and what will not.

Looking back now on these first few days of preparation for our journey in the wilderness, I realise that by far the hardest part of the journey was this initial disentanglement from the forces of tradition. If you are about to alter fundamentally your method of living, you must take care that you are discarding all those accessories which are due to tradition; you must either adopt those evolved by the tradition of the races among which you are about to travel, or you must bring abstract science to bear on the question of how to provide for your immediate wants under the changed conditions. A bare tent in a country where weather is still an interesting topic is a safe place for such reflections; the realities of the situation make one strictly practical. On getting out of bed our clothes were damp with dew and the grass was cold to our bare feet; at the next town we bought the strip of carpet, the idea of which we had rejected at Constantinople.

"Keyf"

Leaving Brusa

A well in the Konia Plains

CHAPTER 2

BRIGANDAGE

Brigandage. The capture of Miss Stone[9], ancient history as it now is, has served to give a vivid meaning to this word in the public mind. We were being continually asked if we wished to emulate Miss Stone. Travelling second class through Bulgaria on our way to Constantinople our fellow-passengers, rough, good-natured farmers, joked about it; but they always added, "No, it will not happen to you." Then they would look at one another and laugh. The capture of Miss Stone did not seem to be looked upon seriously out there.

Then there was the Embassy at Constantinople. They were horribly nervous about international complications. As a matter of fact capture for ransom is a decided danger in the neighbourhood of larger towns in Asiatic Turkey. Not that there are any professional brigands prowling about, but there is a certain class of native ready to become a brigand on the spur of the moment, should they get wind of suitable prey. They are not Turks – no Turk would be bothered; they are, as a rule, Greeks, and always Christians. It is as well, therefore, on any expedition, not to make very great preparations and talk too much of your line of route; but as

---

[9] On the late afternoon of September 3, 1901 between the village of Bansko, Macedonia (now Bulgaria) and the town of Gorna Dzhumaia, an American missionary woman, Ellen Stone, of Chelsea, Massachusetts, was taken hostage with a Macedonian companion. The women's twenty armed captors were affiliated with the Internal Macedonian Revolutionary Organization and led by Yane Sandansky and Hristo Chernopeev.

It is said that the plan for the kidnap and ransom of a high-profile American connected with the missionaries had been under consideration for some time. The immediate demand for 25,000 Turkish lira (about $110,000) to release Miss Stone had been calculated so as to support an erupting revolutionary situation between the Turkish authorities and their subjects in Macedonia. The Ilinden Uprising of 1903 was a manifestation of those troubled times.

The women's fate captured the attention and imagination of most of the Western world and the incident received extensive press coverage. They were eventually released after many weeks in captivity.

quietly and expeditiously as possible get hold of your horses and men and start off before news of your movements has been noised abroad.

It was not at all in our favour that X bore a name well known to fortune hunters; one of her uncles was in the habit of big-game shooting in this district, and his means were fabulously exaggerated.

Calphopolos had been sent with us partly because he could be so thoroughly trusted to take all precautions. He certainly earned his reputation; he seemed to have been born with the fear of brigands in his soul; mere conversation about them caused him to break out into a profuse perspiration. He had talked to us very seriously on leaving Constantinople, as we sat on the deck of the steamer which took us across the Sea of Marmora on our way to Brusa.

"Pour l'amour de Dieu, mesdemoiselles, soyez secrètes; la secrécé, c'est tout.[10]"

"La secrécé" became his byword. If there was one thing he was more afraid of than anything else on earth it was X's surname. He implored her not to use it, but to call herself Miss Victoria. He had all our luggage labelled Miss Victoria; and if in casual conversation the dreaded name leaked out, beads of perspiration rolled down his face and he would glance nervously round to see who was within earshot.

X was rather a reprobate on the subject. On our arrival at Madame Brot's well-known hotel at Brusa, from where we were making our final departure the next day, she marched up to Madam Brot and said, "I think you know my uncle" – mentioning him by name. Calphopolos, who was just behind, explaining that our name was Victoria pure and simple, turned green with horror. With bent back and staring eyes, shaking the same finger in warning which his subconscious self was trying to put on his lips, he endeavoured to attract X's attention from behind Madame Brot's broad back. But X went glibly on, quite oblivious of the panic she was creating. Calphopolos turned to me with the resigned expression of a man on whom death-sentence has been passed.

"It is all over now," he said, "everybody in Brusa will know about us in half an hour. Mesdemoiselles, did I not implore you for the love of God to respect the secrecy? Ah, mon Dieu, mon Dieu, quelles demoiselles!"

And then poor old Calphopolos, who was not without his sense of fun, laughed till the tears rolled down his cheeks.

---

[10] "For the love of God, young ladies, be secretive. Secrecy is everything."

"The only thing left to do," he went on, when he had sufficiently recovered to speak again, "is to pretend we are going to Angora and put them off the scent. Mesdemoiselles, for the love of God please try and remember that it is Angora you are going to. Tell everybody you are going to Angora. The secrecy is everything."

It must be confessed it was very difficult at that time to feel seriously alarmed about brigandage, for we seemed to be moving in ordinary respectable society, and Calphopolos's treatment of the subject merely caused us to think of it as a joke. Still, we fully realised that it was a real risk, against which it would not do to neglect taking ordinary precautions; and this sense was heightened by the extreme alarm of the Vice-Consul at Brusa to whom we applied for the escort of Zaptiehs, without whom one is not permitted to travel in Turkey with any guarantee of safety. He could not understand why we would not drive through to Nicæa in a landau[11] in one day, like the ordinary tourist; this, with a suitable escort, made the journey quite safe, and it is a common thing for travellers to do. But to ride there in three days with our camp, sleeping on the way, was another matter. Every extra hour spent loitering in any one district heightened the risk of being attacked by brigands. X tried to explain that it was for the sake of her health, which only made him more bewildered; surely a landau was more suitable for invalids!

Finding us, however, unmoved by his arguments, he promised to send us two men the next morning and implored us never to leave their sides for a moment. He must have rubbed the same instructions well into the Zaptiehs, for during the seven days which they accompanied us as far as Mekidje on the Anatolian Railway, they never were more than a couple of yards away from us, day and night. This certainly detracted from the sense of freedom we were otherwise experiencing. It seemed at first as if we had only escaped from one form of bondage to fall into another. But the fact that the men were unable to speak any language we understood prevented it from becoming irksome, and one was soon able to become nearly oblivious of the clanking sword at one's elbow.

Calphopolos, however, was not so easily ignored. He had a sort of feeling that we were always running away from him, and tried to check this pernicious tendency on our part by engaging us in constant conversation in his broken French. The more we edged our horses away from his side and tried to put a silent Zaptieh between him and ourselves,

---

[11] A four-wheeled carriage.

the more persistently would he pursue us, propounding some new problem which required an answer. Our behaviour on breaking camp that morning had probably given rise to his state of mind. We had ordained that the start should be made at eight o'clock; but the usual procrastinations had ensued and the men seemed totally unable to get off. Calphopolos kept packing and unpacking his little bag in search of the missing tooth-brush, and tried to keep us calm.

"It is thus in this country, mademoiselle; have no anxiety – we shall go, we shall go."

X and I agreed that there was only one way to go. We had our horses saddled and rode away, in spite of Calphopolos's prayers and entreaties to wait till the whole camp was packed. The Zaptiehs, after the orders they had received, were obliged to ride after us. This left Calphopolos and the muleteers without Government protection, which so filled them with terror that in a very few minutes they also were on the way. Calphopolos came tearing down the road after us, the tails of his long black coat flying out behind, the tooth-brush sticking out of his pocket, and the perspiration rolling down his cheeks.

"Pour l'amour de Dieu![12]" he gasped as he caught us up, "pour l'amour de Dieu!" and then he had so much to say that he couldn't say it and relapsed into laughter and ejaculations of "Mais quelles demoiselles, mon Dieu, quelles demoiselles.[13]"

The second day of our road lay across the great Jenishehr plain. Herds of buffaloes strayed about on the wilder parts, and here and there fields of corn and tobacco, suddenly springing up beside the stretches of rough grass, signalled the approach to an occasional village.

Here also it was very difficult to think of brigands; the harmless look of peaceful cultivators did not suggest them. Besides which the country was so open that you could not be suddenly pounced upon; you would have ample opportunity of considering evil-doers as they approached you across the wide plain.

We encamped that evening near the small village of Jenishehr. The excitement of the novelty had worn off and we had had a long day in the open air. In consequence of this I had fallen into a profound sleep at once on going to bed. Suddenly I was awakened by a noise in the tent, and looking up distinctly saw the figure of a man coming cautiously

---

[12] "For the love of God!"
[13] "What young ladies, my God, what young ladies."

through the tent door. In one moment I had hold of my revolver, kept loaded at the head of my bed, and had it levelled at him, wondering when the psychological moment for pulling the trigger would occur and whether I should manage to live up to its requirements.

"Pour l'amour de Dieu,, mademoiselle! Pour l'amour de Dieu!" came in a terror-stricken voice.

I put down the weapon rather crossly.

"What do you want?" I said.

"Quels sont vos noms,[14]" stuttered out Calphopolos in great agitation.

"What on earth do you mean? I said; "you know our names well enough."

"Pour l'amour de Dieu, quels sont vos noms," he repeated.

"X," I called out, "wake up and tell me what is the matter with Calphopolos – I think his head has been turned by this fright about your name; he is going about jibbering over it."

X had a soothing influence on Calphopolos, and gradually extracted from him that the local Zaptieh had come up for our *tezkerehs*[15] and wanted to know our names. His agitation over the revolver had been so great that he had been unable to explain articulately that it was our *tezkerehs* that he had come for.

The next day the whole character of the country changed. The plain gradually oozed away into a more tumbled country and cultivation disappeared. We were about to cross the range of hills which shut out our view to the north.

The Zaptiehs were very much on the alert here; they unslung their rifles from behind and rode with them across their knees. We were told to keep close together and ride quietly without talking.

The mountains closed in on either side; they were bare, rounded hills for the most part, with stunted shrubs on the lower slopes, which one soon learnt to regard purely as cover for a possible enemy. There was no difficulty about realising possible dangers here; the broad road slowly narrowed, and at every turn in the winding path one almost expected to be confronted by a villain. At the snap of a twig or the rustle of a leaf our Zaptiehs grasped their rifles tighter, and without turning their heads moved their eyes in that direction. Once, on the wider road we had left, a cloud of dust had arisen in the distance, and a long line of camels laden

---

[14] "What are your names?"

[15] Permits

with wood filed slowly past us in twos and threes. Our men exchanged a few monosyllabic words with the drivers, and in another minute or two the tinkling of the bells and the tramp of feet had subsided, the dust settled once more, and we were alone again with the silent hills and the crackling twigs, and wound our way in and out in single file across the rounded hillocks. Here and there the sight of a herd of sheep or goats, tended by peaceful looking natives, relieved the tension caused by our escort's precautions, for it is always difficult to associate danger with such rural scenes. At last there was a break in front; we were through the pass and began to descend.

Calphopolos had been silent all this time; his conversational powers seem to have suffered a severe check. Now he brightened up, mopped his forehead, and murmured "Grâce à Dieu nous voilà.[16]"

Half way down the hillside, perched on a projecting ledge just off the road, stood a lonely coffee-house. The Zaptiehs, pointing at it with their whips, hailed it with delight. They slid off their horses, and holding ours, helped us to dismount[17]. We sat in the porch and sipped thick, hot Turkish coffee; below us the lake Ascanius lay like a blue sheet between the purple hills, its eastern end fringed round with a band of green, in which the minarets and domes of Isnik itself were just visible. All around us the stunted shrubs still formed harbour for the suspected brigands. Our Zaptiehs lay stretched on the ground in front, apparently asleep; but their rifles were never laid aside, and the least stir in the bushes made us realise their state of alert watchfulness.

But not a living creature showed itself, and we rode on down and down the curving incline until we reached the green band of vegetation and our horses trod softly through grassy slopes of olive plantations, whose grey leaves shone like silver as the sun's low rays beat through them. Past the olive plantations lay a stretch of low-lying reedy marsh.

"You shall have a good supper to-night," said Ibrahim; and throwing his reins to a Zaptieh he plunged in on foot. He shot two snipe, and joined us again as we reached the outskirts of the town.

The old city of Nicæa is now represented by a collection of a few hundred miserable houses forming the village of Isnik. But, as everywhere in the ancient towns of Asiatic Turkey, one is confronted at every point with tokens of former splendour. Four great gates in the old

---

[16] "Thanks be to God, here we are."
[17] Both X and the author were riding side-saddle.

Roman walls give access to the town. Courses of brickwork are built in between the large stones of which the bulk of the walls consist; here and there semicircular towers rise up, their ruins still surmounting the ruins of the wall. One, more perfect than the rest, is said to mark the site of the church in which the Nicene Creed was framed.

We fixed on a spot for the camp just inside the walls and outside the present town, where a green field, which merged into a cemetery, lay in the curve of a shallow brook.

The pots and pans were speedily tumbled out of Constantin's saddle-bags and Ibrahim had our tents up with European alacrity; but it was dark before the smell of roasted snipe pervaded the night air. We ate our supper by the light of a lantern hung on a forked stick. The fear of brigands departed and the sleep of the just fell upon the camp. Owls hooted in the green-covered walls of ruined Nicæa, and away in the distance the still mountains kept guard over the dark waters of the lake as they lapped mournfully on the ruins of Roman baths on its stony shore. The Zaptieh on guard poked fresh sticks into the dying fire and sighed heavily between the snores of his companions.

In and out amongst the upright white stones of the cemetery a jackal prowled stealthily and sniffed the smell of snipe bones.

CHAPTER 3

SOCIAL INTERCOURSE

One tree stood out in the middle of the field in which we were encamped. We spread our carpet under it and laid ourselves out for a lazy day. There were letters to write home and plans to make about the journey ahead. It was impossible to do such things comfortably after a day's ride and with the feeling of transitoriness engendered by a short night in camp. So we had decided to spend this Sunday at Isnik.

Constantin got out all his pots and pans to give them an extra cleaning, and promised us a vast meal. He complained that he had never had time to show us what he could do.

Animals and men alike were pervaded with that sense of rest which is in the air on a hot Sunday morning. The horses, after rolling on their backs, stretched themselves out motionless on their sides; and arabajis dozed in the araba. Calphopolos retired inside the men's tent, prepared to make up for the loss of sleep occasioned by anxious nights. We got out our books and papers and thought about all we should get through that day.

We were encamped within the old walls of Nicæa, and from where we sat were in full view of the outskirts of the present town. By and by some native women sallied out in our direction and, skirting the camp, peeped cautiously round our tents; then getting bolder they sidled towards us, smiling propitiatingly. We felt peacefully disposed towards the whole world and smiled back at them. Thus encouraged they advanced nearer and felt the substance of our clothes and examined our hats.

Finally, not finding themselves repulsed, they fingered our hair and stroked our hands. X hunted in her vocabulary for suitable remarks and delivered them at intervals. Meanwhile other women straggled out from the town, and, finding their sisters already so much at home, they also satisfied themselves as to the consistency of our clothes and skin. The earlier arrivals now established themselves on the ground around us, jabbering away amongst themselves and occasionally addressing a single word to us, which they repeated again and again, pointing at each of us in turn. X looked it up, and came to the conclusion that it meant "sister."

So we shook our heads and looked up the word for "friend." The effect was magical; we had established social intercourse.

More and more women arrived and joined the throng settled round us, all new-comers being initiated into the already acquired knowledge concerning us. Soon everybody had a word they wanted looked out in the dictionary, until X became fairly exhausted. We tried "goodbye" and "no more" with disappointing effect, and finally let them sit there gazing at us while we went on with our writing, keeping a sharp look-out on our hats, which every one was anxious to try on. It seemed to please them just as much to look at us as to talk to us, and they sat on in placid content.

By and by Ibrahim hurried up and spoke to the women; they all darted to their feet and fled. We looked at Ibrahim inquiringly. He pointed in the direction of the town, and we saw two men arriving at a slow and dignified pace. Constantin appeared on the scene.

"Gouverneur," he said, "faire visite."

X and I hastily donned our hats and sent for a seat for the "gouverneur." But Ibrahim could only find a saddle-bag. X turned over the leaves of the vocabulary in the hopes of finding suitable greetings. We bowed and scraped mutually, and X delivered herself of the first greeting.

"We are very pleased."

The "gouverneur" bowed and made, no doubt, what was a suitable response; but as we could only attack single words we were no wiser. There was a pause while X collected the words for another.

"Beautiful country," she attempted.

The "gouverneur" bowed very gravely.

"I hope I have said that," said X nervously, "he looks rather shocked."

At that moment Constantin appeared with coffee and cigarettes, which gave us time to recover.

"I should not bother to talk to him," I said. "That is the best of these people – they understand how to sit happily in silence, just looking at you."

But X determined to make another try; it was good practice.

"Health good?" she said.

The "gouverneur" turned to his companion and said a few words in Turkish. The young man looked rather terrified, and began to speak to us in what sounded like gibberish. Constantin came to take the cups away.

"Parle français[18]," he said, pointing to the young man.

We strained our ears to try and catch an intelligible word, but could only shake our heads.

So we all took refuge in silence and looked at one another. There was no sense of *gêne* (embarrassment). The Turk and his companion seemed as content to sit and look at us as the women had been. When he had finished his cigarette he rose, and, bowing once more in Turkish fashion, took his leave.

*   *   *   *   *   *

We picked up our papers once more, then Constantin came and said lunch was ready. We sat on saddle-bags outside the tent and ate chunks of mutton and onions out of the tin bowl keeping hot on the charcoal brazier at our side. Ibrahim filled our cups with water from the brook, and the grass tickled our hands each time we lifted them from the ground. The pots and pans lay about all around, and Constantin, squatting in the middle of them, brought the coffee to the boil three times in the little Turkish pot.

"Sheker, effendi?" he called out, "un, deux?"[19] as he ladled in the sugar. Constantin's language was always of a hybrid nature, consisting of alternate words of French and Turkish.

Then we had returned to the carpet under the tree and sipped the thick, hot coffee out of the little Turkish cups, and sent thoughtful rings of smoke up into the branches of the tree above. And with the rings of smoke went up thoughts of the coffee they were drinking now in the drawing-rooms; the little cups there would have handles, and each one would help himself to sugar off a little tray.

*   *   *   *   *   *

"I guess you find it slow here!"

An American tourist couple from Brusa stood over us. They had seen us off at Madame Brot's hotel, and had then announced their intention of driving to Nicæa in a landau.

---

[18] "He's speaking French."
[19] "Sugar, sir? One or two?"

"We thought we would just look you up and see if you had got here all right, but we cannot stop a minute; we've only had an hour to see the walls, they were so long in getting lunch."

"You ought to see the tower on the site of the church where they discussed the Nicene Creed," said X.

"The Nicene Creed – eh, what?" said the American, as he consulted his guide-book.

"Say, we just ought to have a look at that," he said to his wife.

"We shall miss the *Augusta Victoria* if you do," said the lady. Then she turned to us. "We go on to Smyrna in it t-morrow morning," she explained, "so we must get back to-night."

The landau appeared at that moment; time was up. Smyrna, Beyrout[20], Damascus, Jerusalem, Cairo and Luxor had to be got in during the allotted time, and there had been no provision made for the Nicene Creed. So in they got and dashed away over the plain.

They had come as a whirlwind over from the West, sweeping the surface of this Eastern land and catching up the loose fragments on it; but its traditions were too deeply rooted to be caught in the blast; these had merely bent their heads and let the blast pass by. Strong as it is, it cannot unloose the sway of ancient customs. Even for Americans the East will not move. The natives gazed at the landau, hardly wondering at it; then they forgot it. But we did not forget it so easily. For us an odour of the West was left hanging over the plain – and above all, our sense of time had been offended.

A French engineer with his wife and family were the next to appear on the scene. They were the only Europeans living in the place, and rejoiced over the sound of their mother-tongue. The man poured out volumes of it, and was interesting about his work up to the point when we became fatigued.

"Ah! mademoiselle, what it is to be in civilised company again! We live here from day to day and year after year, and have no one to speak with, no one with whom to exchange ideas. C'est comme la mort.[21]"

"Do you not see anything of the natives?" we inquired. "They seem very friendly, and you can speak Turkish."

"Ah! mademoiselle, what can one do with such people; how can one associate with them? They are canaille[22], mere canaille."

---

[20] Now spelt Beirut.

[21] "It's like being dead."

[22] Scoundrel.

"We were talking to some of them," we said, "and thought them very intelligent."

He held up his hands in horror.

"But, mademoiselle, do you not understand? Certainly there are the Christian races, but for the most part, ce sont des Turques, des infidèles, des chiens. There is Marie there, pauvre Marie! It is bad enough for me, but then I have my work; but Marie, the pauvre Marie, she dies of ennui, [23] she can speak to no one but me and the children.

The pauvre Marie seemed indeed to have lost the power of speech; she sat silently as her husband poured out his contempt of the canaille.

E had found the Greek women very entertaining in the morning, and they too had sat and looked at us in silence. But they had not been ashamed of their silence; Marie was, and felt awkward; so we all felt uncomfortable and tried to talk to her.

One felt then how little actual language had to do with social intercourse. We could not get into touch with Marie, whose language we understood, in the same way that we had got into touch with the native women, whose language we did not understand.

They sa on and on; it was not until the sun began to send out long warning shoots of colour, heralding its disappearance behind the purple mountains, that they rose to go.

And we, won out with this final effort in sociability, gave ourselves up to the quiet of the deserted camp, and watched the shades of night creep once more over the ruined walls and the distant hills, over the houses of the French engineer and the canaille.

---

[23] "They are Turks, infidels, dogs.... Marie, poor Marie, is dying of boredom,"

CHAPTER 4

THE DAWN OF THE BAGHDAD RAILWAY

There is something very weird and uncanny in the terminus of a railway in the middle of a wild and desolate country such as this. The Monster runs his iron fangs into the heart of its desolation and shoots you into it like a ball out of a cannon's mouth. Roaring and hissing and sending out jets of flame, he comes racing through the darkness to a certain definite spot; here he discharges you in the blackness of night and subsides. Next morning when you awake he is gone, and you are left to shift for yourself as best you can.

But there is a certain human friendliness about this Monster while you are travelling with him. He seems to draw all the signs of life out of an apparently dead country and collect them at the stations for you to see. Great warehouses filled with sacks of corn testify to the productiveness of a country which, judging it from the train window after harvest-time, one would dismiss as mere barren soil; an occasional MacCormick's "Daisy" reaper[24] awaiting delivery on a side platform, native carts hanging about, and truck-loads of empty sacks tell the same tale. Groups of peasants, idly gossiping, gathered together by the whistle which heralds the Monster's approach, belie the impression of an uninhabited land; for Turkish villages are carefully designed so as not to attract attention. When one's eye gets more familiar with the seemingly uniform colour of the landscape, varied only by light and shade, one becomes aware of the low, flat-topped, mud-brick houses, which, even at close quarters, often seem but part of the natural rock.

Even the unchanging East is powerless once the Monster's fangs have taken hold; he alone of all influences comes to stay and leave his mark.

Slowly, perhaps, but very surely, he undermines with irresistible persistence the customs and habits which from time immemorial have held their own against religious, educational, or military forces of stronger nations.

---

[24] Cyrus Hall McCormick (1809-1884) invented the first horse-drawn reaper in 1831, which became famous all over the world. In 1851, this reaper won the highest award of the day, the Gold Medal at London's Crystal Palace Exhibition.

This particular spot has long been the battlefield of the East and the West; now one, now the other, has had temporary ascendance; in the long run the East has always conquered.

But already we can see what a power the East has to reckon with in the railway. For one thing it attacks the Eastern in one of his vital points – his conception of Time. Time waited for him when he had but camels to load; but the railway will not wait for him; the Monster screeches and is off. Sunrise or two hours after sunrise is not one and the same thing to him. Relentless as day and night he comes and goes, and there is no cheating him as the Eastern cheats Time.

But the railway is cheating the East out of its time-worn customs and ideas, and there is a certain sadness in the evidences of transition. All down the line picturesque native costumes are being replaced by ugly European clothes. The men wear terrible fancy trouserings from Manchester; the women spend more money on dress – and unfortunately it is European dress – and less on the old-fashioned wedding feasts. The turnover of the shops in the larger towns has increased fourfold in the last ten years. The bazaars are now a medley of stalls exhibiting native manufactures side by side with cheap trinkets from England and loud flannelettes from Italy. The price of wheat has doubled; and with that of wheat the prices of other exports have also risen. Opium, wool, mohair, hides and salt are amongst the products of these great plains.

Two short days' ride from Nicæa had brought us to Mekidje, a station on the Anatolian Railway half-way between Haida Pasha and Eskishehr. The single line went as far as Konia, and one train ran each way every day. It stopped for the night at Eskishehr, continuing the journey next morning.

We arrived at the station some hours before the train was due, and sat in the stationmaster's strip of garden, for there did not seem anything else to do. We said goodbye to the Zaptiehs and to the muleteers who were returning to Brusa, and watched them slowly disappear down the road we had come. Then we heard the low, familiar tinkle of camel bells, and a score or more of laden animals paced slowly into the open ground round the station. They have a more discreet and tuneful way of announcing their arrival than the Monster, and when the appear on the scene they do so in a more dignified, calmer manner. Having arrived also, they do not look as if there were off again the next minute; they look as if they had come to stay for ever, and they give you time to think. One by one, in answer to a word of command, they knelt down in the dust, and the great baskets holding the goods were unfastened and rolled about on the ground. Their owners seemed too slack to do any more. They let them lie there while they looked at the sun. The Monster is slowly replacing these carriers of the East; but their day is not yet done by a long way, for they must feed him from the interior. His life is still dependent on the life of those he is working to destroy.

* * * * * *

At last we heard his distant shriek. Down upon us he came, dashing up all in a minute, in such a splutter and such a hurry, waking us all up. Officials rushed up and down the platform, and swore at the natives who were loading our baggage. Everybody talked at once to everybody else, and the Monster hissed impatiently, noisy even when he was standing still.

There were not many passengers; in a first-class carriage a Pasha travelled in solitary state; all his harem were delegated to a second-class carriage, where the blinds were pulled down. In the third-class were a few natives, who leaned out of the windows and gossiped with the camel owners, idle witnesses of the busy scene.

But the Monster is getting impatient; he hisses furiously and finally gives a warning shriek. Then off he goes, and we take a last look at the kneeling camels, munching away as unconcernedly as if their destroyer had never invaded their peaceful country.

Mekidje is practically at sea-level; Eskishehr is a tableland two thousand feet high; we had therefore a steady rise on the whole journey up the valley formed by the Kara Su, a river which has its source in the neighbourhood of Eskishehr. On each side rounded hills shut out the horizon, save where here and there a tributary valley would reveal, through steep-sided gorges, a distant view of purple ridges with snow-clad tops.

It was night when we arrived at Eskishehr, and we groped our way to the Grand Hôtel d'Anatolie, kept by Greeks. It was at this hotel that we first met Hassan, who was destined to play such a large part in our future travels. He was an Albanian Turk, and had been introduced to us by our friends in Constantinople, whom he accompanied on their shooting expeditions in this district. They had written to ask him to look after us during our brief stay at Eskishehr.

Ibrahim brought him into our room, and there he stood silently, after salaaming us in the usual way.

Ibrahim was a tall man, but Hassan towered above him. He wore a huge sheepskin coat, which added to his massive, impressive look.

X looked up words in her Turkish book.

"They told us you would look after us here?" she said.

"As my eyes," he answered very quietly and simply. And thus began one of those friendships on which neither time nor distance can leave their mark.

Two days later X asked him whether he would accompany us on the next stage of our journey, across the Anatolian Plateau and the Taurus Mountains to Mersina.

"Will you come with us and guard us well?" she said. He dropped on one knee and kissed her hand.

"On my head be it," he said.

*   *   *   *   *   *

Eskishehr, before the days of the railway, was a purely Turkish town; it displayed the usual chaos of mud-brick and wooden houses, with their lower windows carefully latticed over for the concealment of the women; of narrow, winding bazaars, here a display of brightly coloured clothes and rugs, there a noisy street of smithies and carpenters' shops; and rising above it all the minarets of half a dozen mosques.

But the railway's mark is on it to-day. The population has been increased by some five thousand Tartars and Armenians, whose houses, planted together near the line, have a neat, modern, shoddy look, contrasting with the picturesque squalor of the ancient Turkish town.

The railway is slowly attacking the stronghold of the Turkish peasant, extending his operations on the wasted stretches of cultivable land, and slowly opening out dim vistas of prosperity athwart his present apathy. In the same way the railway is slowly affecting the town merchant. But one shudders here at the effect of prosperity unaccompanied by civilising influences. For in the rich merchant of the town you have the Turk at his worst. The simple, hospitable Turkish peasant is made of good stuff; the Turkish soldier of rank and file, if his fanatical tendencies are not encouraged, is equally good; the official Turk is corrupt, but only because the particular method of administering his country's laws obliges him to be so; the educated Turk of Constantinople is rapidly becoming a civilised being.

But the rich middle-class Turk of towns has nothing to be said for him. The Christians have taught him to drink, and he is rich enough to keep a large harem. We had an introduction to one such person in Eskishehr. The polished Turkish phraseology of welcome could not conceal the coarseness and vulgarity of his mind, and we were glad to escape to the sacred inner chambers, where a very young and pretty woman sat in lonely state, the latest addition to his harem. There she sat, draped in the softest silks of gorgeous colourings, surrounded with all the evidences of luxury and comfort, as sulky as a little bear.

We were accompanied by a Greek lady, who talked French and Turkish and acted as our interpreter; but never a smile or more than a word could be drawn out of the cross little thing. She simply stared in front of her with an expression of acute boredom in her beautiful eyes. A good-natured, elderly serving-woman, who stood at the door, explained matters. She had been very much pampered at home, and she had had a good time; she saw all her young friends at the baths, the social resort for Turkish ladies. The rich merchant had been considered a great *parti*[25]; but already she had had enough of it. She never went out except for an occasional drive in a closed carriage. She was tired of embroidery work, she was tired of eating sweets, she was tired of smoking, she was tired of her fine dresses. *Aman*, but it would come all right – and the serving-woman winked and nodded, and stroked her mistress's listless hand.

"Is it always like this?" we asked the Greek lady.

"Ah, mon Dieu! Not at all. This man is very jealous, and she may not see her friends. He heaps on her what money can buy and thinks that is enough. But with the poor it is different. You will see. There is a wedding to-day in a poor family. I will arrange for you to go. Mon Dieu! No, it is not always thus. La pauvre petite.[26]"

The room in which we sat was draped in the usual Turkish manner with magnificent curtains in rich Eastern colourings. Round three walls ran low divans covered in the same way. There was not such a room in Eskishehr, we were told. Had the decorations stopped there, and we had been able to forget the unfortunate prisoner, the general effect would

---

[25] Match.
[26] "The poor little one."

have been decidedly pleasing. But as we sat there our eyes were kept glued, by some horrible attraction, on the glitter of a cheap gilt frame of the gaudiest description, containing a crude coloured print of the German Emperor; below this stood a gimcracky little table covered with a cheap tinselled cloth, on which was placed a glass and silver cake-basked in the vilest of European taste. It hit one terribly in the eye. It was a jarring note in the Monster's work.

*   *   *   *   *   *

We took leave of the sulky little lady, and left her once more to her sweets and her embroideries in the long, weary hours of lonely splendour.

We had only seen the second act of this bit of Turkish drama; when the curtain went down for us we had had enough of it.

But we were about to see Act I in different surroundings. The Greek lady kept her word, and in due course we found ourselves ushered into the house of the bridegroom. The preliminary ceremonies had already begun, in fact they had been going on all day. There sat the bride at the end of a room which had been cleared of everything except the low stool which she occupied alone. She was a lumpy looking girl of seventeen or so, and sat there motionless with downcast eyes. On the floor sat dozens of women, packed as tight as the room could hold. The bride might neither look up nor speak, which seemed hard, for every woman in the room was both looking at her and speaking about her; the hubbub was terrible.

She rose as we entered and kissed our hands; this much is apparently allowed on the arrival of strangers. The Greek lady explained that she was obliged to stand until we asked her to sit down again, and that she might not look at us. This was a good deal to ask on such an occasion; European ladies are not, as a rule, guests at the wedding of the Turkish poor, and we caught one or two surreptitious peeps from under her long eyelashes. We joined the throng on the floor and continued to gaze at her as every one else did. Marriage customs in general and her own affairs in particular were discussed for our benefit, the Greek lady interpreting in torrents of voluble French.

"She may not speak to her husband for forty-eight hours. When he comes in he will lift the veil and see his bride for the first time. Then he puts a girdle round her waist and it is finished. His mother chose her for him. If he does not like her, no matter, he can choose another, for he is getting good wages and can afford to keep two."

By and by a large tray was brought in, piled up with rounds of native bread and plates of chicken. It was placed on a low stool in the centre of us all, and, following everybody's example, we grabbed alternate bits of chicken and bread. Then followed hunches of cake made of nuts and honey.

We were still eating when we heard a noise of singing and musical instruments outside; it became louder and louder and finally stopped by the house.

"They are singing 'Behold the bridegroom cometh,'" said the Greek lady; "the man is being brought in a procession of all his friends."

The food was hastily removed, and all the guests were marshalled into an adjoining room, which already seemed as full as it could hold of babies and children and old hags, who presumably had been left to look after the younger ones. We were allowed to remain while the finishing touches were put on the bride. Her face was first plastered all over with little ornaments cut out of silver paper and stuck on with white of egg; then she was covered over entirely with a large violet veil. And so we left her sitting there, sheepish and placid in the extreme, in strange contrast to the voluble Greek lady and the excited friends. We met the bridegroom in the passage. He kissed his father, and stood first on one foot and then on the other. His mother took him by the shoulders, opened the door of the room we had just left, and shoved him in, Let us hope that the silver ornaments did their work and made his bride pleasing in his sight when he lifted the violet veil. What she thought of him need not concern us any more than it did her or her friends, for such thoughts may not enter the minds of Turkish brides.

The show was over. The curtain of the first act had gone down for us. It gave promise of a more successful drama than the one had had previously witnessed.

* * * * * *

It is 267 miles or thereabouts from Eskishehr to Konia. It took us a good fifteen hours by rail. We were not on the summit of the tableland; the bounded river valley gradually gave way to long stretches where signs of cultivation were more apparent. We were getting into the great wheat-growing district, which the railway is causing to extend year by year. At Karahissar, a town of 33,000 inhabitants, a gigantic rock with straight sides and castellated top rises abruptly out of the plain, and from here another corn-growing valley merges into the great plain stretching away to the north. Mount Olympus, whose base we had skirted on leaving Brusa, could be very dimly discerned on the sky-line.

Then darkness set in, and the Monster ran steadily on with us into the unknown. Towards eight o'clock there was a sudden stop; it had come to the end of its tether.

We had left Calphopolos and Ibrahim at Eskishehr, and now only Constantin remained as a link with civilisation. Hassan had appeared at the station at Eskishehr, prepared to accompany us round the world if need be. He wore a brown suit of Turkish trousers and zouave[27] under his sheepskin cloak. His pockets bulged rather, so did the wide leather belt which he used as a pocket, otherwise his worldly goods were contained tied up in a white pocket-handkerchief.

And so we arrived at Konia. Behind us was the railway, leading back to the things we knew, to the things we should hope to see again; before us was the plain, leading us to strange new things, things we should, perhaps, just see once and leave behind forever.

The iron Monster had dumped us down and was no further concerned with us; if we would go further it must be by taking thought for ourselves.

There were horses and arabas to hire, there were provisions to lay in, there was the escort of Zaptiehs to be procured and the goodwill of the authorities to be obtained. We had letters of introduction to Ferid Pasha, then Vali of the Konia vilayet[28] and since Grand Vizier of Constantinople. He was not as other Valis; he was called the great and the good, and had established law and order in his province. There need be no fear of brigandage while we were within the boundaries of his jurisdiction.

The Government building, the Konak, occupied one side of the square in which stood our hotel, and we sent Hassan across to pay our respects. But Ferid Pasha was away, which caused us great disappointment; we could only see his Vekil, the acting Governor.

---

[27] One of a hardy body of soldiers in the French service, originally Arabs, but later composed of Frenchmen wearing Arab dress; then one of a body of soldiers who adopted the dress and drill of the Zouaves. The author is using this word to describe Hassan's clothing.

[28] One of the chief administrative divisions or provinces of the Ottoman Empire.

Taking Hassan and Constantin with us, we went up the long flight of steps and down a corridor leading to the Vali's room. Peasants and ragged soldiers hung about the passage, and black-coated Jewish-looking men hurried in and out. A soldier showed us the way, holding back the curtains which concealed the entrance to various rooms, and from behind which the mysterious-looking Jews were continually creeping.

The Vekil sat at a table covered over with official documents; a divan, higher and harder than those we had seen in private houses, ran round two walls, on which squatted several secretaries, holding the paper on which they wrote on the palms of their left hands. Beside the Vekil sat an old Dervish[29] priest, and next to him the Muavin, the Christian official appointed after the massacres to inform Valis of the wishes of Christians, and better known amongst those who knew him as "Evet Effendi" (Yes, Sir.)

* * * * * *

X was getting fluent in matters of Turkish greeting; she now reeled off a suitable string in reply to theirs. Hassan stood beside us, grave and dignified, and we noticed that all the men greeted him very courteously. X then endeavoured to explain our desire to travel to Mersina and requested the services of a suitable escort. Owing to limitations in her knowledge of the Turkish vocabulary, the nearest she could get to it was that the Consul at Mersina loved us dearly and wished us to come to him. Matters were getting to a deadlock; the officials appeared to be asking us what was the object of our journey, and we could only insist on the intense love of our English Consul.

Suddenly another visitor was ushered in, and for the first time since leaving Nicæa the strange sound of the English tongue fell upon our ears. The newcomer was Dr. Nakashian, and Armenian doctor living in Konia.

He at once acted as interpreter. Officialdom for once put no obstacles in the way, and an escort was promised us for the journey. The Vekil inquired whether we should like to see the sights of Konia; and on our replying in the affirmative, he arranged that we should be taken round that afternoon; Dr. Nakashian also promised to accompany us.

---

[29] A Turkish or Persian monk, particularly one who professes poverty and leads a very austere life. Some Dervishes perform whirling dances and vigorous chanting as acts of ecstatic devotion.

Accordingly we sallied out later on horseback with Hassan. Dr. Nakashian was mounted on a splendid Arab mare. The Government Protection, in the shape of two Zaptiehs and a captain, followed in a close carriage. We started off very decorously, but the Arab mare became excited and plunged and galloped down the street; our horses caught the infection, and we followed hard; the Government Protection put its head out of each window and shouted; the driver lashed his jaded horse, and the rickety carriage lurched after us in a cloud of dust. The natives lining the streets shouted encouragingly; finally we landed at the Dervish mosque. Dervishes are strong in Konia. Their founder is buried here, and his tomb is an object of pilgrimage. The chief feature of the mosque is its wonderful polished floor, where the dancing ceremonies take place.

At Konia, perhaps more than at Eskishehr, one is struck with the railway's influence in the passing order of things. There are many fine buildings in the last stages of decay in this ancient city of the Seljuk Turks;[30] the palace, with its one remaining tower, the fragments of the old Seljuk walls found here and there in the middle of the modern town, the mosques lined with faïence, beautiful even in its fragments. Contrast with this the squalor and the dirt of the present Turkish streets, the earth and wood houses, enclosed in walls of earth, the apathetic natives, and the general feeling of stagnation and decay.

Then, outside the town, the railway appears; modern European houses spring up round it – offices for the Company and an hotel. A whiff of stir and bustle brought in along the iron fangs of the Monster brings a sense of fresh life to these people, whose existence seemed one long decay of better things, like that of the ruins amongst which they spend their days.

And everywhere there was a whisper of yet closer touch with civilisation. The Anatolian Railway stops at Konia, but its continuation under the name of the Baghdad Railways was everywhere in the air.[31] No one spoke openly about it; its coming seemed enveloped in such a shroud of mystery that one felt there was a sort of halo around its birth. At first one mentioned it baldly by name; and at once the official would put on his most discreet and impressive manner and refer to the will of

---

[30] A Turkish dynasty which ruled in central and western Asia from the eleventh to the thirteenth century.
[31] *The Baghdad Railway is now running as far as Bulgurlu, a point some seven miles beyond Eregli.*

Allah; the merchant would nod mysteriously and then wink with evident satisfaction. "It comes! Oh yes, it comes! But it is better not to talk of it yet." And the Zaptieh would sigh heavily, thinking of his unpaid wages, and say, "Please God, it comes," and then look hastily round to see who had overheard him.

And so at last we also learnt to speak of the Coming of the Monster with bated breath and lowered tones, and were duly infected with the impressiveness of his arrival – the arrival of the Being whose touch was to bring new life into this dead land.

* * * * * *

It was on the morning of the third day after our arrival at Konia that we made the plunge into the great plain from the spot where the Monster had left us. We collected in the square in front of the Konak. There were two covered arabas to convey the baggage, and in one of these Constantin and Hassan also rode; X and I rode horses and had saddle-bags slung under our saddles. Our escort consisted of three Zaptiehs, a Lieutenant, Rejeb, and an ancient Sergeant, Mustapha.

The head of the police accompanied us a few miles out of the town.

Slowly, riding at a foot's pace, we left it all behind, the squalid streets, the modern houses, the scraggy little trees; the lumpy road became a deeply rutted track bordering stubble fields; lumbering carts passed us, squeaking terribly as the wheels lurched out of the ruts to make way for us. The track became an ill-defined path, along which heavily laden pack-animals slowly toiled, raising clouds of dust. Turning in our saddles, all we could see of Konia was the minarets of its mosques standing above a confused blur on the horizon line.

There is a strange fascination in watching the slow disappearance of any object on the horizon, when that horizon is visible at every point round you. The exact moment never comes when you can state the actual disappearance of the object. You think it is still there, and then you slowly realise that it is not. And when you have realised this, you turn round again in the saddle once for all, and set your face steadily towards the horizon in front of you, which for so many hours on end has nothing to show and nothing to tell you, and yet whose very emptiness is so full of secret possibilities and hidden wonder.

* * * * * *

www.horsetravelbooks.com

We had got beyond the point where one met others on the road; we had now become our own world, a self-contained planet travelling with the sun through space. When he disappeared over the horizon line we pitched our camp and waited for his reappearance on the opposite side. At the first glimmer announcing his arrival the tents were hauled down, the arabas loaded up, and by the time his face peeped over the line we were in our saddles, ready once more to follow him to his journey's end.

It is a great half-desert plain, this part of Anatolia; desert only where it is waterless, and very fertile where irrigation is possible. In places it seemed to form one huge grazing ground; now it would be herds of black cattle munching its coarse, dried-up herbage; now flocks of mohair goats, now sheep, herded by boys in white sheepskin coats, tended by yellow dogs. Then we knew that a village would be somewhere about, although we did not always see it; for here too the villages are the colour of the surrounding country and perhaps only visible in very clear sunlight.

Or it might be that we would ride slowly through a cluster of mud huts, and the yellow dogs would rush out and bark furiously at us, while the men and children stared silently, too listless even to wonder. At times we would stop in a village for our midday meal, sitting in the shade of its yellow mud walls. The Zaptiehs would stand round us and keep off the dogs until some of the village men would appear and call them away with a half-scared look – for the Zaptieh is the tax-collector, and they suffered from extortion at his hands.

We visited the women in their houses, and found them always interested and friendly. Turkish was becoming more intelligible to us, and the conversation usually took the same form:-

"Who is your father?"

"He is a Pasha in a far country."

"Where are your husbands?"

"We have no husbands."

"How is that?"

"In our country the women are better than the men, and the men are afraid of us."

Then our clothes are fingered all over and the cost of every thing on us is asked. We rise to go, and hang on us and implore us to come again. But the sun has already begun to dip on his downward course, and we must hurry after him.

Then would follow hours when no attempt at cultivation, or sign of herds and clocks, would be visible, and the desert country was only relieved by wonderful effects of mirage, in which we would chase elusive pictures of mountains and lakes and streams.

One had time to take it all in: the wonderful exhilarating air, the silent stretches, the long, monotonous days of the shepherd boys, marked only by the gathering in of their flocks at night.

How will it be when the Monster comes, roaring and snorting through these silent plains, polluting this clear air with his dust and smoke? At first these haughty, resentful shepherds will stand aloof from the invasion, the yellow dogs will bark in vain at the intrusion. Then slowly its daily appearance will come to them as the sun comes in the morning and the stars at night. Unconsciously it also will become a part of the routine of their lives. They will not cease to look at it with wonder, for they have never wondered. They will accept it, as they accept everything else. But use it? That is a different tale. It will be a long fight; but the Monster has always conquered in the end.

* * * * * *

On the third day we rode into Karaman. A medieval castle crowns the town, and is visible at some little distance across the plain.

The old sergeant, Mustapha, startled us by suddenly greeting it from afar:-

"Ah, Karaman, you beautiful Karaman, city of peace and plenty. Ah, Karaman, beloved Karaman."

And the Zaptiehs, taking up the refrain, made the silent plains ring with "Karaman! Beautiful Karaman!"

* * * * * *

We pitched our tents on a grass plot in the centre of the town. Constantin began preparing the evening meal, and the natives hung round in groups staring at us, or bringing in supplies of fuel and milk and eggs. A seedy-looking European pushed his way up to our tent and began storming at us in French.

"But it is impossible for you to camp here – it is not allowable; you must come at once to my house. There is nothing to say."

X and I tried to rouse our bewildered minds out of the Eastern sense of repose into which they had sunk through all these days.　We concluded that Karaman must possess an urban district council, and that we were breaking some law of the town.

We pressed for further enlightenment.

"But do you not see all these people looking at you?　It is not for you to camp here.　My house is ready for you.　There are good beds and it is dry, but this ..." and he waved his hand at our preparations.　"It is not possible; there is nothing to say."

By this time Hassan and Rejeb, into whose hands we had been entrusted for protection, came up and stood over us, looking threateningly at our gesticulating, excited friend.

"I do not understand," I said.　"Who says that we may not camp here."

"But it is I that say it; it is not possible.　My house is ready; there is nothing to say."

"Who are you?" I said.

"I am an Austrian," he answered.　Then he lowered his voice, in that mysterious manner which we associated with the coming of the Monster. "I am here," he said, in an undertone, "as agent commercial du chemin de fer Ottoman.[32]"

"Very good," I answered; "and now tell us why we cannot camp here."

"But it is damp," he said; "look at the mud."

"Oh, is that all?" I said.　"We are much obliged to you for the offer of your house, but we always sleep out."

"But I have good beds," he said, "and a dry room at your service. There is nothing to say."

At this point Rejeb could contain himself no longer.　He spoke sternly to the Austrian in Turkish.

"What do you want?" he said.　"These ladies are under my protection. What are you saying to them?"

The man poured out volumes of Turkish;　Rejeb and he had a violent altercation, which seemed to be ending in blows.

"Come, come," I said to the man, "enough of this.　We are much obliged to you for your offer of hospitality, but we prefer to remain outside."

----

[32] "sales representative of the Ottoman railway."

He seemed totally unable to understand that this could be the case. "If it is myself you do not care about," he said, in a crestfallen manner, "I can easily move from the house. The beds are clean and they are dry."

We finally consented to spend the evening at his house, and accompanied him through the streets, Rejeb and Hassan following closely on our heels. He showed us into a stuffy little sitting-room. Every corner was crammed with gimcracks[33]; the whole place reeked of musty wool chairbacks.

Then we followed him upstairs; we must at any rate "look at the beds" – he evidently thought the sight of them would prove irresistible.

On calmer reflection the beds were, doubtless, no worse than the ordinary type to be found in commercial country inns; but to us, coming out of the sweet and wholesome atmosphere of the yet-untainted plain, they seemed to be the very embodiment of stuffiness and discomfort. The windows, which had evidently not been opened for some time, were heavily draped, so as to effectually exclude all light and air even when open.

"There, now do you see? It is clean, it is dry. There is nothing humid here; but out there it is exposed, it is damp, it is not allowable."

We waived the question for the moment, reserving our forces for a later attack, and returned to the sitting-room, where a native woman was preparing the evening meal. We questioned our host on the arrival of the railway. He admitted being there to tout for trade *in case* it came; but who could tell, in a country like this, what would happen? Mon Dieu! It was a God-forsaken country, and all the inhabitants were canaille[34]; there was no one he could associate with. He counted the days till his return. "When would that be?" "Ah," then he became mysterious once more and looked round at the door and window: "Ah, God knows; might it come soon!"

The serving-woman appeared and said that our men wished to see us; they had been sitting on the doorstep ever since we entered the house and refused to go away. The Austrian went out to them; high words ensued, and we looked through the door. The Austrian, crimson with rage, was gesticulating violently and pouring out torrents of unintelligible Turkish. Rejeb stood in front of him, hitting his long riding-boot with his whip and answering with some heat. Above him towered Hassan, very calm

---

[33] Showy, useless trifle.
[34] Scoundrels.

and very quiet, slowly rolling up a cigarette and now and then putting in a single word in support of Rejeb.

The Austrian turned to us. "Can you not send these men away, ladies? It is an impertinence. They refuse to leave you here unless they themselves sleep in the house. They say they have orders never to leave you, but surely they can see what I am?"

We calmed him down as best we could, and insisted on our intention of returning to our tents. He could not understand it, and I should think he never will. But we got away, Rejeb and Hassan one on each side of us. When we were out on the road in cover of darkness both men burst into load roars of laughter.

"Have we not done well, Effendi?" they said. "We have rescued you from the mad little man. The great doctor in London, has he not said 'You shall sleep in the tent every night'?"

And, gathering round our camp-fire in the damp and the mud, we rejoiced with Hassan and Rejeb over their gallant assault and our fortunate escape.

*   *   *   *   *   *

Two days' further ride brought us to Eregli. We approached it in the dusk, riding during the last hour through what appeared to be low copse wood. The place seemed to low and damp; we rode past the door of the khan,[35] and the men besought us to go there instead of camping outside. Constantin said he was ill, the arabajis said their horses would be ill. But Rejeb and Hassan took our side and we had the tents pitched on a spot which seemed dry in the darkness. Next morning we awoke to find ourselves encircled by a loop of the river and in a dense white mist. It was so cold that the milk froze as we poured it into the tea. We ate our breakfast with our gloves on, walking up and down to keep warm.

Constantin said that he was still ill; the arabjis said their horses were now ill; but that was because the khan was comfortable. We decided, however, to give them a day's respite and ride out to Ivriz in search of the Hittite inscription at that place.

An hour's ride took us clear of the mists, and the sun came out hot and strong. Our road lay up a gorgeous richly wooded river valley. For the first time on our journey we realised what the absence of water and

---

[35] An inn or caravanserai.

trees had meant. Our horses' feet crackled over brown and red autumn leaves; autumn smells, crisp and fresh, filled the air; brown trout darted from under dark rocks in the steam. Away through gaps in the low encircling hills we got sudden visions of two gigantic white-topped mountain peaks, the first suggestion of our approach to the Taurus barrier.

Ivriz is a good three hours' ride from Eregli and lies high on one of the lower hills. We left our horses in the village and climbed on foot to the spot where the river, rushing suddenly out of the bowels of the earth, has formed a cave in the limestone cliff. Below this the stream had gut its way through the rock, leaving steep sides of bare stone which tell a tale of untold geological age. At one point the ground shelved out on a level with the bed of the stream, and the waters here swept round a corner, so that the face of the rock overlooking them was almost hidden from any one on the same shore.

It is on this fact that the Hittite inscription is carved. A god, with a stalk of corn and a bunch of grapes in his hands, stands over a man who is in an attitude of adoration before him.

There it stands, hidden from the casual observer, visited by no one but the native who comes to cure his sickness in the sacred waters of the cave above.

Away in the desolate hills, off the track of man, the god has looked down on the waters of the river through all those æons since the days of the Hittites, which count as nothing in the time which it took this same river to carve its bed out of the eternal hills. How much longer will its solitude be left unviolated? The "agent commercial du chemin de fer Ottoman"[36] is established at Eregli as elsewhere. When the iron Monster comes bellowing into Eregli his shriek will be heard in these silent hills, and following in his footsteps countless hordes of tourists will invade this sacred spot.

With something akin to a feeling of shame I turned my Kodak on him; and a sorrowful thought of the many who would be following my example in the years to come shot across my mind.

*   *   *   *   *   *

---

[36] "sales representative of the Ottoman railway."

It was the sixth day after leaving Konia, and we were in full view of the Taurus Mountains. We were crossing the same stretch of barren plain, with its occasional patches of cultivation, its hidden villages with the flocks and herds trooping in at sundown. But the bounded horizon changed our conception of it; it was no longer a limitless plain. The nearer ranges stood out in dark purples and blues; behind and above towered the snow-clad heights which, looking down on to the Mediterranean shores, knew of the life and bustle of its sea-girt towns.

We had come out on the other side of the unknown plain and the aspect of things was changed. What drew us on now was not the mystery of unexplored space, but the feeling that here was a great barrier to cross. We were about to share with these heights the knowledge of what lay on the other side. But there was more than this – we were about to do what the Monster might possibly fail to do. As we drew near the barrier, the mysterious allusions to his approach all took the form of pointing at this barrier. "So far and no further he may come," they seemed to say.

As I rode with Mustapha up a long, winding pass on the outskirts of the range he pointed at the valley below us. "The Turkish Railway," he said solemnly.

A long line of laden camels wound slowly up the opposite side; for a full quarter of a mile they covered in single file the road winding up out of the valley. I pulled my horse up, and Mustapha stopped his alongside of mine. We both bent our heads forward and listened. The sound of their tinkling bells came faintly across the valley to us; the low, musical tones, the quiet measured movement, all was in keeping with the towering mountains and the still, clear air. Hassan rode up with the other men and joined us. He put his hands up to his mouth and gave a shrill, prolonged whistle in exact imitation of the engine we had left at Konia. The men looked at one another and laughed. Then they shrugged their shoulders and pushed on up the path.

Kisilkeul

CHAPTER 5

IN THE TAURUS

The Taurus range bounds in a semicircle the base of the plateau we had crossed. We had always been over 3,000 feet above sea-level, and now the heights of the Boulghar Dagh, as this part of the Taurus is called, rose high above us. The pass we were making for measured nearly 6,000 feet, and it looked low in the level of the range. After leaving Eregli we had made a very short day to Tchaym, some four hours' ride across a very barren stretch of country, with the snow mountains always in front of us. The next day was to be our last on the plains, for our destination was Ulu Kishla, well up on the hills. We had always great difficulty in decided what the stages of our journey to be. Maps and guide-books were out of the question, the Zaptiehs had only very vague ideas as to distances, and local informants were hard to understand.

Our destinations and the distances formed fruitful topics of conversation with the men, and generally ended in amicable wrangles.

X having made out from the khanji[37] that it was ten hours' ride from Tchaym to Ulu Kishla, asked Rejeb's opinion on the matter.

REJEB: Eleven hours.

MUSTAPHA: No, no, twelve hours. Tchaym to Ulu Kishla twelve hours.

X: No, no, ten hours.

REJEB AND MUSTAPHA (*in chorus*): No, no, the Pasha Effendi goes like the post.

X: It is ten hours; Rejeb and Mustapha go like camels. (*Roars of laughter.*)

REJEB: It is Mustapha and the little Pasha Effendi who go like camels, *javash, javash* (slowly, slowly).

*   *   *   *   *   *

---

[37] *Innkeeper.*

At Ulu Kishla we lunched in a huge khan, half in ruins, the size of which suggested the almost inconceivable size of the caravans which must have passed in better days. Here we decided to send the arabas on with half the escort, to await us at the next stage on the main road. Taking Hassan and Rejeb and one of the Zaptiehs with us, we branched off to visit Boulghar Maden, the highest village of the Taurus, noted for its silver mines. It was a rough ride up; now over chunks of rock, now along slippery grass slopes, then rock again and sliding bits of stone.

The hills shut is in all round until we neared the summit of the pass; here we reached a level above that of the heights we had skirted on the previous day, and we could see the whole long line of peaks ranging westward to the sea. In front of us the chain of mountains on the opposite side of the valley, whose heights looked down on the Cilician Plain, obscured the view in that direction. We rode towards them in a southerly direction and began the descent into the valley below. Boulghar Maden lies perched on the hillside, and stretches into the valley, so that standing outside the higher houses you looked down on a sea of flat roofs below you. Tall, thin poplar-trees, rising above the houses in rows, mark it out like a chess-board. The great hillside which backs it to the south and keeps off the sun till midday is scarred and marked with the entrances to the mines.

A small party of horsemen rode out of the town and came clambering up the hill towards us. Rejeb confessed to having sent a telegram from Ulu Kishla announcing our arrival to the Kaimakam,[38] and suggested that this was a deputation sent out by him to receive us.

Our spirits sank when we got near enough to distinguish European clothes on the leader of the party; we had been feeling ourselves tolerably safe from "agents commercials" at this altitude. Already from afar we were greeted in voluble French, which heightened our fears. The man was accompanied by a Turkish official and two Zaptiehs. The road was so steep that they dismounted and led their horses, both men and animals panting furiously. Our horses slid down the rough track, scattering the loose stones before them in all directions, and we joined the party below.

"Salutations from Monsieur le Kaimakam, and he bids you welcome to Boulghar Maden." The man took off his fez and bowed. We saw that he was a cut above the enemy we had been fearing and we felt happier.

---

[38] Provincial district governor.

He then explained that he was the representative in Boulghar Maden of our merchant friends in Constantinople, that he was an Armenian, that the Kaimakam was most perturbed lest we should not be received in proper manner, and had commissioned him, Onik Dervichian, at our service, to make all arrangements for our comfort. We were to be the guests of the Kaimakam, and he had caused rooms to be got ready for us in the house of a Greek family, where he would send down the feast he was preparing. But first he was expecting us at the Konak.

We all scrambled down the hill together and rode through the village to the Government buildings. A line of Zaptiehs was drawn up at the entrance and fired a salute as we passed. Then we dismounted, and were led through the usual mysterious curtain-hung doors into the Kaimakam's presence.

With our friend as interpreter, we felt sure the correct salutations would be delivered on our behalf. The health of the King of England and of our fathers, the great Pasha, was duly inquired after. Onik Dervichian then hustled us away to the Greek house. Here we found the women in a great state of perturbation and excitement. Our friend had sent down sheets for our beds, which were being constructed on the divans; would he show them where they were meant to go? Onik Dervichian threw off his coat and set to work on the beds himself, smoothing out the sheets with the fat Greek mother, who argued volubly with him the whole time. The two daughters of the house looked on and laughed; the little fat boy put his finger in his mouth and roared with laughter. We were to sleep indoors, but was it not with Government sanction and under Government auspices? This was quite a different matter from the Karaman experience.

Rejeb was having a good time recounting our adventures to his brother officers at the Konak, whither he had hastened back after seeing us safely landed at the house.

A messenger arrived from the Kaimakam – were the ladies ready for the feast? The dishes had been prepared and the servants were awaiting commands. We invited Onik Dervichian to stay and help us through; for this was not the first time we had experienced Turkish hospitality and suspected that our powers would be taxed to the full.

The little low table was brought in, and Onik showed the Greek mother how to lay it "à la Franka." The dishes began to arrive: curries and pilafs and roasted kid; dolmas and chickens and kebabs, and then the nameless sweet dishes which only Turkish cooks know how to prepare. At the fourth course I made an attempt to strike, but Onik Dervichian was shocked.

"Ah, mademoiselle, pour faire plaisir au Kaimakam,"[39] and he piled up my plate.

At the fifth course he anticipated me.

"Now, mademoiselle, pour faire plaisir au Kaimakam."

At the sixth: "Now mademoiselle."

"No," I said; "Kaimakam or no Kaimakam, I can't."

Onik Dervichian's face was a study.

"Mais, mademoiselle, *seulement* pour faire plaisir au Kaimakam."[40]

"You will have to do it all yourself, then," I said; "he won't know which of us has eaten it."

Onik rose manfully to the occasion and did his best. Only at the last dish did he lean back and, rubbing himself gently, murmur:

"Ah, mon Dieu! Et tout cela pour faire plaisir au Kaimakam."[41]

* * * * * *

There were "written stones," they told us, in this neighbourhood too; accordingly the next day we hired a native as a guide and set off in search of them.

A road roughly cut on the side of the mountain led out of Boulghar Maden down the valley to the east; below it, precipitous sides shot into the river's bed; above it, the range we had crossed the previous day towered overhead.

About a mile outside the village we turned off the road and wound up the mountain-side. Our horses pushed their way through the thorns and brambles which grew in rank profusion in and out amongst the rocky projections, until we had scrambled up to the summit of an outlying hill-top. Here a rocky projection stood out higher than the surrounding ones and shoed a flat face of wall to the midday sun. It was just possible to make out that there was an inscription on this face. We could see that the characters were cut in relief and not incised. The Hittites were metal workers, and this characteristic of their inscriptions no doubt arose from their habit of embossing metal. That they were particularly fond of silver is suggested by the fact that many of their treaties were inscribed on

----

[39] "Ah, Miss, to please the Kaimakam."
[40] "But, Miss, *just* to please the Kaimakam."
[41] "Oh God! And all that to please the Kaimakam."

tablets of that metal. Inscriptions are also found on stones near the Gumush Dagh, where silver-mines have been worked. We may presumably infer that the working of these mines at Boulghar Maden dates from Hittite times.

The view in front of us was one vast breaking sea of mountain tops; the snow-clad heights forming the crests gleamed in sudden flashes of sunlight, like the surf on a rising wave.

*   *   *   *   *   *

We left Boulghar Maden the next morning. The Kaimakam insisted that we should drive in his carriage down to Chifte Khan, the point on the main route where we were to meet our arabas. The road had only been made a few years and they were very proud of it; it was an exquisite road, we were told. The Kaimakam, we were also told, was very proud of his carriage. When he went to visit the mines he had it out; but his horse was led behind, for apparently his pride in it was not so great as regard for his own comfort, not to say safety. But here was an occasion for him to vaunt his pride with none of the accompanying dis-comforts.

It arrived: a springless box on wheels, a hard and narrow seat on each side, the top encased in a heavy roof, with rattling glass windows. The whole was painted a bright primrose yellow, and was drawn by two small Turkish horses.

X and I got in somewhat ruefully. It was a glorious, fresh, sunny day, and we were about to pass though some of the finest scenery of the Taurus district.

Onik Dervichian, who came to start us on the way, and Hassan sat inside with us. The Kaimakam had sent his servants to ride our horses; they and the Zaptiehs followed in a long string behind. For the first mile or two the road was fairly smooth; the vehicle lumbered heavily along; when it struck a loose stone the glass rattled furiously. We peered longingly through the panes, trying to catch glimpses of the surroundings. Pine woods nodded in the light breeze, but the noise drowned their whispers. Valley and hills streaked with laughing shadows beckoned to us to come out and look at them. Every turn in the road displayed new vistas of pine-clad slopes, shooting long tongues of green into the brown-red rocks.

As time went on the road became very rough; great masses of solid rock lay across it, and the carriage, lurching up over them, jumped us about on the hard seats and knocked us up against one another. Hassan took it calmly; he merely ejaculated "Aman" when an extra lurch sent him flying off the seat.

Onik Dervichian, however, was sorely troubled.

"Ah, mon Dieu!" he cried out at intervals, "et tout cela pour faire plaisir au Kaimakam."

At times it was not only painful but positively dangerous. The side of the hill would rise up in perpendicular walls of rock, and a narrow ledge of road, cut at right angles to it, barely gave width enough for the wheels to pass; a jerk in the wrong direction would have precipitated us down the rocks into the valley beneath.[42]

At such moments, Onik Dervichian, pink with terror and excitement, opening with difficulty the door at the back, would scramble out and follow on foot. The crisis over, his sense of humour would return and he would take his seat again, throw up his hands and ejaculate, "Et tout cela pour faire plaisir au Kaimakam!"

Then the carriage came to a dead stop. In front of us the ledge of rock had broken away, and two great boulders, fallen from above, blocked the narrow way.

X pointed down the steep precipice.

"Look, Hassan, look," she said, pretending to shudder.

Hassan looked.

"You go over, I go too," was his reply.

The driver got down and examined the obstruction. We all got out and examined it. The servants, leading our horses behind, dismounted and examined it. The horses stood with their noses on it and stared stupidly. Then everybody took hold of the wheels and lifted and shoved the whole concern bodily over. With the wheels on one side falling well over the steep side, the driver carefully engineered horses and carriages round the corner.

Bruised and exhausted, shaken in body and nerves, we were finally safely landed at Chifte Khan, where we found our men and arabas awaiting us. We flung ourselves down on the grass of a little orchard and thanked God for our delivery from the task of pleasing Kaimakams.

---

[42] **Author's note:** We heard later that the official who had been mainly responsible for the construction of the road met his death in this manner shortly after our visit.

Hassan stood over us and gazed thoughtfully at the yellow carriage standing by the roadside, while the driver devoured pilaf at the door of the khan.

"It is well now," he said; "we have pleased the Kaimakam."

The driver clambered up on the seat again and turned his horses' heads up the road we had left.

"Thank God," said Onik Dervichian, "that we are still alive to see it depart!"

*   *   *   *   *   *

From Chifte Khan we followed a good road, through the gorgeous vale of Bozanti, to Ak Kupru, where we pitched our camp for the night by the side of the river Chakut.

The weather broke suddenly, and we reached the place in torrents of rain.

The wind, tearing in gusts up the valley, shook the walls of the tent, and the ropes strained at the pegs. It drove the rain so hard against the white canvas that it forced the drops through almost against their will. It would have been so much easier for them just to run down the outside slope; but every force in nature seemed to be let loose to make the others worse. I moved my bed a little to try and get a clear course between two sets of drips. X surveyed my endeavours from where she sat, mechanically tilting a pool off her mackintosh rug when the accumulated drops showed signs of flowing in disastrous directions.

"It's no use trying not to be wet," she said, "when there is no way of keeping dry."

A new drip in the centre of the two original ones forced me to accept her philosophy, and we sat silently watching the scene outside. In front of us a bridge crossed the river and from it wound the road we should follow, zigzagging up until it disappeared round a corner. The Taurus Mountains rose like a black barrier in front of us, towering aloft in gigantic walls of rock; then layers of black forest and grassy slopes, then misty tops showing white snow where the clouds parted.

At their feet on the other side lay the great Cilician Plain, covered with yellow crops and brown earth and clothed with mud-coloured villages. On the other side also was the Mediterranean, blue and calm; there was sun and warmth and quiet, and people quietly basking in the heat. But on this side there was turmoil and cold and wet; the earth's face was hard and bare, and over it angry waters dashed in heedless, headlong fury; angry clouds overhead vied with them, shooting down relentless torrents of rain. On the other side, the blue Cydnus wound gently in and out through the level plain, and made marshes of its low banks as its waters lazily crawled round in long, curving loops. On this side the Chakut Su, goaded on by the maddened waterfalls, rushed its black waters impatiently against obstructing rocks, and turning white with fury foamed round them in angry swirls and dashed on through narrow gorges, lashing at their mocking, immovable walls.

*   *   *   *   *   *

We sought refuge in the khan for the evening meal, sharing the fire with ou own men and the Zaptiehs. Onik Dervichian, always merry and full of resources even on such an evening, made the men sit round so as to leave an empty space in the centre of the room. Then he produced a walking-stick and laid it flat on the ground.

"Stand up, oh stick!" he said, waving his hand and addressing it in Turkish.

Not a wound could be heard in the room; all eyes were fixed on the stick, which slowly rose and stood up, apparently of itself.

"Ha! Ha! went round the room in deep murmurs.

"Lie down, oh stick!" said Onik.

For full half an hour did Onik Dervichian, by means of a fine thread invisible in the dim firelight, go through a series of tricks with the walking-stick.

The men never moved or took their eyes off it for a moment, but showed no curiosity about it. They took it, like everything else, as a matter of course.

Hassan and Rejeb, two silent men, talked together the whole night long just outside our tent. What with this and the wind and the rain, and the flapping of the tent and the drips, which, coursing down the canvas, found new points of entry at every moment, we got but little rest.

Hassan greeted us with an anxious look next morning.

"You were not frightened in the night, I hope?" he said.

"No," I answered, "but we did not get much rest."

"Rejeb and I," he went on, "were afraid you would be frightened by the noises, and we talked all night to show that we were close at hand."

* * * * * *

The rain was still coming down in torrents. The khanji said it had come to stay, and he made a big fire, for he expected us to stay.

But X was inexorable. If the bad weather had come, she said, we must push on and get through the pass before we were snowed up; that would be worse than getting a wetting.

We had all got into the habit of doing what X told us; so Hassan went out grimly and packed up the sodden tents. "Aman, aman," he murmured now and again., "it is the whim of a woman." The arabajis dejectedly fetched out the horses, who drooped their heads in the rain and blinked reproachfully. "It is the will of Allah," said the men, and they loaded up the tents. The Zaptiehs and Rejeb fetched their horses and mounted. "It is the will of Allah," said also the Zaptiehs; but their Lieutenant held his peace. The rain might be the will of Allah, but to ride through it was the whim of a woman.

One by one we filed out over the bridge and up the winding road opposite. The arabas creaked; their sodden, wooden wheels squeaked as they lurched along after us; and the khanji stood in the doorway and wondered a little; then he went back to his fire. And we rode up and up silently. Thick rain mists shrouded the heights above us; gradually we reached the forest line, and the grassy slopes were level with us on the opposite side of the valley; and still we rode gently up and up. The rain lessened a little bit, and we raised our heads and told each other so. Onik Dervichian burst into song and made the hills echo with his ringing voice. Then the rain poured down again and we rode silently on into it.

A string of camels laden with merchandise met us just as we were crossing a track, which was being temporarily turned into the bed of a stream for superfluous waters. Their great hoofs slipped on the greasy, muddy sides, and each one paused in its mechanical march as its turn came to slide down the slippery bank.

"Y'allah, y'allah!" shouted the drivers, prodding them, and they resignedly put forward their great hoofs and floundered after their companions.

* * * * * *

The arabas made slow progress up the hill. We were getting wet through and decided to push on ahead with Rejeb and two of the

Zaptiehs. Onik Dervichian announced his intention of returning; he could reach Boulghar Maden that evening if he went no further, and he did not relish the idea of another night such as the one he had just spent.

At midday we arrived at Gulek Boghaz, where we found a new detachment of Zaptiehs awaiting us, for we had crossed the borders of the Konia vilayet and were now under the Vali of Adana. The men took our horses and led them into the stable. Streams of water ran off horses and men alike and collected in pools about the uneven floor. We brushed past the horses' heels and went on into the living room leading out of the stable, where a roaring wood fire blazed at the far end. We lay on the rough divan in the corner and thawed and dried. The men came in from seeing to their horses, and the fire drew clouds of thick steam out of their soaking clothes.

Rejeb sent out a Zaptieh to see if there was any sign of the arabas, but he returned with no news save that of increasing rain. We dozed round the hot fire; the Zaptiehs sat at the far end of the room and smoked; there was no sound but the beating of the rain outside and of the horses munching and stamping in the adjoining room.

More than an hour passed and still no sign of the arabas. We roused ourselves and conjectured all the possibilities of mishap: a wheel had come off; they had stuck in the mud; they had lost their way; the roads were too heavy for the horses after the rain; they had been attacked by brigands.

X, however, had her own suspicions. The arabajis had been very loath to leave Ak Kupru, and they knew of our intention of pushing on after the midday rest. They were dawdling on the road or sheltering somewhere out of the rain – we had passed an open shed – so as to ensure arriving too late for us to get on to the next stage.

She cast round for a method of outwitting them, and at last hit on one.

"You take two of the new Zaptiehs," she said, "and ride on with them to the next khan; I will wait here until the arabas turn up. We cannot leave you alone, and that will be an excuse to make the men come on."

I always did as X told me, and rose obediently from the warm corner. As I drew on my dry overcoat, hot from the fire, and looked out at the drenching rain, I felt strongly drawn in sympathy towards the arabajis. My horse was saddled and dragged outside, as loath to leave its companions as I was. I mounted, and bid farewell to Rejeb and Mustapha, who were returning to Konia. It was a tearful parting, for they had been with us now for eleven days and we were fast friends.

X stood in the doorway of the stable. "When you get to the khan," she called out after me, "say 'Atesh getir.'"

"All right," I said obediently. What 'atesh getir' meant I did not know; but X said I was to say it and that was enough. I was awfully afraid of forgetting it, and it was too wet to make a note, so I kept on repeating it at intervals. The Zaptiehs rode one behind and one before me, for the road was narrow. By and by we entered a defile not more than three or four yards across, where the rocks towered above us quite perpendicularly on one side and overhung us on the other; the road became almost coincident with the bed of the stream, and a large piece of fallen rock nearly blocked the way. The Zaptieh in front of me pointed with his whip at the rock just over our heads and also at the one fallen in the bed of the stream. The rain was pouring over the faces of both and obscured them, but it was just possible to make out that these also were "written stones," and I concluded that we must be riding through the famous Cilician Gates, round which the historical interest of the Taurus centres.

I repeated 'atesh getir' devoutly, and we hurried on. A two hours' ride brought us to a khan on the side of the road. One of the Zaptiehs galloped ahead to announce our arrival. The yard, ankle deep in mud, was full of dripping animals and men. The khanji helped me to dismount, and I said "atesh getir." He nodded and smiled and talked away at me hard as he led me into a vast room, perfectly bare, without even the usual divan. There was a wood fire burning up a tumble-down chimney in the middle, and they fetched me a little three-legged stool to sit on.

I thanked them and said "atesh getir" once more. The Zaptiehs came and turned my hat and coat round and round in front of the fire to dry, as an excuse to dry their own. A boy appeared with more logs of wood, which he threw onto the fire. Every now and then the khanji would come and jabber at me, and I smiled and nodded and said "atesh getir."

It seemed now to have become a sort of joke, for every time I said it the Zaptiehs and the other men laughed, and I caught the words repeated in their conversation amongst themselves. Every few minutes the boy came and threw more wood on the fire, then he would turn and ask me a question. I had nothing but "atesh getir" to say. But I felt a little nervous about the size of the fire. It was exceeding the bounds of the hearth, and I was afraid would soon burn down the rotten old place, for the heat as terrific. So I would point at the fire and shake my head when he threw on the logs, but he only grinned and went off to return with some more.

As I sat there waiting for X, I knew that I should always remember once for all that warmth is the one thing in the world which really matters. I was hungry, for we had not tasted much food that day. There as not much to sit upon, the stool had got very hard; the room was dirty and bare, and the smell of wet animals came up from the sheds below; but the fire made up for it all. One felt one had really got all one wanted, and I would not have exchanged that fire for the best of meals or the downiest of beds.

I was quite content to sit by it and wait for X for ever if need be. She had shipped me off with two strange men to a strange place with two strange words whose meaning I did not know – but there was the fire.

She arrived at last. The men all came tramping in with her and gathered round the blazing logs. Hassan fetched a bundle out of the araba, where the things had kept fairly dry, and made a seat for us. Constantin opened the last tin of sardines, and having demolished them we finished up with native bread and honey.

Hassan went out to look for a place to pitch the tent, and came back to say there was nothing but mud and water outside; should he put it up under an open shed just below the room? The floor was sodden with the smell of generations of passing caravans, but there seemed no other choice, and the tent was the only means of privacy.

Late at night a sudden thought struck me. I turned towards X and saw that she was awake.

"X," I said, "what does 'atesh getir' mean?"

"It means 'get a fire,'" said X sleepily.

*   *   *   *   *   *

We were awakened early by the departure, before sunrise, of the men and animals who, quartered in the yard of which our shed formed part, had not given us much peace during the night. We were not loath, on our part, to leave the tent, which had caught and retained the smell rising up from the sodden earth floor, until we were nearly choked with the fumes. It was still raining, and the peaks we had ridden under the day before were shrouded in mist. We kept on descending slowly, and by and by came out on a piece of open moor land. The sun began to appear again now. We were leaving it all behind, the cold and the wet and the storms of the hills. We were getting into the stillness of the plains again. The men took off their overcoats and rolled them up on their saddles behind. One by one we shed the wraps which had seemed so thin and inefficient under the snowy heights; they were getting unbearable here.

We expected at every turn to get a view of the sea. In spite of this, its first appearance was so sudden as to come as a surprise. We rounded a corner, and there it lay, as we had pictured it on the other side, still and bright, with no suggestion of storm and turmoil. It was not till that moment that we had the distinct feeling of having crossed the barrier. Each step forward now unrolled bit by bit the stretch of plain at our feet. There was the Cyndus winding its easy course through fertile lines as if there were no trouble in its rising waters. There was Tarsus, its flat roofs so sunk in gardens and fruit-trees that minarets and domes alone proclaimed the presence of a large town; and there, too, still faint and dim, but unmistakable, was the thin, moving line of smoke which proclaimed that we were nearing the land of the Monster once more.

Can it be that the day is not far distant when this one will join hands with its brother through the barrier we have crossed; and tearing through these silent plains and the rugged fastnesses of these great hills, destroy the mystery over which they have so long kept their sacred guard?

Hittite Inscription near Boulghar Maden
Mustafa. L. Jebb. Hassan. O. Dervichian. Rejeb.

CHAPTER 6

ROYAL PROGRESS

In the line of country stretching from Tarsus eastward to Urfa, there are a series of stations of the American Mission Board. Travelling as we did, in the direction of this line, we made these stations our stages, and hired horses and men afresh at each place.

At Tarsus we camped in the playground of the mission school, run by Dr. Christie. On the evening of our arrival out of the Taurus Mountains we were eating off spotless cloths with knives and forks, and were singing "Onward, Christian soldiers" with a hundred Armenian and Greek students.

The plunge out of rough travelling into these oases of civilisation is very sudden, and the contrast gives a full meaning to the advantages and disadvantages of both forms of existence.

The missionaries are the embodiment of hospitality. They know also what the discomforts of our journey have been, for they have gone through much the same experience themselves in order to arrive at their present homes; and so we find hot baths awaiting us and fresh supplies of hairpins; buttons are sewn on and clothes sent to the wash. We are started off on the road again clean and tidy, and with a linen bag full of home-made white bread, which will see us through many days. We also carry with us thoughts of the splendid work which is being done by them, and of the hardship and danger many of them have gone through in carrying out this work of education among these Eastern Christians. Gathered round the fire at night we would listen to tales of bloodshed and massacre, of domestic tragedies and individual heroism, of anxiety and hope, all told with that simplicity and quietness which bears the stamp of a personal experience which has come face to face with the real facts of life in a barbaric land.

But, once we were on the road again, we were glad to be there, glad to hear only the sound of the Turkish tongue; glad to lie out once more under the stars and eat our meal round the camp-fire at night.

Occasionally, too, we would get sudden reminders of the institutions we had left. A stray Armenian would accost us on the road with "Who are you? Where are you going? What is your name?" in the English tongue with a perceptible nasal twang.

We would have a momentary unpleasant sense of impertinent familiarity. Then one would pull oneself together and remember the doctrine of universal brotherly love which was being instilled into the minds of mission students, and would try hard not to mind when the individual would proceed to tell us that we were his sisters, that he loved us very much, and would we give him a subscription towards a harmonium for his church.

It was during this stage of our journey, also, that we were taken to be royalties and received at the larger towns with military honours. The idea seems to have emanated from Konia after our departure from there. We had left cards on the officials at the Konak. Now X's Christian name was Victoria, and her address printed on the card was Prince's Gate. To the Turkish mind this was conclusive evidence that she was a relation of the great queen, and instructions for our suitable reception were accordingly telegraphed on. At Adana we found ourselves indisputably "daughters of the King of Switzerland." It was of no use denying it: "naturally we wished to preserve an *incognito*."

We were summoned to pay a state visit to the Vali of Adana, who talked French.

VALI. Welcome; you have come.

X: Gladly we have found ourselves.

VALI: By your features and bearing I can see you are of the high aristocracy.

INTERPRETER: The ladies say that they also can see that you are most high and noble prince. (*Turns to us.* You said that, didn't you?)

VALI: And how do the noble ladies find Adana?

INTERPRETER: The ladies find Adana the most charming and delightful spot in Turkey.

X: Please thank his Excellency for sending the Zaptiehs to meet us; we were very pleased with them.

VALI: The ladies are most welcome; if they should wish for fifty Zaptiehs they would be at their service.

(*Mutual bows and salaams.*)

VALI: And where do the ladies intend to travel after this?

X: We wish to go by Aintab and Diarbekr to Baghdad. Does his Excellency think the road is safe?

VALI: Wherever the ladies go their safety is assured; they are the guests of the nation. There is not a governor in the land who has not received orders to look after them in every way.

(Further bows and expressions of thanks.)

VALI *(continues)*:   The ladies, however, will find it most uncomfortable travelling at this time of year. I would urge them to give up the idea of this journey.

X: We are obliged to your Excellency for your advice, but we do not really mind the discomforts of travel.

VALI *(turns to his Muavin, the* "Evet Effendi" *already mentioned).* This gentleman has just returned from Baghdad; he will tell you how very disagreeable the journey will be.

MUAVIN: Evet, Effendim; the road, of course, is safe as regards the tribes; but do not the ladies fear tigers and the many wild beasts which may be encountered?

VALI: I assure you it is not safe for you. You hear what this gentleman says. If the ladies will wait till the spring I will arrange for them to accompany my brother, the Prince of Kurdistan, in his expedition to the mountains.

Finding it impossible to dissuade us, the Vali then leads the way to the Council chamber, and makes X sit in the Presidential chair, where, he informs us, no one but the Vali has ever sat. He tells X she is now the Vali Pasha, this is her house, and he is at her command.

X promptly seizes the opportunity, and asks for favour to be extended to a friend we had mete in the course of our travels, who had been banished from Adana owing to having incurred the Vali's displeasure.

VALI: Because he was kind to you I will pardon him. He may come back if it will please the ladies.

X: We are much obliged to your Excellency.

VALI: Many people have spoken to me for him, but I would not listen; but to please the ladies I will now forgive him.

VALI: Will it please the ladies to dine with me to-morrow?

X: We thank your Excellency, it would give us much pleasure. But we must apologise for our clothes; we are travelling, and have no suitable dresses for dining with your Excellency.

VALI: *(waves his hand)*: The ladies must not mention it. I can see by their appearance how noble they are, and their clothes are therefore of no significance.

X: We will now say goodbye, and we thank your Excellency for all his kindness.

VALI: It is I that am indebted for your presence. Will you send my love to his Excellency your father? for his is also a Pasha, and we are brothers.

*   *   *   *   *   *

From Adana our next stage was to Aintab. Our luggage had now all to be conveyed on pack-mules, for we were going over tracks where wheels could not pass. This made our party seem larger, for we needed three mules for the baggage, and they were accompanied by three muleteers, who also looked after our horses and the mules ridden by our men. Our escort here consisted of four Zaptiehs and a Captain. This was the lowest number to which we had been able to reduce the fifteen men the Vali had pressed upon us. Nominally, they received no pay from us, but the "baksheesh" which we were expected to give them no doubt compensated for the arrears of pay from which the Turkish soldier invariably suffers.

*   *   *   *   *   *

We had parted with Constantin at Adana. He was not very suitable for really rough camping work, and we had asked the missionaries at Adana to recommend us a less civilised person, who would be more competent in tight places. Through them we engaged an Armenian, Arten by name. He could only speak Turkish, so we were now entirely thrown on our own resources as to Turkish conversation. X, however, had acquired quite enough of the language to be intelligible to Hassan, who interpreted our wants to the others.

We had hardly left Adana before incessant heavy rains came on, which turned the tracks into impassable mud swamps. We struggled on as far as Hamidieh where we sought refuge in the house of an Austrian widow who ran a large cotton mill in the place. For three days the rain came down in torrents. I went to bed indoors with fever; X, however, still preferred to sleep out in the tent in pools of water, which the men vainly endeavoured to keep out by digging trenches all round. On the third day we sallied out again and pitched our camp in the middle of a little green pasture fields in the bed of a lovely valley. Real milking cows strayed about in the little fields, and cocks and hens crowed and cackled familiarly close to us. This was a very different country from the one we had left. In spite of the fact that we had had to exchange wheels for pack-mules, it seemed far more civilised and cultivated. Trees and water everywhere gave one a feeling of life and growing things, unlike the stagnation of the waterless parts.

The Zaptiehs here, in greeting the town or village we were approaching, would always include in their praises its power of providing milk and eggs. Our former Zaptiehs had handed on to them that we had an insatiable desire for these luxuries, and they would use this as an inducement for us to come on to any place where they particularly desired to camp, a desire which generally arose from the vicinity of some large khan where they could spend a sociable evening.

"Oh, it is a lovely village; there are many eggs, there is much milk. The cows they are never dry, and the hens they never cease to lay. The chickens, too, they are not all legs, they are fat and juicy."

But we were getting out of the Cilician Plain and the Taurus was with us again. The branch which runs southwards from the main chain to the coast at Alexandretta, the beautiful Amanus range, still cut us off from the fertile plains of Mesopotamia.

For three days we rode on the outskirts, now climbing gentle, wooded slopes, now winding round a stony valley path; every evening we found ourselves at a higher altitude. We were getting into the Kurdish country. Their handsome women sat on the wide doorstep, which often formed the roof of a house beneath, grinding corn between two flat stones, or baking flat cakes of bread. They wore huge white headdresses, spotlessly clean, covered with silver ornaments, and short crimson zouave jackets. They were disposed to be very friendly, and used to come into our tent with offerings of oranges and eggs.

At one small village we came in for a Kurdish wedding. We happened to arrive just as the bride was being torn, struggling and weeping, from her father's house by the bridegroom and his friends. At first we imagined ourselves witnesses of some domestic tragedy, but we were informed that the display of grief and resistance was part of the ceremony. The bride was plastered over with ornaments and her head was bedecked with a great crown of feathers. She was put, still sobbing, on a white horse, and led away to the bridegroom's village, to the sound of bagpipes and flutes and the shouts and laughter of a hundred brightly dressed natives.

Then we had a precipitous ride up to Avjila, a wild, Kurdish village, 3,000 feet above sea-level. Hidden away amongst the rocks, a few score of shepherds tended their mountain flocks. From Avjila the road wound round grassy hills and through richly wooded slopes, where the crimson berries of the carob-tree hung over our path and the leaves of the golden plane dazzled our eyes in the sunlight. The woodman would be busy, too, and we would hear the sound of his axe in the pine-trees, or brush past a mule loaded with long, scratching bundles of firewood.

The Amanus range slopes very abruptly to the plain on the opposite side. It was not till the tenth day after leaving Adana, owing to our delay at Hamidieh, that we reached the gap in the trees at the summit of the pass which gives you one short glimpse of Aintab on the plain below. The muleteers stopped here to throw stones on a cairn beside the track and greeted the town with expressions of endearment and praise.

"Give us a coin for luck, Pashas," they said, "and that no evil may befall us in the place."

* * * * * *

We rode straight into the Mission compound at Aintab, and found ourselves at once in a very academic atmosphere. The mission has been established here over sixty years and has a brave show of buildings: a college with five professors, a hospital, an orphanage, a girls' and a boys' boarding school, and a church. The women missionaries are mostly graduates of some American University, and one feels rather behind the times in conversation. Their work fills one with respect; there is no proselytising about it; their idea is to civilise by education.

From Aintab it is two short days' journey to the Euphrates. We were now in a country of rich red soils covered with olive groves and vineyards. Near the villages small sized black and yellow cattle, brought in from the pastures, munched maize straw in the rough enclosures of reed or straw round the houses. The road was lined with signs of primitive cultivation and luxurious crops, evident even in these winter months. But the peasants seemed miserably poor. They were partners mostly of city men, who provided the seed and the stock and took two-thirds of the produce in payment.

The Euphrates is visible a long way ahead as it winds southwards. At first you see it as a streak of light across the plain; then slowly you differentiate the banks, the alluvial shores, the flow of the waters. Then

Birejik appears on the opposite side. Its houses, built on a limestone cliff four hundred feet high, rise up above the river tier upon tier; then the black marks on the face of the rock below the houses take on the shape of rock tombs. We descend a long, gentle slope towards the ferry, and find a few buildings on this side also.

We wait while great herds of oxen and sheep going to the market at Killis are ferried across in the great, clumsy, flat-bottomed, flat-sided boat, whose one end rises up in a high, curved keel. Then our turn comes, and one by one our horses plunge into thick mud and up the slippery end of the boat, which lets down to form a gangway. Surely they are not going to take us all at once? Our horses get jammed up tighter and tighter at the far end as each animal enters the boat; they begin kicking and biting at one another. We draw our feet out of the stirrups and hunch them up on our horses' necks to be out of harm's way.

There is no room now for the horses to kick – they are wedged too tight – but they struggle hard. We are shoved off the mud with long paddles, the cranky old boat lurches and wobbles, and we seem horribly near the water. The stream catches us and we are wafted down to a lower point on the opposite shore. Hassan, his great legs stretched up high and dry on his mule's neck, fumbles in his pouch and brings out the little bit of paper on which he writes down our expenses. He slowly puts on his spectacles and proceeds to write, holding the paper on the top of his thumb, and apparently oblivious of the struggles of his steed to kick the horse who is biting his flank behind. Then the gangway is let down and a terrific pandemonium ensues as each animal strives to get its saddle disentangled from the pack-saddle of its neighbour and jump ashore. The hindmost land on the first, who have stuck hopelessly in the mud, the muleteers hit and shout, and we climb slowly on to firmer ground and wind up the steep path to the street at the top.

The next day we ride slowly out of red soils and cultivation. The road is dangerous here, we are told; two extra Zaptiehs and a Yuzbashi are sent with us. We are in a desert plain again. A fearful storm of wind gets up and howls weirdly round us; the sun is getting low, and we have somehow missed the village where we should camp. The small cluster of huts that we pass or see in the distance have no accommodation for the horses, and the muleteers will not let them stand out on such a wild night. The Yuzbashi, who is a mysterious Kizil-bash with a long black beard, gets anxious and makes us push on hard. At last we reach another cluster of huts, where the shepherds are calling in the flocks. It is nearly dark and we can go no further that night. The muleteers are sulky about the shelter for their horses, so we take a house for the purpose and the family cram in somewhere else. The tents are pitched with difficulty in the teeth of the wind. All night long the Yuzbashi, apart from the other men, walks up and down and round and round our tent, muttering in his black beard.

* * * * * *

The next day we ride over a bleak, stony country, exposed to fierce lashes of wind and rain. Smooth faces of rock lie across the scarcely perceptible path, less slippery for our flat-shod horses than the mud in which they are embedded. We can see nothing ahead but low, rounded hillocks covered with broken stone. Suddenly yellow dogs spring from under our very feet and tall figures emerge out of the bowels of the earth. We have stumbled into the middle of a Kurdish village. The huts are hollowed out of the earth and roofed over with the stones which cover the whole ground.

The chief of the village welcomes us at the door of his hut, and we descend the dark passage, blinded by the smoke of the dried camel-dung fire. We sit on strips of felt, thankful to be out of the wind and the rain, and stretch our frozen hands and feet in the direction of the thickest fumes.

The tears run down our cheeks from the smarting of our eyes, but we hardly notice it, for it is heaven to be out of the bluster outside. Slowly our eyes get more accustomed to the darkness and the fumes, and we find the hut is full of arms and legs and motionless bodies, and gleaming eyes fixed on our eyes. But they are friendly and curious, and we feel at home.

Then we crawl out to where Arten has prepared hot Maggi soup in the tent. It has been impossible to pitch ours, but they have tied the men's little tent on to the big stones forming the wall of our house and the roof of another; we can see smoke mysteriously crawling out of the crevices of the ground at our feet. A sudden furious gust shakes the whole tent, and a Zaptieh's rifle, leant against the side, tumbles across and upsets the steaming soup. We pick our belongings ruefully out of the little trickling streams of thick liquid, and make a meagre meal by soaking bits of native bread in what remains. Then we get to bed as best we can, and all night long the wind howls and the tent flaps, and dogs sniff stealthily on the other side of the canvas.

*   *   *   *   *   *

A hard, broad, high-road runs ostentatiously some miles out of Urfa on the side which we were approaching. From the town it looks as if it were going on like that for ever. We stumbled suddenly out of our stony track on to it – where it ends abruptly in the middle of nowhere. The native does not walk on it much; he prefers the soft places at the margin, where the caravans, also shunning it, still make wobbly tracks. At once place, where it passes through a deep gully, the bank has been made up to make a more level run; but even here, as we rode over it, we noticed an old man and a boy driving a couple of mules, slowly crawling up the narrow path down below, which marked the line of the original road.

We could see Urfa some little way ahead of us, and wondered whether the missionaries would have heard of our arrival through their friends at Aintab. For the post travelled quicker than we did; it has passed us days ago, borne at a gallop by two mounted men.

"If ever we wanted cleaning up," I said, "it is at this moment; what with the rain and the mud and Maggi soup and camel-dung fumes, we are almost unfit to be seen even by a missionary."

The words were hardly out of my mouth when a party of some twenty mounted soldiers appeared in the distance. As they got nearer they fired off a volley into the air and ranged up in a line down the road. The Captain rode up and saluted us. There was no mistaking it. We were Royalties once more.

The Captain explained that the Governor was sending his carriage for their Royal Highnesses to make their entry into the town, and that he was expecting to receive them at the Konak. The carriage appeared up the road, a smart landau with red cushions, drawn by two splendid Arab horses, and followed by outriders in uniform.

In we got. It is very difficult under such circumstances to feel the least royal. We were only conscious of our dishevelled looks and dirty clothes. We made Hassan get in with us, for he always had the air of a prince. The driver cracked his whip and we went off at a great pace, headed by the Captain and Zaptiehs, including our own escort, and followed by the outriders. Borne along in the cavalcade came Arten on his mule, looking worse than any of us, in a seedy old black overcoat and a red scarf round his neck. The inhabitants of Urfa lined the streets and waved and cheered lustily. Flags and decorations were hung out. We bow hard – it is getting easier to forget our dirty clothes. I begin to wonder if indeed we are not Royalties. Why not? Hassan looks more princelike than ever, sitting opposite to us, very erect and very gravely gracious, acknowledging salutes.

At the main entrance to the town a smiling Armenian on a mule obstructs the way, and frantically waves a letter. The cavalcade stops, and riding up to the carriage he shoves a well thumbed envelope into our hands. It is from the lady missionary, they tell us.

"The Government," she writes, "are making great preparations for your entertainment, but I hope that you will not despise such hospitality as my house affords, and that you will spend your time in Urfa with me."

What are the Government going to do with us? Once more I become conscious of our outward appearance. We sent a verbal message to say we would call later, and then we are dashed on again; the smiling Armenian whacking his mule and trying to keep pace with the formal, solemn officers.

Finally we draw up in front of the Government buildings. A red carpet is unrolled before us, over which we walk gingerly in our muddy boots between rows of salaaming Turks. Hassan stalks after us, grave and dignified, returning salaams.

We are received by an official, corresponding to the Mayor of the town, and his secretary. X tried to deliver the sentences she had been concocting as we were driven through the streets, but the general bewilderment of the situation and uncertainty as to what we were expected to do was making intercourse more difficult than usual. We were almost at our wits' end when the Head of the Education Department appeared on the scene. He talked French fluently, and explained that rooms had been prepared for us in the building and that the Pasha Effendi expected us to be his guests. After giving us tea, and thereby showing familiarity with the customs of foreign Royal personages, they conducted us to the Vali. He was of a very different type from those we had previously seen. A young, pleasant mannered, intelligent Turk, he received us in a reserved, Western way, with no flowery greetings.

Hassan, in whose hands we felt safe as regards points of Turkish etiquette, had whispered to us that we had better camp outside as usual, for the Pasha's harem was absent at the moment and we could not therefore visit the ladies. For this reason we declined as best we could his offers of hospitality. The Head of the Education Department, instructed by his chief, said the Pasha Effendi was *"désolé"*[43] at our decision. Would we not reconsider it? We were causing his Excellency intense disappointment. His Excellency indeed looked crestfallen, and we would also have enjoyed being royally entertained, but we knew Hassan's judgment was never at fault and thought it best to be on the safe side. We were also conscious of the fact that in all probability this was but a polite form of espionage, for Urfa is the centre of the district where the worst Armenian massacres took place; European visitors, therefore, especially those who say they are "travelling solely for their health," in all the discomforts of winter, are suspected of being mere gleaners of damaging facts.

So we only accepted his Excellency's invitation to dine and, taking leave of him for the moment, were escorted to the Mission-house by the officers and Zaptiehs who had formed our escort, led by the smiling Armenian on the mule.

Thus ended our triumphal entry into Urfa, which some call the ancient city of Abraham – "Ur of the Chaldees."

A Windy Luncheon Place

---

[43] Very sorry

Our Reception at Urfa.

Jacob's Well. Harran

CHAPTER 7

HARRAN: A DIGRESSION INTO THE LAND OF ABRAHAM

"And Terah took Abram his son, and Lot the son of Haran his son's son, and Sarai his daughter-in-law, his son Abram's wife; and they went forth with them from Ur of the Chaldees, to go unto the land of Canaan; and they came unto Haran, and dwelt there."

And it happened that we, sojourning in this land, bethought ourselves of this journey of Abraham; we also, therefore, arose one morning and took two horses of the horses of Ur, and three Zaptiehs also upon horses, and we set our servants upon mules and departed across the plain to visit this Harran, the city of Nahor; and there came with us a lady of the American Mission and her servant Jacobhan and a young Armenian friend; and they also were upon mules. And we all rode together across the plain of Mesopotamia, of which it is written: "When corns comes from Harran, then there is plenty; when no corn comes, then there is hunger." And, even as we rode, the villagers were gathering in the barley, the clean white straw with its well-filled heads; and from time to time we came also upon a couple of sleek-skinned oxen drawing the wooden plough through the soil, making the furrows for next year's seed; and the soil, where it was turned, was of a rich red colour, beside the yellow stubble which was yet unbroken. The villages stood at the space of one hour's ride apart, and by the side of every village, by the side of their bell-shaped huts, we saw great mounds of such a size that they covered as much ground as the villages themselves; and each of these mounds was of a rounded shape. And, looking across the plain as we rode, as far as we could see we saw also many such mounds far distant upon the horizon.

And we said to Hassan, "Wherefore these mounds?" And he answered and said, "Behold, Effendi, you see these villages at the space of one hour's ride apart, each with its cornfields and its unbroken stubble, its pasture and its flocks; so it was in the days when Abraham and Terah passed this way, even as you and I are now passing; but these villages that we see of the bell-shaped huts were not the villages that Terah and Abraham saw, for they are now buried under these same mounds."

* * * * * *

Now Harran is eight hours across the plain from Ur; four hours we rode to Rasselhamur, a village by the side of a stream, where we ate and drank and rested awhile, and yet another four hours we rode from Rasselhamur to Harran.

Now consider the journey of Terah and Abraham. There were his women and his children, his camels, his man servants and his maid servants, his he asses and his she asses, his oxen and flocks of sheep; and they would cause him to delay on the road, for they cannot be over-driven; yet, even as the Arab tribes journey to-day, the caravan of Terah and Abraham would reach this Harran on the second day from the day they left Ur of the Chaldees; and the land of Canaan, the land towards which they journeyed, would still be far distant.

And we, marvelling, pondered on the words of the learned man who has said that the Harran of Herah and Abraham lies not here but at one day's journey from the city of Damascus.

But why should our souls be vexed over the words of learned men? For, whether it be that Terah stayed at this Harran, even the Harran we are approaching or whether he journeyed on day by day over the plains to the city of Damascus, for us, as our noiseless steeds trod the soft earth, these silent plains yet echoed with the tinkling of his camel-bells, the bleating of his innumerable herds, and the cries of his men servants and his maid servants.

* * * * * *

And the sun was yet high in the heavens when the walls of the city of Harran rose up before us; and as we rode through the fields without the city walls we looked, and behold there was a well in the field, and near it were gathered flocks of sheep and herds of cattle, for it was out of that well that they watered the flocks. And it was at the time of the evening, the time that the women go out to draw water; and we drew rein and watched them, even as Jacob watched Rachel. And these daughters of the men of the city were dark eyed and blue smocked, and they balanced their pitchers on their heads; and they went down into the well, down the slippery stones which were worn by the feet of the generations which begat Rachel and Rebekah. And on beholding the strangers some of them ran back, even as Rebekah on beholding the servant of Isaac, and told their mothers; and some of them, even as Rachel on beholding Jacob, emptied their pitchers into the troughs and bade us water our horses. And the herdsmen gathered themselves together and looked at us in silence; and their look was long and straight, like the look of those who have the habit of looking far, as far as where the sun sinks on the horizon; and we, wondering, held our peace. Of what availed it, that we should vex ourselves as to whether this indeed were the Harran where Terah stayed on his way to the Land of Canaan; here are we in the fertile regions, without the walls of a city, by the side of a well where the maidens come down to fetch water and where the flocks are gathered at the going down of the sun. And we bethought ourselves of those ancient days, and we said unto the herdsmen, even as Jacob said unto the herdsmen as they tended the cattle of Laban, "Whence are ye?" and they answered us saying, "Of Harran are we."

And looking about us we saw also the black tents, the good camel-hair tents such as the Arabs use, and they stretched out from the side of the watering-place; and on the ground in front of them the young children rolled amongst the bleating flocks and herds. And the shepherds, haughty and silent amongst men, walked to the right and to the left in and out amongst the bleating flocks and herds; and their cloaks were of sheepskin, long and squarely cut – they hung from their shoulders, reaching nearly to the ankles; and looking at them we thought of Abraham who had left this city for the Land of Promise, of Isaac who sent his servant to seek out Rebekah, and of Jacob who beheld Rachel even on this spot, and who tended the flocks of sheep and herds of cattle for her father Laban on these same fertile plains.

And as we tarried, marvelling on these things, there came out a messenger from the city, and he said, "Why standest thou without? We have prepared a house and a room for thy horses;" and turning our horses' heads we followed him and rode into the city.

Now the people of Harran number at this day over 4,000 souls of the Moslem faith; of men there are 1,900, and of the women 2,300. And some of them live in the city and some of them live without, in the villages. Now in the generations that have passed Harran was a great city of merchants; they went forth to Tyre, they were her traffickers in choice wares, in wrappings of blue and broidered work, and in chests of rich apparel bound with cords and made of cedar.

Harran lay also on the highway from the north to the Land of Canaan, on the highway from the west, from Assyria and Babylonia to the shores of the Cilician Sea; hence also was Harran a great fortified city. And looking about us as we rode through the city, many and ancient were the ruins that we saw, showing that Harran had been great indeed in her time; and there stands to this day a four-sided tower, the walls of which are perfect even now; and at the summit of this tower the bricks are exceeding hard and of a bright yellow colour speckled with black spots withal. And still riding in and out amongst the bell-shaped huts we came at last to the ruins of a great castle; and still riding, our good horses picked their way among the columns which were fallen, of which there were many, and under the massive stone arches which were not yet fallen.

And we came at last to an open space set right in the midst of the castle, and on this space the grass grew green all about in amongst the fallen stones. And, dismounting, we climbed yet a little way further until we came to a room in the walls, well covered in and newly built up with stones, so that neither wind nor rain could enter in. And at the door of this well-built room stood the Sheikh of the Beni-Zeid. And he welcomed us, bowing after the fashion of his country, and we also greeted him, bowing after the fashion of our country; and speaking to Jacobhan, for we knew not his language, neither did he know ours, he bade us welcome, and said that meat and drink would be laid before us, and provender should be found for our horses. And we rejoiced, for we were exceeding hungry. But the sheep was yet roasting on the great fire in a hut in the ruins of the castle below, and we said to Jacobhan, "Send these men away, for we are weary and would rest awhile." And, taking Hassan only with us, we climbed up to where the ruins of a great tower looked away over the plain, even the plain over which we had ridden and beyond also on the other side further than where we had ridden; and sitting down here we rested awhile; and down below the servants tended the horses, and Jacobhan and the lady from the American Mission unpacked the neatly folded bundles – and, further below, lay the ruins of the great city, and between them the little bell-shaped huts; but above us there was nothing but the sky. And looking away from the city, over the walls and over the plain even until the far horizon where the sun was now setting, for the day was far spent, I said unto Hassan; "What think you, Hassan, can this indeed be the city whence Abraham departed, and think you that this is the plain over which Jacob fled with his women and children, his men servants and his maid servants, his asses and camels, his cattle and his sheep?"

And Hassan knit his great brows and pondered awhile, and then he made answer: "What matters it, Effendi, whether this was the city of Abraham, and whether this was the plain over which Jacob fled before the wrath of Laban? Look down below and see these fallen ruins, which are all that is left of the great nations who conquered this city in the generations that have passed; and look down again, and you will see the miserable huts of the people who are left; what do they care for the great people who have lived and died within these walls where you and I are sitting? In a short time they also will be dead, and you and I will be dead, and therefore why should we care whether or not this was the city of Abraham? For, where Abraham is, there shall we soon be also."

*   *   *   *   *   *

As he was speaking we heard a shout from below, and looking down we saw Jacobhan beckoning to us, for the meat was now served. And we made haste to come down, and entered the room. Here on the earthern floor stood a well-filled bowl, all hot and smoking, for the meat was mixed with swelling rice well cooked in fat. Now Jacobhan fetched a little red carpet and spread it on the floor by the side of the bowl, and on this we sat, crossing our legs after the fashion of the country.

On one side of us sat the lady from the American Mission and on the other side sat Hassan.

And they brought us flat cakes of bread, which we dipped into the bowl and scooping out the rice and meat, we ate it thus, for we had neither spoons nor forks. And round about us as we ate sat the dark-eyed Arabs in the white robes. When we had finished eating, one of them rose and fetched a pitcher of water and another brought a bowl, and they poured water over our hands until they were clean. Then, making way for those who had not yet eaten, we caused the carpet to be spread on the far side of the room, where, lying on it, we watched the men eating, gathered round the bowl. Now, when all had finished, one removed the empty bowl and another fetched a brush and swept the floor, for much rice had been spilt about. Then each man folded his cloak together, and sitting back against the wall gazed at us out of the dark corners.

But Jacobhan the Armenian and his young friend, who was also of the same people, had no mind to sit thus quiet all the evening. For they were not as the Arabs are, content to smoke and make no sound. "Give us some song," he said to the assembled company, "that we may make merry, for the night is yet young."

And they pushed forward, out of the far corner, a young man who seated himself at our feet. After looking at us awhile, there being no sound in the room, he began to sing softly, and these are the words that he sang, as they were told to us later by Jacobhan:

"As the swallows from a far country winging their way from the north to the south, so you come to us for the day and on the morrow you are gone. You have the soft eyes of a dove, your hair is of silken threads, and your skin is as the soft skin of the pomegranate. Your little feet they are as the feet of swift gazelles – and they will bear you hence so that your going will be as swift and silent as your coming. Oh, may the snows come in the morning to stay your going away, for my heart will be sick when you are no longer here, and my eyes no longer behold your eyes. The land will mourn and be desolate; the herbs of the field will wither and the waters of the river will dry up in the wilderness."

When the words of the song were finished, a silence fell upon us all; and the silence was so long in the quiet stillness of night that many of us fell half asleep sitting there in the dark room. And one by one the company glided out softly into the night until we were left only with our own men. There numbered thirteen of us in all, and wrapping ourselves each in his blanket we lay on the hard floor until morning.

* * * * * *

Now on the morrow the son of the Sheikh came to us and said:

"My father sends you word he will be absent until evening, for he rode away this morning two hours before the rising of the sun. To-night, however, he prepares a feast for you and will return, Insh'Allah, with glad tidings for his people. He bids me meanwhile to ask of the ladies what their pleasure will be to-day, and I am at their commands."

And we said to the son of the Sheikh:

"Take now they father's lance and these our horses, and we pray thee call out one of your companions and let us see how the men of your country fight their enemies."

And the young chief, nothing loath, fetched the long spear which stood at the door of his father's house, and he mounted one of our horses; and he called another youth from amongst the many that would ride with him, and they rode out together into the field, without the city walls. And we climbed up upon the high walls of the castle which looked over the field that we should have the better view. And the two young men set their lances and rode their horses hard at one another, first to the one side and then to the other, now wheeling round, now holding the spear aloft, shouting with loud cries. And their cries were mingled with the cries of all the assembled company, and we also shouted with the others. For the space of an hour or more did they fight thus with one another until they and their horses were weary, but we were not weary with watching them.

*   *   *   *   *   *

Now as we were feasting that day at the time of the setting of the sun, the Sheik entered the room where we sat and greeted us.

And we, speaking through Jacobhan, said to him, "Has your business been well?" And he said, "Very well; to-day is a great day for myself and for my people."

And we said, "Tell us, we pray thee, how that is?" And he seated himself in our midst, and he told us how his tribe, the tribe of the Beni-Zeid, had offended the great Kurdish chief, Ibrahim Pasha, head of the Hamidieh, who lived not far distant at Viran-shahir. For some amongst them had stolen camels and mules belonging to his people. The wrath of Ibrahim Pasha was very great, and he caused his men to harass their men, and their beasts were no longer safe. Now the Sheik knew not which among his people were the offenders, but after a year had gone by there came certain of the tribe to him and said, "Behold these camels and mules, are they not those which were stolen from Ibrahim Pasha? We pray thee restore them that we may no longer live in fear of having ours stolen." Thus it was that on this same day the Sheik had ridden out with his men, driving these animals, and had delivered them back to the Pasha at Viran-shahir. Insh'Allah, now they would no longer live under fear of his displeasure. For those who offended Ibrahim Pasha had no mercy at his hands; but those who pleased him had much kindness shown to them.

And we and the whole company rejoiced together over the good deed that had been done that day, and there was much feasting and singing that night.

*   *   *   *   *   *

www.horsetravelbooks.com

On the morrow we mounted our horses once more and rode away through the bell-shaped huts and past the ancient ruins, over the rich plains, back again into the city of Ur, at the foot of the grey hills.

CHAPTER 8

THAT UNBLESSED LAND, MESOPOTAMIA

We were encamped in the khan, the native inn, at Severek, a dismal town in the dismal wilds of Mesopotamia ; the weather and the depth of mud made it impossible for us to pitch our tents outside, and the dirty, windowless sheds round the courtyard, which afforded the only sleeping accommodation, were not inviting, so we had fixed our tent in a covered passage by tying the ropes to the pillars supporting the roof. The Zaptiehs deputed to guard us for the night hung about the door, plying Hassan and Arten with questions as to our sanity. Why should two foreign ladies choose the depth of winter to travel between Urfa and Diarbekr along the caravan route which had been long deserted owing to the raids of the Hamidieh Kurds? I had often asked myself the same question during the last few days, but had not yet thought of an answer.

A pale, dishevelled young man in semi-European clothes slouched into the courtyard and joined the group. The Zaptiehs spoke roughly to him and he gave a cringing reply. He forced his way past them up to me.

"Moi parle Français,"[44] he said, with an accent corresponding to his grammar.

"So it seems," I answered, in the same language.

"To-morrow I travel with you," he went on.

"Indeed!" I answered, with more of interrogation than cordiality.

"Yes, you and my mother and sisters will go in an araba and I and my brother will ride your horses."

I made a closer inspection of the individual, but could detect no signs of insanity to harmonise with his utterances.

"Who are you?" I said.

"I am an Armenian," he answered. "I have a travelling theatre. We want to get to Diarbekr, and have been waiting here for weeks for an opportunity to join a caravan; the road is so unsafe that no one dares pass this way now, and if we do not go with you we may be here for months yet. You will start at seven to-morrow morning, and we shall do thirteen hours to K----."

---

[44] "Me speak French"

"We shall start when it suits us," I replied, and stop when we have a mind. We never travel more than eight hours, and shall not do the regular stages to Diarbekr. We shall be three days on the way."

"You must go in two days," he persisted; "we cannot afford to be so long on the road."

I began to get angry.

"Go away, strange young man," I said, "and don't bother me any more."

"I will have everything ready," he said.

"You may make your own arrangements for yourself," I rejoined, "if you wish to follow us on the road. It is a public way, but understand that we have nothing to do with you. We start when we like, stop when we wish, ride our own animals, and call our souls our own."

"My soul is Christian," he said anxiously, as I moved off; "are you not my sister?"

"Young man," I said sternly, "we may be brothers and sisters in spirit, and we may be travelling along the same road to heaven; but please understand that we travel to Diarbekr on our own horses and not in our sisters' arabas."

Next morning we left the khan at sunrise, and outside the town we found the whole of the Armenian theatre party ready to accompany us. A covered araba concealed the mother and daughters – we caught glimpses of tawdry garments and tousled heads. Another araba was piled with stage scenery and cooking-pots. Three or four men were riding mules and there were an equal number on foot. The men were dressed in flimsy cotton coats, showing bright green or red waistcoats underneath, and tight trousers in loud check patterns; they wore Italian bandit-looking hats, and their shirts seemed to end in a sort of frill round the neck, suggesting the paper which ornaments the end of a leg of mutton. The whole get-up seemed singularly inappropriate as they plunged ankle-deep through the mud. Patches of snow lay in the hollows of the road, a furious gale was driving sleet at right angles into our faces; it was bitterly cold.

We rode for hours through a dreary country of broken grey stones with no sign of vegetation or life of any kind. At last we arrived at a collection of tumble-down deserted huts, built of the stones lying round, and hardly distinguishable from the rest of the country until we were actually amongst them. We were cold and wet and had hardly come half-way to our destination, but as neither of us could stand long hours in the saddle without rest or food, we called a halt here to recruit. The Zaptiehs forming our escort begged us not to stop. They could not understand the strange ways of these mad foreigners, who not only travelled in such weather, but sat down to picnic in it instead of pushing on to the shelter of the khan at the journey's end. But we were inexorable, and they reluctantly fastened the horses on the sheltered side of the remaining walls, against which they stood with their backs tightly pressed, drawing their ragged coats closely round them.

The village had been but lately ransacked and destroyed by Ibrahim Pasha, the redoubtable Kurdish chief; he was still abroad in the neighbourhood, and any detention on the road increased the chances of our falling in with him or some of his stray bands. The knowledge of this and the discomforts of the journey made the men fretful and anxious.

We picked out the least dilapidated looking house and clambered over fallen stones and half-razed walls until we found a roofless room which boasted of three undestroyed angles. In one of these the cook tried to make a fire with the last remnants of charcoal; we huddled in another to avoid, if we could, the blast which rushed across the broken doorways and whistled through the chinks of the rough stone walls. The arabas, accompanied by their bedraggled followers, rumbled heavily past us; the noise gradually died away as they disappeared in the distance; desolation reigned on all sides; the howling blast moaned weird echoes of destruction round the ruined walls.

We managed to boil enough water to make tea; and then, yielding to the men's protests, we mounted and rode on. Hour after hour passed; the driving wind hurled the hailstones like a battery of small shot right into our faces; the rain collected in small pools in the folds of my mackintosh, and I guided their descent outwards and downwards with the point of my riding-whip. The drop which fell intermittently from the overflowing brim of my hat had been the signal for a downward bob to empty the contents, but now the wet had soaked through and I let it run down my face unconcernedly. We were a silent and melancholy band. X rode in front with her chin buried in her coat collar; her face was screwed up in her endeavour to face the elements; the hump in her shoulders betokened resigned misery. The soldiers' heads were too enveloped to allow any study of their expressions, but the outward aspect of their bodies was a sufficient indication of their inward feelings; the very outline of their soaked and tattered garments bespoke discomfort and dejection.

The pale-faced little officer, straight from the military school at Constantinople, urged his horse alongside mine. "Nazil?" he said. It was a laconic method, essentially Turkish, of saying "How?" *i.e.,* "How are you?" "How's everything?" "Hasta" (ill), I answered. "Amān," he groaned. "Kach Saat daha?" I asked (how many hours more?). "Jarem Saat, Insh'Allah. Bak, khan bourda" (Half an hour, Insh'Allah. Look, the khan is there).

I raised my head to follow the direction of his pointed whip; the jerk sent a trickle of wet down the back of my neck and the rain blinded my eyes. I dropped my head again. It was not worth while battling with the elements even to look upon our approaching haven of rest. I was too familiar with the aspect of the country to be particularly interested in the scenery; it had not altered at all for many days. If you looked in front you saw an endless tract of slightly undulating country, the surface of which was a mass of stones; there were stones to the right, there were stones to the left, there were stones behind; you rode over stones, slippery, broken, loose, sliding stones; and now stones, stones of hail, were hurled at you from the heavens above. The very bread we had eaten for our midday meal seemed to have partaken of the nature of the country. I had accidentally dropped my share, and had to hunt for it, indistinguishable among the other particles on the ground. We were rapidly turning into stones ourselves. One seemed to be riding on a huge, dry river-bed, the waters of which had been drawn up into the heavens and were now being let down again by degrees.

The officer gave an order to a Zaptieh. The man tightened the folds of his cloak round him, wound the ends of his kafiyeh into his collar, and, digging his heels into the sides of his white mule, darted suddenly ahead. The crick in the back of my neck made it too painful for me to turn my head to look, but this must mean that were near the khan and that he had gone on to announce our arrival. Visions of being otherwise seated than in a saddle faintly loomed in my brain; I hardly dared wander on to thoughts of a fire and something hot to drink. We turned at right angles off the track and plunged into a bed of mud, which led up to the door of a great, square, barrack-looking building with a low, flat roof and a general air of desolation. The Zaptieh stood grimly at the door. "Dollu" (full), he said. Nevertheless we forced our way through the narrow entrance and found ourselves in the usual square courtyard lined with dilapidated sheds. The whole enclosure, inches deep in mud and indescribable dirt, was crowded with camels and mules and haggard, desperate-looking, shivering men, with bare legs and feet and dripping, ragged cloaks. The officer laid about him right and left with his riding-whip and ordered up the khanji (the innkeeper).

"You must find room for us," he said; "I am travelling with great English Pashas." The khanji waved his hand over the seething, jostling mass of men and animals. "Effendi," he said, "it is impossible; I have already had to turn away one caravan. If we made way for the Pashas there would still be no room for their men and horses. But they are welcome to what shelter there is."

We gazed with dismay at the reeking scene.

"How far is it to the next stage?" asked X.

"Two hours," was the answer.

"We had better get on to it, then," she said, and turned her horse's head outwards. We followed in silent dejection. The wretched animals, who had been pricking their ears at the prospect of approaching food and rest, had literally to be thrashed out on the road again. We waded back through the mud and turned our faces once more to the biting blast and driving rain.

The track we followed was apparent only to the native eye; to the uninitiated we seemed to be going at random amongst the loose stones. One had not even the solace of being carried there by an intelligent and sure-footed beast who could be trusted to pick its own way. The hired Turkish horse has a mouth of stone and his brain resembles a rock. Left to himself he deliberately chooses the most impossible path, until it becomes so impossible that he stops and gazes in front of him in stupid despair, and you have to rouse yourself into action and take the reins in your own hands once more. His one display of originality is a desire not to follow his companions, but to veer sideways until you are in danger of losing sight of the rest of the party and become hopelessly lost off the track. I struggled to keep straight and in pace with the others. Weariness and disgust had made my stupid animal obstinate and more stupid, and I finally gave in and lagged behind, letting him go at his own pace. The officer pulled up and waited for me.

"We must push on, Hanum" (lady), he said, "or we shall not get in by sunset."

"My horse is tired," I answered, "and I am tired," and I showed him my broken whip. It as the third I had worn out on this obstinate brute's skin.

He called back one of the Zaptiehs and muttered to him unintelligibly in Turkish. The man crossed to the other side of the road, and he and the officer, one on each side, urged my horse on with continual blows behind. I dropped the reins almost unconsciously, and, all necessity for action of mind or body being removed, sat between them numb, petrified, and hardly conscious of my surroundings.

Pitter, patter came the rain on the saddles; click, clack went the horses' hoofs on the stones; clank went the captain's sword; whack came the men's whips behind; each noise was hardly uttered before it was rushed away in the driving wind.

Expectation of something better had made the present seem unbearable in the earlier part of the day; now that one no longer held any hope of alleviation, the general misery had not the same poignant effect; or was it that weariness from long hours in the saddle, and the pains consequent on exposure to cold and wet, had numbed one's senses? Jog, jog; one was being jogged on somewhere, one did not care where and one did not care for how long.

* * * * * *

The men were saying something; the sound fell vaguely on my ears, but the meaning did not travel on to my brain. Then we stopped suddenly and the jerk threw me forward on the horse's neck. I felt two strong arms round me and was lifted bodily off the horse. "Brigands at last," I thought vaguely; "well, they are welcome to all my goods as long as they leave me to die comfortably in a heap."

"Geldik" (We have arrived). It was Hassan's voice; we were at the door of the caravanserai. He deposited me on the floor of a bare, black hole on one side of the courtyard and carefully arranged his wet cloak round me. I was conscious of a motionless heap in the dark corner opposite.

"X?" I muttered interrogatively.

"Hm," came from the corner.

"Hm," I responded.

The muleteers came and flung the dripping baggage bales promiscuously about the floor. We were soon hemmed in by sopping saddles, bridles, saddle-bags, wet cloaks, and muddy riding-boots.

Hassan sat on a pile of miscellaneous goods, smoking reflectively and giving vent to great groans as he looked from one corner to the other, where each of his charges lay in a heap. The cook cleared a small space in the middle of the room and tried to make a fire with dried camel-dung, the only fuel to be had. The whole place was soon filled with suffocating smoke; there was no window, no hole in the roof to let out the fumes; We opened the door until the fire had burnt up, and a sudden gust of wind tearing round the room and out again drove the smarting fumes into our eyes, causing the tears to roll down mercilessly.

Another caravan was arriving, and the animals passed through the narrow passage by our open door, on into the courtyard beyond. Mules bearing bales of cloth or sacks of corn; camels laden with hard, square boxes stamped with letters that suggested Manchester; donkeys carrying their owners' yourghans, quilts which form the native bed, damp and muddy in spite of the protection afforded by a piece of ragged carpet thrown over them, the whole secured by a piece of rope which also fastened on a cooking-pot and a live hen. The procession wound slowly through to the sound of tinkling bells, until the whole caravan had entered the enclosed yard, which now presented a chaotic scene of indescribable crush and dirt.

Kneeling camels, waiting patiently for the removal of their loads, looked round beseechingly at their own burdened backs; mules munched the straw out of each other's bursting saddles; slouching yellow dogs sniffed about the fallen bundles. The theatre ladies, in gaudy plushes and silks covered with tinselled jewels, sat about on the piles of stage scenery flirting with the young men in the bright waistcoats; stern Mahomedans wrapped in long, severe cloaks, gazed with contemptuous disgust at these unveiled specimens of the unworthier race, while the short-coated and less particular muleteers and menials stared at them with open-mouthed, grinning wonder.

Our little captain sat unconcernedly in a sheltered corner, deftly rolling up, with his delicate, finely shaped fingers, endless piles of neat cigarettes; a Zaptieh, with his face to the wall, bowed and murmured over the evening prayer. Each pursued his reflections and employments with that disregard of his neighbour'' presence which is so impressive in any crowd in the East.

Apart from these by-scenes, the dominating human note was one of quarrel, in strange contrast with the silent waiting of the dumb animals, for whose shelter in the limited accommodation their respective owners were fighting with clenched fists and discordant, strident voices. Then the hush of mealtime falls on all; men and animals, side by side, are busy satisfying their bodily needs. It is a strange mingling of men and beasts, where the man, in his surroundings and mode of life, savours of the beast; and the beast, with his outward aspect of patient and beseeching pathos, is tinged with human elements.

We had shut the door on the scene, finding smoke preferable to cold and publicity. It suddenly burst open, and a camel's hind-quarters backed into the room, upsetting the pot of water on the fire. We had been anxiously waiting for its boiling point with the open teapot ready to hand. The men threw themselves upon the animal and pushed it back; they pushed and hit and swore; it was ejected; the fire hissed itself out and the smoke cleared. A dishevelled looking official in uniform peeped through the door: "The Governor's salaams, and do the Princesses require anything?"

Hassan courteously returned his salute. He was now seated cross-legged by the dying fire, sorting nuts from tobacco which had been tied up together in a damp pocket-handkerchief. With the air of a king on his throne he graciously waved his hand towards a slimy saddle-bag; "Buyourun, Effendi, oturun" (Welcome; sit down). The man sat down, carefully drawing his ragged cloak round his patched knees.

"The ladies' salaams to his Excellency; they are very pleased for his inquiry and send many thanks. They have all they require."

The quiet dignity of Hassan's appearance and utterances seemed to dispel any sense of incongruity the visitor might have entertained as to the limitation of our wants and the methods of our Royal progress; he merely thought we were mad.

He departed, no doubt to glean information from the more communicative members of our escort. The cook came in with a pleasing expression.

"What will you have for supper?" he said.

"What can we have?" we answered, with the caution arising from long experience of limited possibilities.

"What you wish," he said, with as much assurance and affability as if he was presenting a huge bill of fare. I knew what one could expect in these places.

"Get a fowl," I said.

"There is not one left here," he answered.

"Eggs, then," I suggested, with the humour of desperation.

"No fowl, how eggs?" he answered with pitying superiority.

"Well we will have what there is," I said faintly.

"There is nothing," he answered cheerfully.

"Miserable man!" I said, "how dared you begin by holding out hopes of lobster salad and maraschino croûstades?"

Was there nothing left of our stores? I rummaged in the box which held them. Everything was wet and slimy; a few bars of chocolate were soaked in Bovril[45] emanating from a broken bottle; a sticky tin held the remains of pekmez, a native jam made with grape juice; two dirty linen bags contained respectively a little tea and rice; a disgusting looking pasty mess in what had once been a cardboard box aroused my curiosity. Could it be – yes, it had once been, protein flour, "eminently suitable for travellers and tourists, forming a delicious and sustaining meal when no other food is procurable." It had been the parting gift of our respective mothers, along with injunctions to air our clothes. I calmly thought the matter out.

"X," I said, "will it be best to eat chocolate with the Bovril thrown in, or to drink Bovril with the chocolate thrown in?"

"Don't talk about it," said Xo, "cook everything up together, and let us hope individual flavours will be merged beyond recognition."

We put a tin of water on the fire and threw in the rice and protein. The chocolate and Bovril were added, after carefully picking out the bits of broken bottle. Hassan fumbled in the wide leathern belt which he wore round his middle; the space between himself and the belt served as a pocket where he carried all his goods. With an air of unspeakable pride he produced a small, round, grimy object, which he held aloft in triumph.

"Soan?" (Onion) we all shouted simultaneously in excited, ungovernable greed. He nodded ecstatically, and pulling the long, dagger-like knife out of his belt, he proceeded with great deliberation to cut the treasure into slices, and let them fall one by one into the bubbling pot. The cook sat stirring it all together with a wooden spoon; he kept raising spoonfuls out of the pot, and as the thick liquid dribbled slowly back again he murmured complacently:

"Pirinje war, chocolad war, Inghiliz supper war, soan war, su war" (There is rice, there is chocolate, there is English soup, there is onion, there is water).

When the moment of complete mergence seemed to have arrived he lifted the pot off the fire and placed it between us. "Choc ehe, choc"

---

[45] A savoury hot drink.

(Very good – very), he said encouragingly, and handed us each a spoon. X swallowed a few mouthfuls.

"We must leave some for the men," she said, with a look of apology as she put the spoon down. She picked up a piece of leathery native bread and started chewing it.

"Try a cigarette," I said sympathetically. I could not find it in my heart to tell her the history of that identical piece of bread, which I had been following with some interest for several days. It was always turning up, and I recognised it by a black, burnt mark resembling a figure 8. It had first appeared on the scene early in the week; we had been enjoying a lavish spread of chicken legs and dried figs, and with wasteful squander I had rejected it as being less palatable than other bits. The men had tried it after me, pinching it with their grimy fingers, but being unsatisfied with the consistency they had thrown it, along with other scraps, into a bag containing miscellaneous cooking utensils. The next day it had appeared to swell the aspect of our diminishing supply and had been left on the ground. But as we rode away Hassan's economical spirit overcame him; he dismounted again and slipped it into his pocket, where it lay in close proximity to various articles not calculated to increase the savouriness of its flavour. I was determined to see its end, and when X laid down half – no doubt meaning it for my share – I threw it on the fire.

"It's hardly the time to waste good food," said X.

The cook picked it out, blew the ashes off, and rubbed it with his greasy sleeve. He offered it to me.

"Eat it yourself," I said magnanimously, "I have had enough." But he wrapped it carefully in one of the dirty linen bags and put it on one side.

"Jarin" (to-morrow), he said.

And so we sit; a mass of wet clothes, saddles, cooking-pots, remains of food, ends of cigarettes, men; unable to move without trading on one or other of them; tears rolling down our cheeks from the fumes of the fire, thankful we cannot see what dirt we are sitting in or what dirt we have been eating.

We roll our rugs round us and lie on the sodden earth floor. Hassan turns the men out and stretches himself across the doorway. Dogs moan, men snore; outside the storm rages unceasingly.

In the middle of the night I wake with a start; something had hit me on the face and now lay in the angle of my neck. I knew what it was; a piece of plaster had fallen off the walls, and the plaster, like the fuel, is made of dried camel dung.

"The age and time of the world is as
it were a flood and swift current,
consisting of all the things that are
brought to pass in the world. For as
soon as anything hath appeared and is
passed away, another succeeds and that
also will presently be out of sight."

PART II

DOWN THE TIGRIS ON GOATSKINS

CHAPTER 9

AFLOAT

We rode into Diarbekr on Christmas Day, arriving just in time to share the plum-pudding at the house of Major Anderson, the Vice-Consul.

They say of Diarbekr that its houses are black, that its dogs are black, and that the hearts of its people are black – and they say so truly. The first moment that one catches sight of it in the distance one is impressed by the blackness of its walls, built of a black volcanic stone. When one gets inside, the people look dourly at one, and the Zaptiehs ride closer together. But this may be because they have no other choice, the streets being often only four feet across. It is quite easy to cross a street from on high by jumping from one roof to another; and it is certainly cleaner, for down below we are ankle deep in mud, in which great boulders are embedded – relics, presumably, of ancient pavement or fallen houses.

If you want to take the air at Diarbekr you walk round and round the flat roof of your house and watch the life of your neighbours on adjoining roofs; or else, closely accompanied by armed cavasses[46], you ride out into the bleak, stony country, and follow up some mud stream in the hopes of getting a shot at wild duck and snipe.

*   *   *   *   *   *

A week later we sat on the banks of the Tigris by the Roman bridge which spans the river just below the black walls of Diarbekr. The raft on which we were about to embark was moored to the shore and the men

---

[46] Armed porters

were loading our belongings. A dancing-bear stumped about to the tune of a bagpipe made of the skin which answers so many purposes in the East. When inflated they can be used either for carrying water for people inside, or for carrying people on water outside. We were using 260 of them in this latter way. They were tied on to two layers of poplar poles put crossways, forming a raft about eighteen feet square. At one end were two small huts made of felt stretched across upright poles; the fore end was weighted down with bags of merchandise laid side by side across the poles to form a rough floor.

The Kalekjis (raftsmen) waded in and out with a great seeming sense of hurry but without appearing to accomplish anything.

"Can't you hurry the men up?" said X.

"No," I answered, "we are in the East."

"You might try," she said; "you always leave me all the talking to do."

"They do not understand my Turkish," I said apologetically.

"It would not take you long to learn enough for that," went on X.

"I do know the swears," I answered humbly, and I stood up amongst the men and delivered myself of them.

"Quick! Quick! The Pasha is angry!" said the men.

Our crew had assembled; there were our two personal attendants, Hassan and Arten. Hassan was now our interpreter, for, although he could only talk Turkish, he could interpret our signs to other Turks until we learnt the language. Arten, we found, was more Armenian than cook, and sang us Christian hymns in his native language when we felt low after meals.

Then there were two kalekjis in charge of the raft; they were Kurds; we had yet to discover their qualifications. Two Zaptiehs forming our escort made up the number. We did not yet look upon them as individuals, but as part of an abstract regime in the country with which we now felt tolerably familiar; the outward aspect of it was a ragged uniform and an antiquated rifle, which served many useful purposes but had forgotten how to eject bullets.

"Hazir dir, hazir" (Ready, ready), shouted the kalekjis. The owner of the dancing-bear hurriedly thrust his fez under our noses.

"Don't give him anything," I said, "a bear has no business to be dancing in this country; he ought to be trying to eat us in a cave."

"The demoralisation of the bear comes from the West," said X, who was studying the primitive habits of the natives, "we must pay for it."

"Does this abuse of the hat emanate from the same source?" I inquired, as she dropped a coin into the fez.

"That would be an interesting point to inquire into," said X, and she made an entry in her notebook.

The worst of X was that you never knew whether she was laughing at you. It is a most uncomfortable position, which men as a rule resent. But I was another woman, and took it philosophically, especially as X accused me of the same failing, and we never see ourselves as others see us.

We boarded the raft: the coil of rope which had fastened it to the shore was hauled in, and we drifted slowly out into the centre of the muddy stream. We were followed by another raft, laden up with bags of merchandise, which was coming with us to share the protection of our escort.

We went into the sleeping-hut to ascertain the length of its possibilities. Boards had been nailed across the poles to form a floor, and on this was spread a thick native felt mat. Dwellers on land little know the feeling of luxury recalled to my mind in writing these words: the luxury of being able to drop all the things addicted to dropping, especially when dressing, with the knowledge that they would not disappear for ever in the depths of the Tigris waters; the luxury of being able to walk in the ordinary biped method of placing one foot in front of the other.

This was not the case in the open part of the raft, where the floor, formed of poles and sacks, exhibited a network of rounded interstices. The water gurgled and spluttered, below them: one's foot invariably slipped into them when cautiously manipulating a journey across the raft by hopping from a slippery pole to a sliding sack; and unattached articles dropped through them on to the skins below, and were occasionally rescued in a dripping condition before they were washed away altogether. The water showed spiteful discrimination in its washing-away proclivities. I recall certain chinks in the more roughly boarded floor of the hut where we had our meals, through which the cook had a habit of brushing his cooking refuse, and where, if one was rash enough to look, there could be seen an accumulation of tea-leaves and bones and bits of decaying delicacies which one associated with meals of past ages.

The felt walls of the hut were lined on the inside with white cotton tacked on the poles. There were two small glazed windows, one of which opened. The door was a single width of felt tied with tape. There was just room inside for our two camp-beds – with a space between, which would admit of one of us occupying it at a time. At the foot of each bed stood our two Eastern sacks, which contained all our worldly goods.

I feel constrained, on mentioning this form of baggage, to say a word of warning concerning it. In one sense it is easy to pack, because you need not fold anything up, but can simply stuff it in and give the bag a shake; and it is easy to unpack, if you do it in a wholehearted manner – standing in the centre of a large room or vast desert where you can turn it upside down and spill everything out on the ground. But under ordinary circumstances the bundle of hay with a needle in it is nothing to this sack with your clean handkerchief in it. X and I had a mutual understanding, owing to which we never attacked a sack while the other was within hearing; but whenever she appeared in a half-fainting condition and asked the cook why on earth tea was so late, I knew what she had been doing. She had asked me, as a personal favour (the only one I've ever known her ask) not to attack my sack in the morning, because it was a pity to have the whole day spoilt, and if I did it in the evening to go to bed before she did.

But to return from this digression. Having examined our quarters, I arranged a rug on the open part of the raft and sat down to take in the surroundings.

Arten was unpacking cooking-pots in the second hut, the other men sat about on the sacks smoking silently. The boatmen sat on a pile of sacks in the middle and manipulated the oars which served to steer the raft and keep it in the fast part of the current. The oars consisted of single young willow-trees, with short strips of split willow bound on one end with twigs, forming the blade; they were tied on to rough rowlocks made of twisted withies wound round heavily weighted sacks.

The Tigris at this point is singularly hideous. There was not a single blade of vegetation to be seen anywhere; the country was a stretch of mud hills and stony desert, and the mud banks of the river were only relieved by the hosts of water-birds that darted in and out or waded in the shadows. The high black escarpment, crowned by the massive black walls of Diarbekr, and fringed by a swampy tract of willow gardens, rose up sharply above the mud flats. As we were carried along the winding course of the sluggish river a higher mud bank shut it altogether from our view, and I felt we had severed that link with the world which one feels so strongly on arriving in any town of a distant uncivilised land, where a European mail occasionally arrives and a telegraph wire eliminates the isolation of its natural position.

We were drifting into an unknown world at the mercy of these unknown Kurds. We were alone with the birds and the mud banks and the rippling waters.

Our Raft below the Roman Bridge. Diarbekr.

CHAPTER 10

HELD UP

The snow-capped mountains of Kurdistan were just visible on the horizon line; toward them rolled wave after wave of low brown tracts of land, utterly destitute of any form or sign of life. Behind, as in front, like the coils of a shining serpent, wound the thin white line of the Tigris bed, the one response to the light overhead, imparting a sense of wearing pursuit in its never-ending course. Fresh coils unwound themselves ahead as we toiled after new yet familiar spots on a never changing horizon. Now and then the raftsmen dipped their oars quietly into the water, and with a few strokes twisted the raft into the straightest part of the river; otherwise, we were helpless, in the hands of an arbitrary current which made us bide its time as it slunk pensively round unsuggesting corners, or sped us faster when it gurgled impatiently over a long reach, where grey rock vied momentarily with the endless grey mud.

We had given ourselves up completely to Time, and sat all day contemplating one stretch of bank after another as we swirled along. The ripple of the water, the intermittent splash of the oars, the crooning songs of the raftsmen all added to the sense of drowsy contemplation already established by the surrounding view. Everything was in contemplative harmony; isolated herons fished from slippery stones, gazing with such intentness into the passing water that they hardly deigned to raise their heads towards us, and, if they had deemed it wiser to move out of our way, they would do so by a very deliberate walk on to the shore, after fixing a resentful, half-wondering stare upon us.

Flocks of black ducks, suddenly disturbed round a corner, would rise in silent indignation, and with a sharp whirr would pass over our heads and drop quietly down on to the waters behind, smoothing out their ruffled plumage.

Fat, ungainly penguins, sitting in white rows, like surpliced choirs, on the shallow shore, would scuttle further back along the mud flat, and taking up attitudes of doubtful interrogation would stare us out of countenance.

www.horsetravelbooks.com

One and all they condescended to no notes of fright or alarm, and where any sound was uttered it impressed u only with a sense of resentful indignation or of mocking inquiry. We were intruders in specially reserved spots, and could only offer apologies to our unwilling hosts by showing our appreciation of their mode of life in a respectful silence; indeed, to have uttered any sound in such places would have seemed a crime against Nature.

So we floated on, casually returning the stares of the would-be enemy, while we listened with lazy indifference to their taunts and threats. At times, when there was complete absence of life on the shore, we confined our attention to more personal reflections.

We were a strange assortment of human beings, whom accident had thrown together to live the same life for an allotted time in such close companionship on a small space. Here sat the Moslem in friendly relation with us, Western Christian infidels; the Armenian broke bread with the hated oppressor of his race and religion, while the Turk, on his side, had to endure the presence of his despised enemy. The Arab Zaptiehs and the Kurdish boatmen represented tribes whose traditions told of constant deadly feuds and warfare. The whim of one among us had gathered us together.

What casual observer would realise what we had in common? For difference of language, custom and appearance counts for little when all are equally exposed to the chance of circumstance; and the bonds that united us all with a common feeling were the hardships we endured alike from hunger, cold, and danger. We shivered together in wind and rain, and basked in the sun together; we suffered pangs of hunger together, and rejoiced together over meal; we faced the same perils with the same chances of escape or annihilation. Whomsoever Fortune had chosen for her favourites in the ordinary run of life stood here on the same level as their less fortunate companions, to take their chance under the same conditions.

We each had our several occupations when we felt that it was possible to snatch any time from contemplation. Hassan would retire into the hut at one end of the raft, and, sitting cross-legged on the floor, would chop up tobacco; whilst one of the Zaptiehs, seated at the door, would roll up cigarettes. Now and then he would reach out one to me – "Will you smoke, Effendi?" – and the other Zaptieh, seated outside, would strike me a match.

Arten might easily have worked all day, but he seemed to spend most of his time contemplating the brazier on which he occasionally cooked something. At intervals he blew up the live charcoal with measured puffs; or he would sit perilously near the extreme edge of the raft contemplating the sky, with the tails of his dirty black overcoat dangling in the water, holding the dishes in the river until most signs of the last meal were removed from them. Being an Armenian he was endowed with a more restless nature, and the apparent contemplation in his demeanour was but the dejection resulting from a broken spirit. When not engaged in his own pursuits he would break in on the silence by pointing out what he considered objects of interest.

"Look! Look! There is a bird," he would say; and the true Easterns would gaze on without moving a muscle, neither looking at him nor the bird. Arten would look nervously round, knowing from long habit that he was being despised, but unable to understand the grating, silencing effect of allusions to the obvious at the moment when the obvious is being most thoroughly appreciated.

The two raftsmen were obliged to concentrate a certain amount of attention on the business of navigation, but they seized every moment they could spare from the task of guiding the raft, and, leaning on their oars, would devote it to contemplation. They too pointed out objects of interest, but only in their capacity as local guides, and in a monosyllabic manner in complete harmony with the occasion.

"Christian village," they would say, without looking round, pointing a thumb over their shoulders in the direction of a group of mud huts; or "Arab" when an encampment of black tents appeared on the bank. Hassan and the soldiers would respond by slowly turning their eyes in the particular direction; perhaps even going so far as to give vent to a sudden, sharp "Ha!" if the occasion was one of particular moment. Arten, however, would jump about the raft.

"A Christian village! Look, it is there; do you see, did you hear? A Christian village."

No one would answer him.

"Did you hear, Hassan?"

A minute of absolute stillness, and then Hassan's deep, deliberate voice, with no suggestion of impatience.

"I heard."

But we did not always drift along in a smooth and idle manner; the mud banks gave way at times to steep, rocky sides, between which the waters flowed more rapidly, and careful steering with the oars was required to avoid rocks and whirlpools. And here there were not infrequent signs of life: rock-tombs were cut in the walls of the rock, and we would have liked to stop and examine them further, but it was impossible to land the raft at such places, and the current hurried us on almost before we were aware of their existence. There was a certain relentlessness about the way we were torn past all objects of interest; it was like dealing with Time. We were conscious that things passed now were passed for ever, and that we should never have another opportunity for realising them. Evidences of ancient civilisation, episodes in the everyday life of the present tribes, all seemed to sweep past in bewildering, incredible swiftness; we found it hard sitting there to believe that it was we who swept past them.

Now we would catch sight of a wedding procession on the bank – the bride, plastered with feathers and ornaments, being escorted to the bridegroom's village amid a din of music and shouting, the sound of which would follow us long after they were lost to view.

Now it would be a group of women washing their clothes at the river's edge, beating them on large, flat stones.

Now a solitary horseman would stand motionless on the cliff above, his coloured cloak flowing over his horse's back, barely concealing the brilliant hues of his embroidered saddle; he would watch us out of sight and then turn and pursue his lonely road.

Now a shepherd boy would be driving in the flocks of sheep and goats at sundown; and his weird calls, and the answering bleat of the animals, would echo and re-echo right away across the distant hills.

Men and women on the bank hailed us as we passed; we could only cast one look at them and wave back a hurried and kindly greeting; they knew we must not stop and talk; we came out of a different world from theirs, and they paused for a moment to gaze at us and then returned, forgetful of the fleeting vision, to their own pursuits.

Meditative oxen, chewing their cud, surveyed us wonderingly from the shore. "Why in such a hurry?" they seemed to say, and we answered, "We are not in a hurry, but we have no power to stop."

And the eagles overhead peered in contemptuous security at us, vaunting with arrogant flaps the great wings with which they flew whither they listed, while we were being swept along uncertain currents. A hidden bird would pour forth his sweet song to cheer us on our way, and the owls utter a dismal note of warning as of unknown dangers yet to come.

And there was some possibility of danger, for we were still in the land of the Sultan's irregular troops – the Hamidieh. Our friends, however, had been decidedly encouraging as we bad them goodbye. "You will probably meet with Kurds," they said, "but if they do shoot at you it will only be for the fun of sinking the raft; they may rob you and strip you, but if you don't resist they won't kill you."

We felt distinctly elated. We still clung to ideas of life; our clothes and provisions were a convenience, but no doubt sheepskins and rice would be always forthcoming if the worst happened. "What would you mind losing most," I said to X, on the third day, as we lay on our backs on the raft, the muddy water rippling very close to our ears and the muddy banks swinging round as the current changed.

"My hot-water bottle," answered X reflectively; "and you?"

"My camera first," I said, after a pause, during which I had pictured X alone with the hot-water bottle, "and then my stylo.[47]"

"Yes," said X sympathetically, "I really don't see how you could get on without them; but perhaps," she added consolingly, "if you persuaded the men that there was an evil spirit inside they would let you keep them."

This was a decided inspiration. I booked it for possible contingencies; a hot-water bottle and a camera were obvious resting-places for the evil eye.

We drifted on; the whirls of a slight rapid caught us – the top end of the raft where we lay dived suddenly into the water and then rose again, the bottom end followed suit, we became bowed for a second, then we were flat once more, and loose things which had started jumping about, lay still. I shook the water off my sleeve; X stretched out a hand, without turning her head, to feel whether the "Oxford Book of English Verse" had been washed away.

"Mashallah, the Pashas like water," volunteered one of the kalekjis, a little, round-faced Kurd in a brightly striped coat.

"The Pashas are English," answered Hassan, in a tone of dignified rebuke. "The English fear nothing; why should they fear water?"

---

[47] Probably *stylus* "an instrument for writing."

The kalekji paused in his work; he was plying the two poplar poles, with which he guided the raft past shingles and kept it in the open part of the river. He started rolling up a cigarette.

"May it please Allah to spare us from an attack from Ibrahim Pasha," he said devoutly, "or even these Pashas may have cause to fear."

Hassan looked at him sternly and with some contempt.

"The Pashas are English," he repeated, "and the Pashas are not afraid of Ibrahim Pasha."

Reasons are superfluous to the Oriental mind; statements are conclusive; the kalekji lit his cigarette and resumed his task. The two Zaptiehs, Ali and Achmet, who had been aroused to a slight attention during the conversation, became listless as before and puffed away in silence after a simultaneous murmuring of "Aha, aha, Ibrahim Pasha." The remaining occupant of the raft, Arten, alone looked disturbed and uncomfortable. He was continually scouting the horizon, and retired behind the door of the hut whenever a black spot was visible. He burst into roars of forced merriment, "Ibrahim Pasha! Who is afraid of Ibrahim Pasha? Let him come, and we shall give him a warm welcome!" His companions gazed in front of them in stolid, silent contempt.

Silence reigned again – only the splash of the oars was heard and the beating of the water against the skins. Nothing broke the monotony; the river wound its way slowly in and out round mud banks; the country as far as one could see was unbroken, endless mud; the water one drank and washed in and floated on was diluted mud; the occasional village on the banks was built of mud, the inhabitants were mud colour; the very sky gave one a feeling of mud.

It was time for a diversion. Away in the distance, since early morning, there had been a black smudge on the horizon which was slowly taking more definite shape as we followed the course of the shiny loops of the river, the one break in this endless, monotonous waste. We had lazily fixed our eyes in its direction. Almost imperceptibly it had evolved itself into great masses of solid, black, limestone rock; a few more turns of the river and we shot right under them and were suddenly shut inside a narrow black gorge. Bare walls of rock rose straight up on either side, and above a narrow stretch of sky-line, with its broken edges formed by the turreted ends of rock, and in a row, on every point, silent, motionless, awe-inspiring, sat peering down at us, like sentinels on guard, great brown vultures of the desert. I fidgeted uneasily; an armed brigand flesh and blood could stand, but this penetrating, undivulging, inhospitable gaze was too uncanny. To appear unconcerned I took out my field-glasses and stared back; with deliberate scorn, and of one accord, they slowly spread out their great wings, shook them, and soared up in the air, dropped down the other side of the rocks, or took up a fresh standpoint a little further removed from the intruders.

We floated rapidly through the gorge. Already, on one side, the rocks were giving way to mud banks, though on the right bank the sides rose steeply in high, jagged cliffs. I lay back with a sense of enjoyment of life and peace; my thoughts had strayed to Western scenes. We turned a sharp bend in the river, and I vaguely noticed a native woman carrying a child in her arms. All of a sudden the atmosphere seemed disquieted, the two Zaptiehs had seized their rifles and dropped on one knee as if marking prey; even the imperturbable Hassan was handling a dangerous and antiquated looking weapon. There were men on the shore hailing us, and our boatman was shouting back vociferously.

"Pashas," said Hassan in a solemn voice, "put on your hats."

I slowly woke to the situation as I obediently donned the insignia of our nationality. There were men each side the bank; they were armed men, and their arms were pointed us.

"Why, X," I exclaimed ecstatically, "we're held up!"

X looked at me with a pitying expression. "You've been rather a long time taking that in," she said. This was not the moment for feeling snubbed; I wished to show that I was now acting with cool deliberation.

"X," I said, "before leaving England we took some trouble with revolver practice; with much inconvenience we conscientiously wore our revolvers all through the wilds of Mesopotamia and Armenia; for some weeks we slept with them, loaded, under our pillows in the Taurus Mountains; they are now hanging discarded on the walls of the hut. Do you not think the moment has arrived for giving ourselves some little return for all the bother they have been?"

"They have been a bore," assented X; "perhaps it is our duty to have them now.

I went and fetched them and solemnly handed X hers.

"They are loaded," I said, "but they seem rather sticky and rusty; I wonder if they will go off."

"Please point the other way if you are going to try," said X.

I could not allow this challenge to my want of knowledge in firearms to pass, and replied with dignity, "Remember to aim at the middle of the man – then if you miss his heart you have a chance either way at his head or his legs."

"I do not think I shall fire," said X, "because I cannot do it without shutting my eyes. I will just point."

The river had become very narrow, though the current was slow; the men could keep pace with us at a walk; they were masters of the situation. I gathered my wits together and debated our chances; the Kurds did not alarm me, but I cast nervous glances at Hassan.

"X," I said at last, "if Hassan fires that blunderbuss, he cannot fail to hit either you or me."

X surveyed the situation critically.

"I don't think it will fire," she said; "he was trying to shoot with it one day and it would not go off." I breathed more freely.

"Effendi," said one of the soldiers to Hassan, "tell the ladies to go into the hut."

"Pasha," said Hassan, "you would be more out of the way in the hut."

X laughed, Hassan laughed, the Zaptiehs laughed, we all laughed, except Arten, he did not laugh – yet. Meanwhile, the Zaptiehs and the boatmen had been yelling and shouting at the brigands as they kept pace with us on the shore. As they spoke Kurdish we were unable to know what negotiations were going on, and could only await developments. They were a fine set of men, dark, handsome, well set-up, their long, black, curly hair worn down to the collar. They were dressed in bright colours, and armed to the teeth with long knives and pistols, besides the rifles they were flourishing.

"There do not seem any villages near," said X. "We shall be very cold if they take our clothes and we cannot get sheepskins."

"Yes," I said, "and very hungry if we can get no rice. We have longed for this moment, but there do seem to be inconveniences connected with it." My heart suddenly warmed within me. "X," I said, "isn't this a splendid piece of luck!"

"Glorious!" said X; and we gave ourselves up to the full enjoyment of the situation.

We had got into a faster bit of current, and the men had to run to keep up with us. They seemed to be yielding to the importunities of our escort; one by one they dropped behind, and finally, with a few parting yells, stood and gazed at us as we floated on. Indignation swelled in my veins.

"X," I said, in a voice struggling with emotion, "they are letting us go!"

X's face reflected my disappointment and disgust.

"And they did not even fire one little shot!" she said bitterly.

"Or try to burst our skins," I gulped. X tried to take a cheerful view of the situation.

"Never mind," she said, "cheer up, we may have another chance; we are not out of their country yet."

But I was not so easily comforted; I wanted some outlet for my rage and disappointment, and seizing my revolver I fired six shots up into the air and flung the weapon across the raft. The reports rang out loud and clear, and the echoes slowly died away in the answering rocks. Arten's white face peered through a chink in the door.

X turned to the Zaptiehs and demanded of them a full account of their conversation.

"Effendi," said the officer, "it is merchandise they want; they dare not touch the personal effects of the English; they have had some good lessons."

"But," I interrupted, "we are loaded with merchandise."

"Effendi," said the officer, "we swore by Allah that it was all your luggage, and that if they took it the English Padishah would send his soldiers and kill them all.

"Yes," broke in the other Zaptieh, "and we swore that his Excellency the English Consul was on board, and that if they fired a shot he would come out with his great weapon and blow them all into the next world."

The little boatman's face beamed with radiant smiles. "Ah! the English are a great people," he said; "with you English we are safe. I have been down the river scores of times, and always at this place I have been robbed. You saw the solitary woman as we turned the corner; she was put there to signal when the rafts were coming; if you see a woman alone on a bank you know what you are in for. The river here is narrow and the current slow – you have no chance. On the one side the banks are low, and they can draw the rafts on shore and unload the merchandise while the men on the other side, high up on the cliffs, cover you with their guns.

"Why do you not carry arms?" we said. The man smiled sadly.

"Pasha, what are we against these men? If we float on, they sink the raft by shooting at the skins till they burst, and we lose raft and merchandise and all; if we submit quietly, they take what they want and let us go peaceably. Should we fire back at the men on the low bank within our range, we are at the mercy of the men on the cliffs who have good ambush. No, Allah wishes it. Why should we resist?"

There was silence for a few minutes. The Oriental's first refuge from the ills of the world is in his subservience to the will of Allah; his second is in his tobacco; our boatman slowly rolled up a cigarette.

"It is not you English they will harm," he said, "they are afraid of punishment. It is we poor ones, who can get no redress. They take our little all, and know we must submit and they are safe."

"Surely you can appeal to the local authorities?" we persisted. The man laughed – a low, quiet laugh.

"The Governor!" he said; "poor man – he is no better off than the rest of us. He has no authority over these Hamidieh. Only last week he was set on and robbed himself by a party of them. They stripped him and threw him over a bridge; he was picked up half dead by a passing caravan next day. Amān – it is the will of Allah," and he took long, serene puffs at his cigarette.

During the conversation Arten had emerged from his retreat, and, after casting furtive glances in all directions to make sure of the enemy's absence, he seated himself amongst us on the raft and started winking and giggling.

"Ach, Pasha!" he said, "we scared them well. We are under the protection of God. Their shots came whizzing round our heads but none could hurt us; they fell round us in the water like hailstones and the air was black with them, and when we shot back we left them dying in hundreds on the bank and they were afraid to follow. Ah, ah, it was a great fight, and we shall be heroes in Stambul."

"X," I said, "I fear this poor creature's head has been turned with fright; do you think a little quinine would be of any use? We have only that and the eye-lotion left in the medicine case."

X looked at me reprovingly. "You know you only hate him because he is an Armenian," she said; "you will not make allowances for his belonging to a down-trodden race. It is only natural he should boast when he knows what a coward he has been."

X was putting new ideas in my head; I transferred my thoughts from insanity and quinine and looked with fresh interest at Arten. He as a typical specimen of his race – sallow complexion, dark hair and eyes, and a huge hooked nose. He was closely buttoned up in a long, thin, black overcoat, which had evidently descended on his shoulders from those of a missionary; on his head he was a dirty red fez, bound round with a still dirtier coloured handkerchief. He sat hunched up, shivering with cold or fright, and his eyes wandered about uneasily.

I looked from him to Hassan, and the contrast was indeed striking: Hassan was the embodiment of strength; there was strength in the massive, well-balanced proportions of his huge frame; there was strength in the poise of his head and in the keen level look of he eyes; there was strength in the quiet repose of his mind and body. If these two men were to be taken as typical specimens of their respective races, there was indeed cause to reflect on the result of one race dominating and crushing another through the course of generations.

I sat down to reflect about it. It was getting dark; the waters were very still; we hardly moved. The sun was setting behind us, and the intense redness of the sky made the rocks underneath look absolutely dead black; the moon had arisen and cast a silver glimmer over the dark waters – dark from reflecting the blackness of the rocks; the kalekjis felt their day'' work was over and crooned a low song. We drifted to the shore and made fast the raft with large stones laid on the ropes. A very unsavoury smell of cooking alone kept our thoughts well on the solid earth. Arten appeared at the door of the hut.

"Supper is ready, Pashas," he said. So we ate our supper that night.

CHAPTER 11

A RECEPTION AND A DANCE

Hassan Kaif is the first place of any interest along the banks, and we arrived there early on the fourth day, having floated about eighty miles in that time.

As we approached the village the banks of the river rose perpendicularly in a wall of rock which as simply riddled with tombs. Many of them seemed to be quite inaccessible; those which had any sort of approach from the land side appeared to be inhabited by Kurds. We passed between the ruined buttresses of a Roman bridge of four arches, and then had a view of the whole village on the right bank. The mountains curve away from the river at this point and leave a semicircular level space, which is occupied by the ruins of an ancient Christian town. At the back, extending right up the curving side of the hill to where the topmost peak, surmounted by a castle, crowns the river, is a vast necropolis. The natives live in the tombs and in caves cut out of the rocks.

We landed here and slowly toiled up the stony paths on the face of the rock, which led over the roofs of one habitation to the next above it. Near the top we were met by a local Zaptieh, who guided us to the house of the Mudir.[48] We were not sorry to have this opportunity of examining the interior of the dwellings. The house consisted of a single room, into which we stumbled down a dark passage; the walls were roughly levelled off inside, the marks of the chisel everywhere apparent. A low divan ran down each side of the room. In one corner the rock had been hollowed out to form a cupboard, inside which, through the chinks of a rough wooden door, we caught glimpses of his Excellency's bedding – for the Oriental keeps his bed in a cupboard in the day-time and spreads it on the floor at night.

With all the instincts of a wandering tribe, the Turk, however permanent his abode, conducts his household exactly as if it were in the nature of a tent. He lives in one room, sleeping, eating, and doing

---

[48] *Local Governor.*

business. Should he wish to eat, his meal is carried in on a little low table, beside which he squats on the floor; the meal over, the table is carried out and the floor swept. Should he wish to write, he discards the rickety table occasionally found in an official dwelling, and writes upon his hand, balancing the ink-pot upon his knee as he sits cross-legged on the floor. When it is time to sleep, his bed is pulled out of the cupboard and laid upon the floor; his slumbers over, it is rolled up and put away again.

The Mudir received us with salaams, and taking X by the hand led her to the seat of honour at the top end of the divan; our men ranged themselves below in order of rank, and a few ragged soldiers hung about the door. A servant appeared with cups of coffee and we were offered cigarettes.   Then watermelon and sweets were handed round. Conversation was limited by our small knowledge of Turkish; but X was by this time proficient in the formal modes of greeting.

MUDIR: How do the ladies like Turkey?

X: We think Turkey is a very fine country, and everybody has been very kind to us.

MUDIR: How could they be otherwise;   are the ladies not the honoured guests of the Sultan? Have the ladies a kalek[49] in London?

X: No, we never saw one until we came here. We find it very comfortable. We should like to take one back with us.

MUDIR: The ladies are sisters, then?

X: No, we are friends; we were educated at the same college.

MUDIR: The lady's father, is he a great Pasha?

HASSAN: He is a very great Pasha and a friend of the Queen of England.

(Mutual salaams.)

MUDIR: Your father, the great Pasha, has he many sons?

X: Yes, he has five sons.

MUDIR: Mashallah! God has been good to your father.

(A pause, during which we were closely scrutinised.)

MUDIR: Have the ladies no husbands, then?   Why are they not married?

HASSAN: In England the ladies do not care about husbands. In that country they rule the men. If anything were to happen to these ladies, the Queen of England would send her soldiers out here to revenge them.

----

[49] Raft.

(The whole room gives vent to murmurs of "Mashallah," and every eye is fixed on us.)

MUDIR: The other lady *(nodding at me)*, is she a servant that she does not speak?

HASSAN: No, she too is a Pasha, but she cannot speak Turkins.

MUDIR: *(incredulously)*. No Turkish?

HASSAN: *(scornfully)*. Well, only such words as "hot water," "tea," and "be quick," and "is my horse ready?"

The Mudir then inquired calmly "how many times" we had been held up by brigands in his district, a strange satire on Turkish methods of government. There was not a doubt in his mind that we had not been waylaid and robbed.

He then took us to visit another house which boasted of three rooms, all leading out of each other. The first one appeared to be the general living- and sleeping-room, absolutely bare save for strips of felt ranged down the far end and a pile of native quilts in a corner; the second room, which could only be reached through the first, was dedicated to the animals; and the third, which was almost pitch dark, was a larder and store-house. We were received by several women, who held us fast by the hands while they displayed their abode with great signs of pride. One of them was a strikingly handsome dark girl, dressed in gorgeous coloured native silks and velvet, and literally plastered with ornaments from the face and hair downwards.

On returning to the raft we were somewhat puzzled (one is never *surprised* in Turkish dominions) by finding it taken possession of by two women, magnificently dressed and closely veiled, accompanied by a man and a woman servant. They were sitting in a row on our beds examining all our belongings complacently.

"We are very pleased to have a visit from the ladies," said X to the local Zaptieh who had accompanied us back to the raft, "but they must go on land now, as we are starting at once."

"But they will travel with you," said the Zaptieh.

"That would be very pleasant," said X, who never forgot to be polite, "but the raft is so small, I am afraid there will be no room for us all and they will not be comfortable."

"Oh, there is plenty of room," said the man reassuringly. "The ladies need not trouble themselves."

X turned to one of our Zaptiehs.

"Will you explain," she said, "that the raft is ours, and that we are very sorry but we are afraid we cannot take the ladies with us?"

"It is an arrangement of the Mudir's," explained Ali; "he has been waiting for an opportunity to send the harem of a great Pasha to a neighbouring village, and he ordered them to travel with you. They will land before evening."

As there seemed no choice in the matter we expressed our tremendous appreciation of the honour, and instructed Hassan to keep an eye on their pockets. Hassan, who had looked somewhat perturbed from the outset, had resolutely ensconced himself at the furthest corner of the raft with his back turned to everything. He refused to change his position, and explained to us that the ladies were such very great Pashas that it would be "shame" for him to look in their direction.

Towards evening we reached a spot where two armed Kurds, with long black curls and magnificent striped coats, stood waiting with saddled horses. The servant woman carefully wrapped the great ladies up in their gaudy silk cloaks, and the man servant helped them off the raft on to the backs of the horses. The little party rode away up a lonely looking mountain pass, and as we floated on we caught occasional glimpses of their bright colours in and out of the rocks until they disappeared entirely over the crest of a distant hill.

That night we moored the raft at Sheveh, a village backed by high hills, the last spurs of a great range of snow mountains, at whose base we had been winding in and out. We arrived at sunset, just as the women were trooping down, with jars on their heads, to fetch water from the river. I went and sat on a rock above them, and one by one, having filled their jars, they filed up past me, and, stopping for an instant, fingered my garments and gently stroked my hair. Many and various questions they asked me, of which I could understand nothing beyond the note of interrogation, and they sailed on with that free and graceful carriage which is the gift of uncivilised races, balancing the jars at an angle on their white-veiled heads.

We had finished supper and had stretched ourselves out on the raft under the stars, enjoying the quiet and beauty of the scene. The boatmen belonging to the two rafts had joined forces and pitched a tent on the shore close by. Most of the village had straggled down to the river and were flitting mysteriously about in waving white garments. All of a sudden a wild, savage noise of screaming and singing arose.

"The men have bought a piece of meat," said Ali, "and are singing to it."

It was a weird sight; a roaring fire blazed in the gloaming; in the centre hung a large black pot containing the meat which was the object of this adoration. The men had joined hands and were dancing round the fire in a circle, dark figures in long white flowing robes which waved about in the semi-darkness as their owners flung their feet up or swung suddenly round. All at once the men dropped on the ground with a prolonged dwindling yell, which finally died off into an expectant silence. The head boatman fished out the meat and began to tear it to pieces with his hands, distributing it amongst his companions. A deathly silence reigned while the carcass was being consumed. This gave place, as time went on, to a murmuring ripple of satisfaction, which developed a little later into bursts of contented song. Then they sprang to their feet and flung themselves once more into a dance.

"Let's join in," said X.

We each seized a Zaptieh by the hand and were included in the circle. We sprang and kicked and stamped; we turned and hopped and stamped. One man stood in the middle clapping the time with his hands as he led the song. It was a war-dance; the circle broke into two lines and we dashed against one another. Then the lines receded and the song became a low murmur as of gathering hordes, whilst our feet beat slow time. The murmur swelled and our feet quickened; louder and louder we shouted, quicker and quicker we moved, and finally with a great roar the two lines dashed against one another. We gave one great stamp and a roar, then a hush, and the lines receded. Thoroughly exhausted, I fell out of the line while this proceeding was repeated.

By this time the moon shone out bright and strong. On one side a great desert stretched away into the starry night; on the other the waters of the Tigris swept darkly past us. The wild shrieks flew up into the clear, silent air. X danced furiously on between Hassan and Ali. Her face was strangely white lit up by the moon, amongst the dark complexions of her companions. They sprang and hopped and stamped, they turned and hopped and stamped; a white robe here, a red cloak there, a naked foot and a soldier's boot, hopping and turning and stamping.

"X," I said to myself, "you are mad, and I, poor sane fool, can only remember that I once did crotchet work in drawing-rooms."

A feeling of wild rebellion took hold of me; I sprang into the circle.

"Make me mad!" I cried out, "I want to be mad too!"

The men seized me and on we went, on and on with the hopping and turning and stamping. And soon I too was a savage, a glorious, free savage under the white moon.

Chapter 12

An Encounter with an Englishman

Between Hassan Kaif and Jezireh, a distance of thirty-five miles, the scenery is very fine. The river winds through narrow gorges with steep walls of limestone rock riddled with rock tombs. Here and there in the black gorges the high turreted rocks would be skirted below with bands of vegetation; little spurts of glistening water shooting over the rocky tops, as they dashed down to join the river, shot between masses of ferns or trickled through beds of green moss. It was months since we had seen anything green, and we feasted our eyes and senses on the unaccustomed luxuriance. All the grim bareness and desolation of the stone and mud country through which we had passed seemed to serve a purpose now in heightening the intoxication of this scene.

Reluctantly I had been compelled to admit, on more than one occasion, that Nature could be positively revolting in places where absence of life and colour were not relieved by any sense of stern ruggedness or the freedom of space; where day after day we had journeyed through a country of little meaningless hillocks strewn with grey stones, only getting round the corner of one to be confronted with another of the same appearance; where it seemed as if Nature had chosen a spot, far from the eye of man, to dump all the clinkers of life, all the stony refuse which even she could not turn to any profitable account – she, the great mother, of whom men say she knows no waste. We had discovered her ugly secret hidden away in this far corner; and now she was using her chief weapon, contrast, to make us feel the true extent of her power. She had wearied and revolted us, and now she seemed to make use of this very fact to give us an intenser appreciation of her best.

"Pretty view, isn't it?" said a voice in the native tongue at my side. Startled from another world, I turned round. Arten was rubbing some spoons with a dirty cloth and waved his hands towards the banks.

"Got anything like this in London?" he asked affably.

I looked at him in silence. He dived into the hut with a scared look, and complained later on to X that the other Pasha had an uncertain temper.

The spell of enchantment was broken; but sentiment was in the air with the smell of wet earth and the sound of drinking vegetation; oleander bushes with bright red blossoms stood out against the dark rock, water-birds darted in and out and vultures hovered overhead. I had a sudden desire, awakened by Arten's interruption, to share the emotions called up by the surrounding scene. I glanced at X. She looked fairly sentimental, I thought, lying motionless in her favourite place at the extreme end of the raft, with a dreamy, far-away look in her eyes.

"X," I murmured softly, "what does this make you think about?"

X was one of those rare people who always know what they are thinking about. She did not fail me on this occasion.

"It reminds me of Scotland," she said without hesitation. "Why, what does it make you think about?"

But I had stopped thinking about it, and agreed that I had seen places like it in Scotland.

"Pasha," said Hassan, "the boatmen want you not to sit so near the edge of the raft."

"Why," laughed X, "do they think I shall roll over?"

"No," replied Hassan, pointing ahead, "but we are going to shoot a rapid and they say you will be frightened."

"I would sooner be frightened than go through the awful exertion of moving on this raft," said D, and she gazed placidly at the line of foaming waters which we were rapidly nearing. There was only just room for the raft to rush between hard, sharp-edged boulders of rock, and it seemed as if we should inevitably be dashed to pieces or stranded at an acute angle on one of them.

The Zaptiehs helped with the oars, they and the boatmen keeping up one prolonged yell of "Allah! Allah!" They exerted themselves strenuously, a strange thing for Easterns to do; the raft creaked and rocked and plunged; there was a very disturbing sense of fuss and unseemly exertion on board; the cook was saying his prayers inside; Hassan, with an air of total unconcern or even apparent perception of what was going on, was laboriously adding up his accounts; and X, with equal unconcern, was mending her gloves. On such occasions one thinks of one's past sins and the future; I thought of the future. I stood up and leaned my back against the wall of the hut to steady myself.

"X," I roared above the din, "I wonder what there is for supper to-night."

X looked at me with a bored expression. "The same, I should think," she said, "as we had last night and the night before and the night before that. Why this sudden interest in your food?"

"Because," I said, "I have an idea I shall enjoy my supper to-night."

"Yes," said X (she was always sympathetic), "this sort of weather does make one hungry."

Further conversation was prevented by a sudden leap of water and raft right into the air, and with the leap went up a loud cry to Allah as the men threw themselves, with one great determination, on the oars. We shot head downwards into the dark waters past the white froth of foam; there was a moment of turmoil, then everything became very still; the men rested exhausted on their oars, the roaring waters sounded faint in the distance.

I looked round: Hassan was still at his accounts; X had finished her gloves and was lying back with her eyes closed; the cook's prayers had ceased; we were through. The cook came out rubbing his hands jocosely.

"Arten," I said, "your prayers have saved us from some inconvenience."

Arten looked conscious. "What danger has there been," he said; "was the Pasha afraid of the waters?"

"No, indeed," I returned; "it was not the Pasha who was afraid of the waters, but she was afraid he might not get her supper to-night."

"The Pasha is hungry," said X; "we must have onions as well as potatoes to-night."

We arrived at Jezireh, without further adventure, at noon the next day. The River Jezeer runs into the Tigris at this point, so that the town can only be reached by wading through the water.

We were making preparations to go on shore when we observed a little man being carried across the water on the back of a half-naked Arab. He had that incongruous look made up of the European overcoat with a fur collar, the black trousers, and the brown boots, all surmounted with a fez, which we had learnt to associate, curiously enough, both with the office of local Governor and with that of the native Christian Man.

In this case our visitor was the Kaimakam. He was spilt off the Arab's shoulders on to the raft, and landed in rather an unofficial position. We went through the usual pantomime of salaams, and after inquiries after the health and rank of our relations he invited us to come on shore and visit the town.

Jezireh is a stronghold of the Hamidieh Kurds; the ragged soldiers about the streets bore their distinguishing mark, a silver star on the forehead. Their chief Mustafa had been murdered but a year ago, after devastating and burning the whole country round, and under the rule of his weaker son there was a temporary lull in hostilities. But Mustafa's name was still only mentioned in whispered words of awe, and this not by plundered natives alone, but by Turkish regulars and Turkish officials alike.

On returning to the raft we heard that an English Pasha had just ridden into the town and that he was coming to visit us. He had met Hassan, who had been buying supplies in the bazaars, and the following conversation had ensued, which Hassan now repeated for our benefit.

ENGLISH PASHA: Who are you?

HASSAN: I am a cavasse.

ENGLISH PASHA: Who is your Pasha?

HASSAN: Victoria Pasha.

ENGLISH PASHA: Where is he?

HASSAN: She is sitting on the raft.

ENGLISH PASHA: What is she doing there?

HASSAN: She is floating to Baghdad.

ENGLISH PASHA: Where did she come from?

HASSAN: She came out of England.

ENGLISH PASHA: Is she alone?

HASSAN: No, she has a friend, who is not her sister, neither is she her servant.

ENGLISH PASHA: Give the ladies my salaams and say that I will call upon them.

X and I looked at one another. The meeting of an Englishman under such circumstances is no doubt, in one sens, an excitement; so would it be to meet a tiger in an English country lane. In a jungle, now, one expects a tiger, and, being prepared for his attack, does not resent it. In the same way one is prepared to meet an Englishman on common ground in England, but, in an Asiatic wild, one is not prepared for the onslaught and one is therefore taken at a disadvantage. It was ten days since we had seen ourselves, as the Man would see us, in a glass (and then it was only a missionary's glass), and we had lost nearly all our hairpins in the crevices of the raft.

"Is my face as red as yours?" said X.

The question was evidently the outcome of the thoughts which assailed her mind during the few moments' silence in which we had gazed at each other, wondering whether we really looked like that too.

"Your face is all right," I said, "it's only red in patches; but your hair is disgraceful. How's mine?"

"It's all right," said X, critically, "it's only coming down in patches. But there is no time to do anything; here it is; we must brazen it out."

A young Englishman was boarding the raft; he was very spick and span, shaved, brushed, a clean collar, and polished boots.

"You must excuse me for calling upon you in this dishevelled manner," he said as we shook hands, "but travellers have to come as they are; I daresay you can sympathise," and he glanced round at our *ménage*.

X laughed. "Oh, as far as that goes," she said, "we are all in the same boat."

"Raft," I corrected in a nervous flutter.

The Young Man looked at me and smiles. I realised that he thought I was trying to make a cheap joke, such as one might have been capable of in the country lane.

"I must introduce myself," he want on. "I am Captain T —— of V——. I am on my way there now. It's strange you should just have arrived to-day as I was crossing the river…"

I murmured something about tea and fled into the men's hut, where Arten was boiling the kettle.

"Arten," I stammered out in broken Turkish, "the English Pasha will have tea with us. You must bring the cups clean. The English never have dirty cups."

Arten smiled back very genially; he breathed into a cup and wiped it vigorously with one of his dirty cloths, by which I concluded that he understood what I had said to him. I had learnt up all the words about dirt and the desirability of washing.

It was raining slightly and we had to ask the Young Man under cover. X and I sat down on one of the camp-beds and the Young Man sat on the opposite bed, sticking his long legs out through the door.

"You speak Turkish, then?" he said to me as I returned.

So he had heard my injunctions! I hastily denied any claim to a knowledge of the language. Arten came in with the tea, which he placed on the floor between the Young Man's top-boots.

"The Pasha," he said, addressing X, "said you wanted something for tea which the English always have, only I did not understand what it was."

"Oh," said X, turning to me, "what was it?"

I kicked X.

"Biscuits," I said.

:No," said Arten, persistently, "it wasn't biscuits; it was something which you don't usually have."

I gave Arten the look which he had learnt to associate with the advisability of his own retreat. The Young Man smiled again and looked the other way.

"Yes," he said, "I don't know where we should be very often without biscuits in this country; they are so easy to carry."

I knew then that he had heard.

The Young Man stayed about half an hour and then rose to go. His camp had gone on, and it was a two hours' ride to the place where they would spend the night.

When he had departed X and I thought it over.

"You bet," I said fretfully, "he will have a five-course dinner to-night, on a table with clean plates and knives for each course, and probably a camp-chair to sit on."

"Yes, said X, "and a looking-glass hung on the wall of his tent, and hot water and a clean towel."

And that's what a man calls roughing it!

CHAPTER 13

THE CREED OF THE KORAN

We left Jezireh early next morning. The scenery was now much tamer; the banks of the river were low; stretches of conglomerate and red rocks were interspersed with grassy slopes. The river was no longer disturbed by rocks and rapids, and our two kalekjis had been replaced by a bright-faced youth who was going to take us single-handed as far as Mosul.

"Am I not a good kalekji?" he kept on saying to us, "see how quick I make the raft go. When you get to Mosul you will remember what a good kalekji I was," and, standing up on the raft, grasping the two oars, he would throw himself right backwards, causing the raft to shoot on through the slugging stream. Then when we had got into a faster bit of current he would lean on his oars and roll up a cigarette, talking all the time.

"The ladies like me, do they not? They see I am a good kalekji. They surely like me better than their other kalekjis?"

Six rafts laden with merchandise had followed us from Jezireh, and one with a hut similar to ours, and flying the Turkish crescent, was conveying a Turkish Yuzbashi with his harem to Mosul. The women were shut inside the hut the whole time, and occasionally, when the rafts drifted alongside, we caught glimpses of them peering shyly at us through the little glazed window. Did they envy us, sitting boldly outside, unveiled, open to the stares of all this crowd? Or, knowing no other lot, did they merely regard us with astonished curiosity, these so-called women from a strange land, who dressed like women but went about like men?

The fat little officer in his smart uniform sat outside most of the day, smoking with Oriental listlessness or playing with his little fat boy, a miniature counterpart of himself, dressed in uniform with a toy sword.

One some of the merchandise rafts the kalekjis were accompanied by their families. The sacks were piled up to form a rough shelter, under which the women and children crouched all day and cooked their masters' food. More rafts joined on to us further down, until we numbered thirteen. All day we floated in and out amongst each other, the rafts twisting and turning with the vagaries of the current; the kalekjis yelled and shouted at one another, they raced for the fast bits of current ahead where only one raft could pass at a time; they jostled one another or got entangled in shallow places, and the other rafts passed them with jeers.

Our little kalekji put forth all his skill.

"See, Pasha," he would say, excitedly, "see how we leave them behind! You have the best kalekji; do you see I always have the best of the river?   Yah, yah, yah," and he roared derisive laughter at his pursuers.

At night we all moored together and the kalekjis would land and sleep in the caves under overhanging rocks, or light a fire on the banks and stretch themselves out round it, taking turns at the night watch.

No sooner was the raft drawn up along the banks than X and I would land to get as much exercise as possible in the remaining hour of daylight. The Zaptiehs, who were obliged to accompany us, wrung their hands over this display of energy.

"Amān, amān. These English have strange habits. They land all in a minute, and before you know what they are doing one has rushed in one direction and one in another, and perhaps both are lost in the darkness, and we have orders from the Government never to lose sight of them. If the Government only knew what they were asking!"

The first evening after leaving Jezireh, Ali and I climbed to the highest point near the river, from where I obtained a good view of the surrounding country. The top of the hill on which we stood was a mass of stones and bulbous plants with withered leaves and tufts of rough grass. The country stretched away all round in strong, firm undulations to a distant horizon.

To the west was the full glory of an Eastern sunset, intensifying the reddish hue of the rolling hills until they merged into blackness in the shadows.

To the east the terminating range was snow-clad and the setting sun, casting a pink glow over the white peaks, gave a graduation of colour which caused them to melt imperceptibly into the sky and mingle with the pale reflection of the sun's setting rays on the opposite horizon.

What villages, what life lay concealed in the hollows of these rolling hills I do not know. To the eye there was nothing visible but the hill-tops in their naked immensity and intense desolation; on one side the flaming colours of the setting sun, on the other its pale reflection on the snowy peaks, and over it all the vast, inscrutable sky.

We were alone, Ali and I, with "that silence which some call God." I liked Ali's companionship on these evening walks; his nature, truly Eastern, was in keeping with the country. He had been chatting away merrily all the way up, trying to teach me Turkish words; and now we both lapsed of one accord into silence and his merry face took on something of the sternness of the surroundings. He laid his rifle on the ground and, moving away a little distance, went through the evening prayer. Now upright, now bending, now on his knees, a misty black form in the dazzling red light, he murmured inaudibly the prescribed words, words which at that same hour were being uttered alike by so many thousands in the fevered rush of busy towns, on the house-tops and in the crowded chambers. A form, a ritual of empty words this prayer may be, but up here, in Nature's loneliness, the prayer and the man seemed strangely relevant.

Was it not in such a place as this, alone with the great forces of Nature, that Mahomet formed his conception of God as an Irresistible Power?

"Has there come to thee the story of the overwhelming?" he cries out at one time, and again;

"Does there not come in man a portion of time when he is nothing worth mentioning?"

The great need of man is for expression; in places such as these his own insignificance is forced upon him by the overwhelming might of primeval forces. Alone with the great silence which his voice cannot fill, with the great space in which he, as a physical being, is lost; with the great mountains against which to measure his strength, with the stars which he cannot reach, and the floods which he cannot stem, his own personality seems so trivial that he doubts its very existence, until a strong feeling of participation in the forces themselves, of his own share in them, gives a truer sense of his own proportion; and the reaction of feeling, from this realisation of his own impotence to that of his own magnificence in being part of them, produces an overwhelming desire for utterance.

Was it under such influences as these that Mahomet's longing, awe-struck soul first heard, "Cry, what shall I cry?" and subsequently gave forth that long blazonry of Nature's beauty in the Koran? There is something in the grand simplicity and childish acceptance of the unspoilt

Eastern character at its best which seems to be a counterpart of the feeling inspired by Nature in this Eastern land itself. That it should be so seems natural when we remember how Mahomet was continually conjuring his followers to look at Nature and understand great things.

"Look at the heaven how it is reared, and at the mountains how they are set up, and at the earth how it is spread out ..."

"Verily in the creation of the heavens and the earth are signs to you if you would understand ..."

"Lift up thine eyes to the heaven; dost thou see any flaw therein? Nay, lift up thine eyes again; thy sight returneth dim and dazed ..."

The murmuring words of Ali's prayer had stopped; the sun sank behind the distant line of hills; a breeze sprang up and stirred the tufts of withered grass, whispering in the "still of night."

We retraced our steps to the edge of the hill and dropped into the hidden valley, where the Tigris rushed along unheeded and unseen from above.

Arten's voice rose with the sound of the waters, singing the well-worn words of an Armenian Protestant hymn.

The kalekjis had lit fires at the mouth of the caves, and crouched round the black pot which contained the evening meal. From the far corner of one cave came the wail of a new-born infant.

Under "the splendour of the Night tar" we too retired to rest.

*   *   *   *   *   *

We were already afloat when I woke next morning. From my bed I could see the banks shooting past the little window of the hut. The reader must not imagine a continuous view, such as one would get through the window of a more civilised vehicle of locomotion. The banks at one moment would move straight past the window in the orthodox way; then they would be suddenly shooting past in the opposite direction, or we had a view of the river behind.

It requires in many ways a certain amount of practice to live in a state of equilibrium on a raft. One is constantly being made aware of the truism that there are two sides to everything. First of all there are, as one would expect, two sides to the river; and owing to the particular method of our progression we were always being reminded, in a most irritating way, of this purely geological fact. No sooner had we become aware of the scenery on one side, and had decided that it was the right bank, than

– swish – round went the raft, and the whole length of the right bank would be shot before our view like a circular panorama, and before you could take it in you were looking at the left bank; moreover, you would be looking at it moving past you upwards, though you were perfectly certain the raft could only be floating downwards.

There was hardly time to reason this out when – swish – round you go the reverse way again, the left bank swings past you downwards and you are travelling up the right bank, although the raft, you are persuaded, is still pursuing its downward course. If you stood outside and fixed your eye with strenuous determination on some fixed and immutable spot of heaven or earth you might be able to keep your bearings with a strong mental effort. But when you observed the features of the landscape through the small window of your hut you gave it up – and simply gazed at the view as you would at a magic-lantern slide being slowly withdrawn through the porthole of an undulating steamer.

It was equally difficult to look steadily ahead from a mental point of view. Travelling by yourself you might be able to arrange your own philosophy, but it is upsetting when the other person sees the side which at any particular moment you do not happen to be looking at. When, for instance, we were delayed later that morning repairing burst skins, X was perfectly happy dwelling on the romance of navigating this noble and ancient river in the same way as those heroes whose feats were recorded on the tablets of Nineveh, until I unwittingly disturbed the harmony of these thoughts by complaining that I was unpleasantly reminded of a punctured bicycle on a lonely road of civilisation.

"How delightful this is," I said, in exuberant laziness, when we were floating on once more, "to be able to lose all conception of time and float on, as it were, to eternity."

"Personally," said X, "I find myself counting the days with a most unpleasant conception of the lapse of time, for we have only food enough for one day, and owing to this delay there is no possibility of renewing our supply for two."

I felt an injury had been inflicted on me by being reminded of absence of dinner when I had been inflated with great thoughts. But I had not long to wait for my revenge.

"What a picturesque man the kalekji is," X exclaimed suddenly; "I take such a delight in watching him shaking out his flowing garments and folding himself up in such graceful attitudes."

"Personally," I said, with some malice, "it gives me no pleasure since I became aware that he is only engaged in hunting for fleas."

X made no answer: I felt we were quits. She would have to think of the presence of fleas while I thought of the absence of dinner.

We floated on very quietly that day. The banks were flatter and the patches of grass became more frequent. At long intervals we passed villages of mud huts built on the sides of the river where the banks rose to a higher point.

Towards evening we swung round under a rocky prominence, on the top of which stood the village of Hassoni. There was no possibility of mooring the craft anywhere near it for the night. The banks rose up in a straight wall of rock, of such a height that the inhabitants of the village, peering down at us from above, seemed like pigmies on the sky-line. We floated on until the hills curved and the banks sloped down to a muddy flat. The other rafts were already moored along the shore and we drifted alongside of them.

Ali and I landed, and we set off to walk back to the village in the hope of getting some eggs and milk to eke out our supply of provisions. We had some difficulty in scrambling up the wet, grassy places between edges of rock where the water oozed out and trickled down to the river below; and on reaching the top we found ourselves on the edge of an extensive tableland which ended abruptly in the escarpment under which we had floated. Below us we could see the river winding ahead through a low-lying country to the east.

We walked for half a mile across the flat table top towards the village; a long procession of black and yellow cattle were sauntering along in front of us, lowing quietly in answer to the shrill calls of a boy who stood motionless on a little hillock, a weird figure in the straight, square-cut sheepskin cloak of the natives.

From all sides flocks of goats and sheep were coming in and filled the narrow streets, sharing the homes of their masters as a protection against the raids of Hamidieh chiefs. It was a partly Kurdish, partly Arab village, and the inhabitants mingled their curiosity at my appearance with fright at that of Ali's. Long experience had taught them that a visit from a Turkish Zaptieh meant extortion of some sort. A child in our path screamed aloud, rooted to the spot with terror. Ali's bright, laughing face clouded over.

"That is what the children are taught to think of us," he said, "and I have my own little ones at home."

Our demands for milk were received with sullen grimness, until the sight of the unwonted coin caused the faces to clear, and a further present of tobacco established quite a friendly footing. I sat down inside an enclosure of maize stalks at the door of a larger hut, where the cows were being milked, and the natives, clustering round, plied Ali with questions. One of the villagers offered to walk back with us and carry the milk.

It was dark before we reached the edge of the tableland again, and I shouted down in the hopes of getting an answer which would guide us to the encampment below. The village boy held up his hand with a scared look: the call was only answered by its own echo, and the stones, slipping under our feet, rattled noisily down the steep slope.

"Hush!" said Ali, "who knows but what Ibrahim Pasha may hear you," and we slid silently down the slippery banks in the darkness, until the light of a camp-fire gleamed out a welcome signal.

CHAPTER 14

THE EVIL ONE

At noon on the tenth day after leaving Diarbekr and the fourth from Jezireh we caught sight of the minarets of cupolas of Mosul, and floated for a couple of miles under the chain of limestone cliffs, on the end of which the town is built. We had hardly got within sight of the town itself when a fearful cannonading met our ears, accompanied by piercing screams and savage yells. It sounded as if the walls were being attacked by battering-rams, and all along the shore line at their base we could faintly distinguish a seething line of human beings brandishing some form of weapon. We were evidently going to be eye-witnesses of a tribal disturbance which would cause diplomatic unrest in Europe, and who knows but what our participation in it would not brand us with fame for the rest of time. I determined to make full use of the opportunity and prepared my camera and notebook.

The Zaptiehs, however, seemed quite unconcerned, and we understood from them that there was no cause for alarm, and that this sort of thing was of weekly occurrence in Mosul. On floating up to the scene of action we realised that it was indeed only Mosul's washing-day. All along the shore, as far as we could see, under the walls of the town stretched a continuous line of women beating clothes with flat sticks on the stones at the water's edge; and the screams resolved themselves into the ordinary sounds usually emitted where women congregate in large numbers.

Truly, the men of the East are wise in their generation. They had thus solved the problem of washing-day and all its horrors, and were left in peaceful and undisputed possession of their hearths and tempers. The women were there in their hundreds, and, as we approached the bridge of boats which crossed the river lower down, we floated past a small army of them on the opposite shore, where a flat stretch of mud was covered with gaudy rags laid out to dry.

Mosul, I believe, derives its name from the manufacture of muslin carried on there, and the guide book informs us that it is chiefly remarkable for the Assyrian mounds found near it. I am bound to confess, however, that it is indelibly impressed on my mind solely in its connection with the vulgar art of washing.

We had to wait several days at Mosul while a new raft was being constructed, on to which our huts were bodily transferred. The skins on which we had floated so far were deflated, and the kalekjis would return with them to Diarbekr by land on donkey back.

We spent the time visiting the historic mounds of Koyunjik and Khorsabad, for detailed information on which I must refer the reader to the works of Layard and Botha and King.

The site of Nineveh to the uninitiated eye is represented by the great mound of Koyunjik, which rises out of the flat country on the opposite side of the river to Mosul; it is surrounded by smaller tumuli representing parts of the ancient walls. Here and there are patches of cultivation, and at the time of our visit the bare brown earth was beginning to show promise of being covered by a scanty vegetation.

Of winged bulls, of lettered slabs, of cylinders, of all the wondrous contents of the palaces of the ancient Assyrian kings, now ensconced in the museums of Western cities, the only indication we had on the spot were the subterranean tunnels, now choked with fallen débris, from which these evidences had been removed; and the broken bits of masonry and pottery which were strewn promiscuously about the surface.

From the summit we obtained a comprehensive view of the country: of Mosul at our feet standing on its limestone cliffs at the further side of the Tigris, and of the distant country through which the river wandered southwards; a great plain dotted with vollages round which patches of cultivated land were already green with the rising corn. Long strings of mules laden with cabbage and other vegetables came in from the outlying villages and swelled the motley coloured crowd at the stalls established on this side of the river, or passed on over the rickety wooden bridge to the bazaars inside the town.

The exertion of living on land for these few days had seemed so very great that we were not sorry when we found ourselves afloat once more on the new raft and with a new set of men. Achmet and Ali had bidden us a tearful farewell, and we now had one Zaptieh only as escort, an Arab also named Ali. He was a Chous,[50] and I will give him his full title to distinguish him from our late friend.

---

[50] *Sergeant.*

A picturesque kalekji is almost an essential in such close quarters as a raft, and up till now we had rejoiced in the brightly-striped Kurdish coats and turbans of our first kalekjis, and the clean, flowing white abba of our Jeziireh friend. The two men who were to take us from Mosul to Baghdad presented a very different appearance. Unlike most Arabs, they were both huge, stout men, and were dressed in rough brown camel-hair cloaks over unwashed white undergarments. One of them we nicknamed at once the Evil One; he had the most excruciatingly wicked face imaginable – and the terror of it was considerably heightened when he tried to super-induce a conciliating smile on his hideous expression of wickedness.

The country below Mosul was decidedly tame; the dry brown plain was fringed by the already green banks of the river. The river itself was now much wider, and here and there its course would be divided by islands with low, swampy banks, round which the waters would lose themselves in marshy tracts, where herons waded in and out and innumerable black ducks dived and spluttered amongst the rushes. The jungle round was the haunt of the wild boar, jackal, and hyena.

It was hard to believe that a few weeks later the first spring sun would call forth wild masses of gorgeous flowers and long, rank grasses, and that the whole country would be teeming with succulent vegetation.

It was, indeed, a monotonous bit of country. The sun had not yet melted the snows of the distant Armenian hills, which later on would cause a rapid flood to the river, and we progressed very slowly in the low, sluggish waters. Our two kalekjis displayed no desire to hurry matters by their own exertions, and leant on their oars all day, disturbing the general harmony by constant quarrelling in harsh, grating voices. Now and then Ali Chous, who was fat and meek, would address himself to them in a soothing, almost pleading tone of voice. The purport of their remarks were lost to us, as their conversation was carried on in Arabic, and we found it hard to extract any information out of Ali, who could communicate with us in Turkish.

"Tell them they must stop talking and row," I said; "we are hardly moving at all."

And Ali Chous would answer:

"They will row, Effendi, indeed they will row." And the kalekjis rested on their oars as before, and the Evil One would smile at me, distorting his evil countenance with a diabolical green.

Finally, Ali informed us, in his anxious, conciliating tone, that they had brought no food with them and that they were hungry. If the Pashas would give them bread they could row; now they were faint. This was a favourite Eastern dodge with which we were well acquainted by this time. The kalekjis were always engaged with the understanding that they fed themselves, and knowing the fatal results of giving in on such points we hardened our countenances.

"Tell them we cannot help that; they knew they had to bring their own food, and if they starve it is not our fault." And the Evil One, on hearing this through Ali's no doubt modified interpretation, gave us another grin, even more diabolical than before.

When we retired into the hut for our next meal I took the precaution of cutting a hole in the felt wall, and peeping through it saw them comfortably ensconced at the furthest end of the raft, eating bread and scraps of meat out of a dirty linen bag, which they hastily sat on when we reappeared.

Arten was terribly afraid of them, and I knew what that meant.

"Arten," I said to him early in the day, "if you dare to give these men any food without my leave we will land you at the next village."

Arten hastily disclaimed any intention of giving them food, but he evidently cherished the thought as quite a good idea; after all, he was more alarmed of them even than he was of me.

Early on the second day we arrived at a small village, where it seemed as if we were expected. There was a crowd on the banks, and one of the men was waiting with a large sack. Ali explained to us that it contained the kalekjis' bread, and that we must land to take it on board.

The Evil One waded to shore with the rope, which he made fast to a rock. A little further down the bank were several natives making a raft, and I strolled down to have a look at them.

One man sat on the ground with a pile of skins beside him. The skins had been cut off above the hind legs, and the man was engaged in tying up this end, and the openings of the forelegs, with string. One end of the string was tied round his big toe, and he worked the other end up and down the gathered end of the skin until the tied ends were quite air-right. Then he threw the skin to another man, who blew into the open for end until it was inflated, when he tied it up. A third man stood in the water, tying the inflated skins on to the poplar poles with the ends of the same strings that had served to tie up the openings.

After watching them a little time I returned to our raft. By this time the whole village had turned out, and a great uproar was going on.

"What's up?" I said to X, who had not left the raft.

"I've been trying to find out," said X. "The Evil One has displeased them somehow and they will not let him go."

We instructed Ali Chous to insist on our going on. The second kalekji, Jedan by name, seemed only too delighted; he kept winking at us and pointing derisively at the Evil One. He untied the rope and shoved off. A man on the shore promptly seized the rope and held us back.

"Get a stick," said X, "and give him a smack on his head."

X was of a peaceable disposition, and I daresay she was laughing at me. She enjoyed seeing me get angry. But it was in our contract that I should do all the manual labour connected with keeping order, so I obediently seized a long pole and let it descend gently on the offender's shoulder. He turned round and stared, dropping the rope with an astonished grin. The crowd burst into joyous shouts and pointed at the Evil One, who still stood expostulating angrily in their midst.

"Hit him!" they yelled, "he is the one to hit!" and quite believing them I transferred my attentions, along with the end of the pole, to his shoulder.

"Come!" I shouted. It sounds tame, but it was the only Arabic word I knew. The raft slowly drifted down-stream and the Evil One, dashing in up to his waist, clambered on board.

Al explained to us that he refused to pay enough for his bread, and that the crowd would not let him go until he had done so.

The Evil One grinned, and, diving into the bag, offered me a dirty piece of native bread in his still dirtier fingers. He would share his food with us, although we refused to do so with him; a typical Eastern method of putting one in the wrong.

The waters were still sluggish, and the men seemed determined to do no work.

"I am beginning to think they are in league with some one on shore," said X. "It cannot be to their advantage to be so long on the way, as they are paid a lump sum to get us to Baghdad, and we are not feeding them. I quite expect we shall be held up and robbed before evening."

Finding that orders and threats were of no use and learning from Ali that Jedan, the second kalekji, was afraid of the Evil One, who would not allow him to row. I sat down facing them and produced my revolver.

"Tell the bad kalekji," I said to Ali Chous, "that if he does not row I will shoot him."

The Evil One, greatly to my astonishment, appeared to believe in the possibility of bloodshed and set to work at the oars. All the rest of the day I sat with my revolver at his head. It was a most fatiguing, if effectual, process.

"Supposing he does stop rowing," said X, "will you shoot him?"

"I cannot think what I shall do," I said; "the only way will be to fire over his head and pretend I've missed him."

"Mind you do miss him," said X languidly.

"Sure to," I answered, hopefully.

Some hours before sunset we were held up in a manner which admitted of no blame being attached to the Evil One. A strong head-wind arose, before which the raft refused to make headway, and we were forced to take refuge on a dreary mud bank which sloped down to the water's edge under a low line of shaley rocks.

The men sat about cross and disconsolate. It was very unsafe, they said, to spend the night so far from a village. We should certainly be attacked; the Evil One had arranged this – wind and all. We might be there for days, and what should we do for food?

Tired of looking at all their sulky faces, I clambered up the cliff above to see what I could see. The top of the hill was as level as if it had been flattened out by a giant with a hot iron. A low line of hills with equally flattened tops at a little distance hid the further view. I walked to the top of them, led on by the sort of fascination which makes one wish to see what is hidden between one and the horizon.

Having reached the top there was nothing to be seen but repeated lines of naked, flat-topped hills. The dreary loneliness of the place, its utter nakedness, in which one seemed shut off from all the real things of life, colour, sound, space, and growth, descended like a physical weight on one's senses. It was all like one great senseless punishment, which from its sheer callousness held one, with mingled fascination and terror, rooted to the spot.

With an effort I turned to retrace my steps, when my eye caught sight of a dark object on the same line of hills on which I stood, which made my blood turn cold. A wild-looking, half-naked Arab, who seemed to have dropped suddenly from the sky, was standing motionless gazing at me from a little distance. For one moment I stood transfixed with nameless dread; the whole feeling of terror which had been established by the mere aspect of this country seemed now to be concentrated and personified in this sudden apparition. What hordes of like beings might not be concealed behind this mysterious hillocks?

He moved one step towards me and I turned and fled, down the slope and across the level plain to the edge of the cliff under which the raft was moored. The apparition pursued me silently. On reaching the edge of the cliff I peered over and could see the crew of the raft still occupying the disconsolate positions in which I had left them.

My senses now slowly returned, and I sat down to await the arrival of the apparition out of consideration to my own self-respect. He was still some distance from me and, on seeing me sit down, he also sat down and we gazed at one another. The comic element in the scene asserted itself. A savage and I holding each other at bay like two dogs preparing for a fight on the top of the cliff, and down below X sitting unconcernedly on the raft reading the "Meditations of Marcus Aurelius."

I laughed out loud; the savage sprang to his feet with a yell, brandished his arms in the air, and darting up a neighbouring slope disappeared behind it as suddenly as he had appeared.

I slid down the cliff and joined X.

"Where have you been?" she said. "I was just going to send Ali to look for you; he says it is not safe to go out of sight of the raft."

"I was only on the top," I answered, too ashamed to enter into further details.

We discussed our general situation in bed that night.

"X," I said, "if you met a savage all alone in a wild piece of country what would you do?"

"Why, go up and speak to him, of course," said X; "it would be awfully interesting. What would you do?"

"I don't know," I answered; "I want to go to sleep now."

The wind dropped in the night, and at the first break of day we were off once more.

Chapter 15

Arab Hospitality

Fifty-three pairs of dark eyes were fixed upon us in unwavering scrutiny; it was dark and there was silence. The eyes, as they gleamed out of the darkness, might have belonged to a herd of wild beasts watching their prey; but we were privileged guests of the Arab Sheikh in whose tent we were sitting, and the gaze was but that of friendly curiosity. We had been placed on the seat of honour – a rush mat at one side of the tent; opposite to us squatted our host, a venerable old man with a white heard which flowed over his bare, wrinkled chest; with one arm he supported a small boy, who played with the beads round the old chief's neck.

Between us, in the centre of the hut, glowed a dying fire, and beside it, silently watching the pot on the ashes, sat the coffee-maker. Now and then he scraped the ashes together round the pot. A thin veil of smoke rose up slowly and dispersed itself under the low roof of the tent. The silence was almost religious; the darkness suggested witchcraft rather than night; a hobgoblin might have sprung out of the coffee-maker's pot and not been found out of keeping with the natural sequence of events.

All at once, at the back of the tent, a hand was raised and a bundle of fine brushwood came down on to the fire; in sudden blaze it momentarily lit up the fifty-three dark faces, flared an instant, flickered, then as rapidly died away, and we only felt the gaze we had seen before. We silently watched the coffee-maker and our host, who, being nearest to the fire, was dimly visible in its remaining light; the attention of the one was concentrated on his pot; that of the other, in common with his companions, was on us. There was no call for speech, for we spoke in tongues unintelligible to one another, and the only sound which fitfully broke the ghostly silence was that language understood by all nations alike, the wail of an infant in its mother's arms.

"Salaam Aleikum," we had been received with as the Sheikh stood up to welcome us on our arrival, unexpected and uninvited, in the midst of his tribe. We had been guided to his tent by the long spear which stood upright at the door, and when had offered us that token of Arab goodwill

– the cup of coffee – we knew that we were among friends. He waved us to our seats, and then, seating himself, pulled the child towards him; he patted his own chest, and then pointed to the lad with pride.

"His youngest child," interpreted Ali, who accompanied us, and who understood a few words of Arabic.

We nodded back our looks of appreciation and, these preliminary acts of courtesy having established the requisite good feeling, all need for further converse seemed at an end, and a comfortable silence fell upon us all.

The whole village had followed us into their chief's tent as a matter of course, and those for whom there was no room inside herded together at the door. The Eastern standard of ideas, which allows respectful equality with one's superiors, was responsible for the total absence of ill-mannered jostling which would have characterised a civilised crowd under similar circumstances on the reception of strange foreigners.

The coffee-maker reached out his hand without turning, and one amongst the crowd at his back handed him a massive iron spoon on to which was chained a copper ladle. The Sheik's little son, obeying a nod from his father, pulled a bag out of a dark recess behind him; another bundle of brushwood was thrown upon the fire and by the light of its sudden, almost startling blaze, the lad untied the bag and carefully counted out the allotted number of coffee-berries. The coffee-maker dropped them into the spoon, for which he had raked out a hole in the ashes.

The slight stir caused by these proceedings subsided, the blaze died away, and the attention of all was again riveted on us, save that only of the coffee-maker, who, sitting close up to the embers, now scraped the white ashes round the pot, now turned the roasting berries over with the ladle chained to the spoon. The Sheikh's hand stole on to the little boy's head, and the boy, looking up, stroked the old man's beard. On we sat in the dark silence, learning from these true masters of Time how neither to waste it nor to let it drag, but going step by step with it, to lay ourselves open to receive all that it had to give.

The silence was so prolonged and so intense that, silently as time flies, we could almost hear its moments ticking away. It has been said that we take no note of time except when we count its loss. It might be said of all Easterns that they are unconscious of the time they lose, because they take no note of it; they live unconsciously up to the fact that, the past being beyond recall and the future unfathomable, the present only is in our power. And the Eastern is master of Time because he spends it absorbing the present.

Meanwhile the berries had blackened, and the man emptied them into a copper mortar. As he pounded them he caused the pestle to ring in tune against the sides of the bowl. The child laughed gleefully and pointed at him; the stern old man smiled and shot a proud glance over at us.

"Fiddle away, old Time," rang out the tones of the metal pestle. It seemed to give voice to our joyful derision of Time; here was Time trying to weary us with himself and we only laughed at him.

> "Fiddle away, old Time –
> Fiddle away, old Fellow!
> Airs for infancy, youth and prime,
> Tunes both shrill and mellow.
> Fiddle away,
> Or grave or gay,
> For faces pink or yellow –
> Scrape your song a lifetime long,
> Fiddle away, old Fellow!"

Not a soul moved. Outside in the dusk a stunted black cow thoughtfully chewed the maize stalks of which the enclosure round the tent was built, and a kid rubbed his head up and down against a child's bare leg. Beyond this the darkness had nothing to conceal. We were in the middle of a bare, largely uninhabited, desert land known only to a few wandering Arab tribes. Outside, the mysterious open vault of the dark sky with its many hundred points of light; inside, the mysterious recess of the dark tent with the fifty-three pairs of gleaming eyes, every one fixed upon ourselves. Now and then, as a flash of lightning in the sky at night will expose the immediate surroundings to view, so a sudden spark from the fire revealed the setting of the eyes – the solemn, dusky, Arab faces.

A splutter on the fire as the pot boiled over put an end alike to the tune and to the meditations called up by it. The man transferred the ground berries to a copper jug and, pouring the boiling water on to them, placed this second pot on the hot ashes. We had been sitting there for an hour watching these preparations, and it seemed as if we might now reasonably entertain hopes of tasting the results.

Our expectations in this direction were also enhanced by the appearance of three tiny cups which had been unearthed from a dark corner, and handed to one of the men nearest the fire. He proceeded to rinse them out one by one with hot water, displaying a care and absorption in the process which contrasted strangely with the simplicity of his task.

The coffee on the fire came to the boil, the coffee-maker poured it back into the original pot, which he again set on the ashes. He then handed the empty jug to the cup-washer, who rinsed each cup out carefully with a few drops of the coffee left for this purpose. Very quietly, very precisely, he placed each cup on the ground within reach of the coffee-maker, and retreated into the background.

The coffee on the fire boiled up; we straightened ourselves in expectation as the coffee-maker reached out his hand. But he emptied the boiling liquid back again into the original pot and replaced it on the ashes.

The fire now burned very dimly. Even the man's form bending over the glowing ashes was discernible only as a black shadow. The stillness for a few moments was so great, and the concentration of all so centred on the bubbling coffee-pot, that one felt as if all the meaning of life, the past, the present, and the future, was being distilled in the black liquid, and that an incantation was only necessary for the future to take shape and, rising out of the pot, become visible to us all in this mysterious darkness.

Again the coffee boiled up. Again the man emptied the boiling liquid back into the other pot and replaced it on the fire.

The stillness and the concentration became more intense. Outside, a lamb's sudden cry and the mother's answering bleat rang out sharply in the black night, a distant reminder of a far-off world; it died away, and the broken silence was all the more intense.

The coffee boiled up.

By this time one had ceased to associate the drinking of coffee with the end of these mysterious rites. The coffee of Cook's hotels, the coffee of crowded railway stations, whole coffee, ground coffee, French coffee, coffee at 1s. 8d.[51] a pound; the clatter of black saucepans, the hot and anxious cook, the bustling waiter, the impatient people of the world with only a minute to wait – calling for instantaneous coffee; what had coffee

---

[51] One shilling and eightpence – approximately eight modern British pennies.

and all those associations to do with this? And so it was with a certain shock that we looked at this magician pouring the result of his black art into the cups, a few carefully measured drops only.

Two are handed to us and one to the Sheikh. We sipped the oily black drink slowly and thoughtfully. A liquid which had been prepared with so much deliberation could not be quaffed down with the reckless indifference ordinarily displayed in the process. It was thick and bitter. We drained the last drop and returned the cups. Another spoonful was poured in and they were passed back to us. Etiquette required that we should not refuse till the third time of offering; then the remainder of the coffee was handed round to the rest of the company in order of rank.

There was a stir among the crowd round the door, and a woman forced her way through with a baby in her arms. She squatted in front of us, and held the child down for our closer inspection by the fire-light.

"Khasta," (ill) said Ali Chous; "she wants medicine."

The mother pointed to the sores on the child's face and body, the pleading eloquence in her dark eyes rendering unnecessary any explanations on the part of our interpreter.

It was a pathetic instance of the suffering induced by man, even when living so akin to Nature, when he tries to superimpose his own crude ideas of beauty and expediency on to the human frame. The baby, though only a few months old, had been pierced in the nose and ears for the reception of the ornaments which were to enhance its charms in after-life, and of the blue bead which would ensure its safety from the one recognised enemy – the Evil Eye. The wounds were healing badly, and the irritation set up had caused fever.

"Tell her we can give her medicine," we said to Ali, "but it is not medicine to drink, it is to wash the wounds with. If the baby drinks it, it will die."

The message was interpreted. "Aha, aha, Mashallah," was murmured all through the crowd. The baby became an object of intense interest. Ali threw back his head and pretended to swallow, then he pointed significantly to heaven and to the unconscious victim at his feet.

"Ha! ha!" murmured the crowd.

Hassan meanwhile had begun to fidget uneasily.

"There are fleas here," he said, "you must not stop any longer."

We rose, and silently salaaming our host, passed out of the tent. It was lighter outside; the moon had risen, casting mysterious black shadows round the huts, where weird black and white forms flitted stealthily in and out.

Owing to the shallowness of the water on the low shelving mud banks we had been unable to bring the raft right up to the shore, and it had been moored at a little distance out in the water. The kalekjis had carried across on their backs and had returned to cook their evening meal on board. We now shouted across the water to them to come and carry us back. As we stood waiting, a woman came up to us dragging a child by the arm, who hid his head in his mother's dress and refused to allow himself to be examined.

"He is ill too," said Ali, "like the other child."

"We will give them some medicine when we get on the raft," we said; "tell them each to send a cup."

"And this one says he is ill," the man went on, as a tall, sheepish-looking youth touched me on the arm; "they will all say they are ill now that they know you have medicine."

"We can only give to those who are really ill," we answered; "what is the matter with this one?"

"He has fever, he cannot eat, and his head hurts."

I had some quinine pills in my pocket, and I gave three to the boy.

"Tell him to take two now, and not to keep them in his mouth," I explained, "but drink some water and swallow them down; then, when the sun has risen one hour to-morrow, let him take the other one."

A dozen interested spectators at once went through the whole process in pantomime; a pill was swallowed, and its downward course indicated by stroking the chest. "Ha!" was ejaculated all round. Then the second pill was swallowed with equally suggestive signs. The rising point of the sun was indicated, and one finger held up, and the third pill swallowed.

"Mashallah!" went up through the crowd, staring with bated breath.

We boarded the raft, and had scarcely established ourselves in our sleeping-hut when Hassan staggered to the door with a huge clay pitcher, capable of holding several gallons; he deposited it at our feet.

"For the medicine," he said gravely.

"We said that the woman was to send a cup," we said; "the few drops of lotion will be lost in that."

"For the medicine." He answered, imperturbably.

"We had better send it in one of our cups," I said, and I measured out some lotion. Hassan took it; a few minutes later he returned laden with cups, jars, pitchers, and bowls of every size and description.

"For the medicine," he said, as he deposited them beside us.

We looked at one another aghast.

"Say that we have no more," we said.

"I have told them" he said, "but they will not go away."

We went outside, where a tremendous hubbub had arisen. Our men were standing round the edge of the raft resolutely pushing would-be intruders back into the river. Up to their waists in water, hanging on to the raft at every point, shouting out their ailments, pointing to their throats, their eyes, their heads, were the whole male population of the place. In vain our men strove to keep them off; the raft was besieged at every point.

In desperation we unmoored and floated out into the middle of the river; the most determined swam out after us, and holding on to the raft with one hand stroked their chests and pointed to the absent sun with the other. Finally, as we drifted down-stream, they gave up, and the last sight we had was that of a row of disconsolate invalids, suddenly endowed with great evidence of health and strength, careering wildly on the mud flats in the starlight round a discarded heap of empty bowls and pitchers.

CHAPTER 16

A STORM AND A LULL

The men were still very quarrelsome; the whole day their grating voices never stopped. They seemed, however, quite anxious to row now, and proposed at sunset that we should not moor to the shore as usual but, as the night was not very dark, keep on and make up for lost time. We had been in bed a little while and were dropping off to sleep, in spite of the ceaseless quarrelsome voices, when a worse outbreak than usual thoroughly awakened me.

"They are having a fight on board," said X, sleepily; "I suppose we must leave them at it."

I peered through the chinks of the door. Jedan had taken off all his clothes and was trying to jump off the raft into the middle of the river. Hassan and Ali were holding on to him for dear life, and the Evil One sat at the oars screaming with rage. Arten was offering him the remains of our dinner. Jedan seemed finally to yield to the other men's entreaties and sat down on the raft, the tears rolling down his cheeks. Ali sat beside him, holding his hand and murmuring soothing words. The Evil One occupied himself with devouring the dinner. General peace seemed, in fact, restored, and our slumbers were not again disturbed.

Next morning we threatened them both with dismissal at Tekreet, where we hoped to arrive that day, and which we know was the seat of a Mudir, to whom we could make a show of appealing if the worst came to the worst.

The cause of the disturbance was put down to Jedan, whose native village was close by, and who had threatened to leave the raft altogether if the Evil One bullied him any longer. Jedan begged to be allowed to visit his home, and it so happened that the wind rose again to such a pitch just opposite the place itself that we were compelled to put to shore. It was another Arab encampment, a collection of black tents with maize enclosures. Jedan at once disappeared amongst them and, later on, as we strolled round the village, we came across him seated just inside a tent with two small children on his knees. He invited us to come in and sit down. The tent was full of his kindred. In the far corner a child shared with a bleating kid the quilted covering which constituted the bed of the establishment. A woman beside him was spinning wool and another one at the door was grinding dari for bread. A grown-up son sat opposite, industriously working the wool from his mother's wheel on to a leather sole for sandals.

Jedan appeared in quite a new light in the centre of his family circle; he suddenly seemed endowed with a dignity becoming his present position as monarch of all he surveyed. The children on his knee clung to him and stroked his beard, and he softly patted their heads. All the gruff surliness and cringing hatred of the expression with which he regarded the Evil One on the fact had disappeared, and he smiled with benign content on his domestic surroundings. He sent the boy out into the village with orders to get some delicacy in our honour. In a few minutes the lad returned with a raw turnip, which was cut into chunks and offered to us with much ceremony. Then a bowl of youart[52] was produced, and we felt compelled to drink out of the common stock.

At midday the wind had subsided and we insisted on starting off at once, with the hope of reaching Tekreet before evening. It was five days since we had left Mosul, and we had scarcely covered one hundred miles. As we had counted on reaching Baghdad in that time, our supply of provisions had got very low. The river was now deep and broad, and the strong current carried us along at a good pace. Jedan's visit to his family had put him in a very good humour, and even the Evil One, who had participated in the feast of raw turnip, worked quietly at the oars.

Every moment took us further from the snow mountains and the bleak country of the north and nearer the sunny south. Already the sun's hot rays poured down soothingly, and everybody was in that state of quiet contentment, known as "kief" in the East. Hassan, seated cross-legged with his back against the hut, dozed at intervals. Ali was rolling up long, fat cigarettes by the door, and Arten, stretched full length inside, was making up for his disturbed slumbers of the past night. X lay on a rug at the edge of the raft and I sat beside her, reading aloud the Prophetic utterances on Nineveh.

The Bible is one of the few books that one can read in this sort of wandering life. This is, perhaps, because we are in the land where people live in rock houses, and hew their tombs in rocks, and wear girdles, and say "Aha," eat honey a lot, and go out to desolate lands, and

---

[52] Yoghurt.

say their prayers on the housetop. We were living with the shepherds who divided the sheep and goats and nightfall and watered their flocks at sundown; with the women who came down with their pitchers to the wells, and with the elders sitting at the gates. One felt that any other book made too great a demand on one's mental powers. Even now the sound of one's own voice was disturbing, and for some time we sat listening to the silence and imbibing the sun.

A sudden chill crept into the atmosphere and a blackness covered the face of the waters. I looked up at the sky. A line of angry, black clouds had overtaken the sun, gathering up the scattered white fleeces in its path, and was advancing rapidly over our heads. An ominous sound of rising winds seemed to herald its approach. In less than three minutes we were swept up in the arms of a howling gale; sudden gusts caught the walls of the hut and swirled us round, the playthings of a merciless, raging force, at one moment tearing us into the middle of the stream, and the next dashing us with redoubled vigour against its rocky sides.

The rain came down in blinding torrents, and the waves, breaking over the surface of the raft, made it seem as if we were being submerged altogether under the water. Then we rose on the crest of a wave once more, which dashed us against a wall of rock rising precipitously at the side, with a force which seemed as if it must shatter asunder all the bending, creaking poles of the raft. Ali and Hassan stood on the edge, trying to break the force of the blows with the butt end of their rifles, while the kalekjis struggled fruitlessly at the oars.

The lowering black sky, the raging black waters, the unyielding black walls of rock gave a grim setting of darkness to this struggle, which proved to be no less than a fight with death itself. Our companions, the birds, clung huddled up with fright to sheltering walls of rock, or crept into niches, where they cowered together, hiding their heads under their wings. Even the noise of the wind and waters could not drown the wild, terrified shriek of startled crows when we were dashed against their hiding places, and they flew close past our heads to seek a fresh shelter.

This, then, was to be the end of our interlude of peace. It seemed as if the jealous gods, conscious of our forgetfulness of their authority, were proclaiming our powerlessness against their decrees. They tossed us ruthlessly about until we were reduced to a state of subordination, and then, as if repenting of their anger, they caused the wind to lull and shot out a gleam of sunshine through the dark clouds. We passed out beyond the walls of rock, on which the wet drops now gleamed like bits of silver, and drifted in a broad, slow stream with low, shelving banks. On the last ledge, with downcast heads, sat three great vultures, disappointed of their prey.

Hassan thoughtfully rolled some cigarettes; he lit one and handed it to me; then he lit another and handed it to X. She shook her head. "Smoke," he said sternly. X took the cigarette and, all need for action being over, we resumed our attitudes of contemplation. But the atmosphere of lazy indifference seemed to be dispelled. Where were we drifting to? Were we at any moment likely to be snatched from this state of peaceful acquiescence in our surroundings, and be hurled to destruction with no word of warning or choice in the matter?

"Ah, well, kim bilior?" (who knows?) I said out loud.

"Who know what?" said Hassan.

"What is going to happen to us?" I said.

"Kim bilior?" repeated Hassan. "Allah bilior" (God knows), and then, after a minute's silence, he repeated:

"Kim bilior? Allah bilior!"

I looked up at him.

"It is so," he said, nodding his head solemnly; "Kim bilior? Allah bilior!"

The influence of the Eastern mind asserted itself; the future had no interest for them. Allah had arranged their destiny; it had nothing to do with them, and no thought or effort on their part would make any difference. Nor had the past any interest for them. They lived in the present, enjoying the pleasant places and accepting the unpleasant ones with no fear or resentment.

The storm was over and they sat about drying their clothes and making preparations for the evening meal. Jedan slowly unwound his keffiyeh[53] and wiped his head all over, then he spread the coloured rag out to dry. Ali and Hassan rubbed their rifles carefully and hung them up inside the hut. Then Ali spread out his cloak on the far corner of the raft and went through the midday prayer; this over, he borrowed a needle and thread from me and began darning a tear in his ragged uniform.

The sun shone brightly and our clothes were soon dry. Birds appeared on the bank shaking their feathers and stretching out one limb after another. The lull that follows a great storm reigned over everything; all nature seemed resting after her exertions.

---

[53] A Bedouin Arab's headdress

Ali Chous finished his darn and began to sing; the kalekjis joined in the chorus, clapping their hands. An element of cheerful carelessness established itself on board. I went inside and began to invent a pudding for dinner. Arten was not enlightened in his profession as cook, and I was trying to supplement his deficiencies by the light of nature, for Arten did not seem to have that sort of light. I tied the mixture up in a handkerchief and set it to boil in a pot on the brazier. One by one the men came in and sat round the fire, gazing silently at the pot as they smoked away. After a time I took the lid off and examined its contents.

"Is it really going to be a pudding?" said X, with an agonised expression.

I tried to recall what puddings looked like in England, and then remembered that I had never seen one at this stage.

"I cannot say till it is finished," I said.

The pudding still clung ominously to the handkerchief; I had greased it well and have since heard that you only grease pans. I gave it a few minutes longer, then, as we were all hungry, I fished it out of the pot and untied the handkerchief.

"Bak!" (Look) said Arten.

"Bak!" said Hassan.

"Bak!" said the kalekjis.

It was a moment of extreme tension.

I slipped it on to a plate.

"Now look," said Arten.

"See now what a cook she is!" said Hassan, "a wonderful cook."

"Mashallah," said Ali.

"Mashallah," said the kalekjis.

"It *is* a pudding," said X, "a real pudding."

We all gazed at it for several moments in ecstatic excitement. I handed X a spoon and we each took a mouthful; then we looked at one another.

"It is a pudding," said X again.

It almost seemed as if she were trying to persuade herself of the fact against the dictates of reason. When we had finished, the men shared our spoons in turn; each one cautiously raised a spoonful and smelt it, then they swallowed it, very much as one remembers swallowing jam in the nursery when one knew there was a powder inside.

"Ehe," (Good), they said very deliberately, nodding their heads, and then, as they handed the spoon to their neighbour, "Inghiliz" they added.

One felt that the first word was Turkish politeness; the second was a veiled warning to their brethren.

But on the whole it seemed a success; we had a sense of repletion; how often had we not swallowed bowls of rice and been only conscious of a great internal void.

The men carried our rugs outside and we stretched ourselves lazily out on the open end of the raft. I began to reflect upon Time and Destiny. No shadow of a cloud appeared to disturb the horizon, no obstruction in the river affected our steady onward course down the slow, wide stream; we took the current where it served, and so were not delayed in the shallows where the waters dallied about the banks; they in due course would arrive at their destination and pour themselves, unquestioning and unquestioned, into the oblivious sea.

But what would Time, that unremitting, relentless current, do with us? Was it going to hurl us too into oblivion? Whatever it had to give was ours, and et, because we could not stop it, we were not master of it. We could moor to the shore and let the river go on without us; the current did not wait for us, but we could pick it up again when we were ready for it and go on without loss; but in the current of Time, when we stay on one side and let the moments go past us, we have lost for ever what those moments had to give, and our arrival at our destination has not been delayed; it is so much the nearer.

"X," I said, "where do you think we are floating to?"

"Baghdad," said X.

"I wasn't thinking geographically," I answered, "I was thinking whether it was Eternity or Oblivion. Being hurried along by this current gives me an uncomfortable feeling of not being allowed any choice as regards time, which I resent. Do you mind it at all?"

"No," said X, "I feel that I have lost all conception of time, and that we are floating on, as it were, to Eternity."

"Do you?" I said dubiously; "I feel it's Oblivion we are getting to."

"But we are only three days off Baghdad," insisted X.

"Well," I answered, "I devoutly pray that we may get there first."

We arrived at Tekreet just before sunset, and at once sent Ali up to the Mudir with the request that he would help us in the dismissal of the Evil One.

"Tell the Mudir," we said, "that we cannot sleep for the noise he makes at night, and our heads ache from the noise he makes in the day time, and that he has guided the raft so badly that we have spent five days getting here from Mosul."

Ali obediently disappeared. He first communicated the substance of our remarks to the kalekjis, who, after putting their heads together, landed and strolled down a rambling street of Arab huts. We also went on shore with Hassan, and wandered about along the rocky paths amongst labyrinths of tombs which ran down to the water's edge. Tekreet boasts of one palm-tree, the first we had seen on the river, and an old castle, the ruins of which stand on a rock above. The town is a tumble-down sort of a place, inhabited chiefly by Arabs, who ply rafts with merchandise between Mosul and Baghdad.

Ali returned with the news that the Mudir had given orders for new kalekjis to be ready in the morning. He apologised in the name of the Sultan for the discomfort we had experienced in his Highness'' domains. We asked what had become of the others, and were informed that they were frightened of being punished and had run away.

"That's curious," I said, "I should have thought that no Eastern would put fright before baksheesh, or mind what a Mudir said in this district."

Later on an emissary arrived from the Mudir with a piece of sheep and a message that he would travel with us the next day as far as Samarah. Accordingly we sent back word that we were starting at sunrise.

We went to bed that night with a greater sense of security than we had felt since leaving Mosul. We came, moreover, to the conclusion that there was, perhaps, a slight advantage in being under Government patronage, when we really had to apply for that protection which his Highness the Sultan so anxiously proffers to all travellers in his well-regulated country.

CHAPTER 17

AN ENCOUNTER WITH FANATICS

It was long after sunrise when we awoke next morning; the raft was still tied up and the men showed no signs of moving.

"Hi!" shouted X to Hassan through the felt wall, "why haven't we started?"

"The Mudir has not arrived yet, Effendi."

We waited another ten minutes.

"Hi! Hassan, has the Mudir come?"

"No, Effendi, he will come soon."

We turned over and had another doze.

"Hi! Hassan, if the Mudir has not come we shall go without him. Send Ali to say we must start now."

"Yes, Effendi, he will go."

Turkish acquiescence, especially when very polite, is suspicious. I got out of bed and peeped through the door. Ali was sitting on the bank chatting with a local Zaptieh.

"Hi! Hassan, send Ali at once."

"Yes, yes, Effendi, this minute he goes."

From my point of observation I reported that neither Hassan nor Ali were making any move in the matter, so we decided to dress and become strenuous about it.

I relieved my feelings at intervals by trying to express in my best Turkish to Hassan, through the wall, what I thought of the Mudir who dared to keep great English Pashas waiting beyond the accustomed two hours which one conceded to Eastern ideas of punctuality.

Before we had finished dressing a sudden rocking of the raft and general bustle outside announced our departure. Through the window I took a last look at Tekreet and thanked my lucky stars that departure from it meant also deliverance from the Evil One.

"Do you think the Mudir will be angry with us for leaving him behind?" I said.

"Let us hope not," said X, as we emerged from the hut for breakfast; "we owe him something for ridding us of the Evil One."

The words were hardly out of her mouth before we became aware of the Evil One himself, sitting between the oars in his usual place. He greeted us with a bland smile. Beside him, instead of Jedan, sat a grinning boy.

We turned on Ali for an explanation.

"Ach, Effendi, he is good now; he will not speak; he will not say a word; he is changed; he is now a good kalekji. The ladies can now sleep at night."

The Evil One nodded affably at us and put his finger on his sealed lips. The grinning boy understood Turkish. "I am a good kalekji, Effendi; I do not talk, I never say a word."

We had become sufficiently Oriental to reconcile ourselves to the dictates of Destiny; there was no getting rid of him now, so we had to be content with threats of no baksheesh if a word was uttered on the way to Baghdad.

We caught sight of a stranger in the men's hut.

"Who is that?" I said.

"The Mudir, Effendi."

"How long has he been there?"

"Since sunrise, Effendi."

"Why did you say he had not come?"

"Ach, Effendi, the kalekji's bread was not ready; they could not go without bread."

So all this time the local magnate had been sitting listening to our abuse of his person. There is only one way to live in the East, and that is to accept it. Its ways are stronger than your ways, especially when you come out freshly armed with the ardour of the West. Your best reasoning is worsted by gracious irrelevancy; your protesting attacks are turned by acquiescing politeness; and the East moves on its smiling, unalterable way.

The country below Tekreet began to have a more civilised look; there were plantations of cucumbers and melons on the banks and roughly constructed windlasses for raising the water in skins into irrigating channels. We passed several ruined villages, and caught sight in the distance of the remains of an old castle.

At noon, after floating about three or four miles, we arrived within sight of Samarah, a town which was made conspicuous by the huge blue dome of its mosque and which, we learnt later on, was a place of pilgrimage for Mahomedans of the Shia sect. We drew up opposite it to land the Mudir, and Hassan announced his intention of landing also to replenish the store of charcoal.

"Then I'll get off too," said X, "I want to see inside that mosque."

X had a mania for looking at mosques; we had seen inside hundreds of them and she never seemed to get tired of them. I connected the process chiefly with having to unlace your boots, a proceeding I detest, and dawdle over cold floors in your stocking feet. Then you had to remember to cross your hands in front; if you put them behind your back or in your pockets you were a marked infidel.

The raft was run along the shore and we walked up to the town. It was enclosed by a high mud wall which was defended by towers and bastions. We entered through a large gateway and found ourselves amongst a collection of falling mud houses lining the usual dirty, narrow streets. Hassan went in search of charcoal, and we, accompanied by Ali Chous, strolled on to the mosque.

We were followed by the usual crowd of curious-minded inhabitants, but being by this time quite used to these attentions, we did not notice them particularly. X was in front, and advanced towards the low line of chains which barred the entrance to the building; she was in the act of stepping over the chains when an excited-looking fanatic rushed at her and hurled her across the street with what appeared to be effusive execrations.

In one moment we were hemmed in by an angry, buzzing mob; there was no mistaking the glaring menaces of their expressions and the significant handling of the long knives worn by all natives in their belts. We realised in a flash that we had unwittingly aroused the dangerous side of Eastern fanaticism.

Resistance was out of the question; a sign of fear would have been fatal. All day-dreams were at an end: I recalled the vague forebodings the storm had first aroused in me. Was it only the day before that X had said she felt like floating to Eternity and I had maintained that we should be hurled into Oblivion? Were we only joking then? Now we were face to face with grim reality. Hassan's words rang in my ears, "Kim bilior? Allah bilior!" (Who knows? God knows!) We stopped and looked over the crowd. Ali Chous, our only protector, stood beside us white and trembling, appealing to some of the leading men, who hesitated and glared at us in wavering suspicion. Hassan was nowhere in sight.

"Let's stroll on as far as the end of the street," said X.

"Yes," I answered, "that seems a good idea."

"Don't let's hurry," she said.

"No," I replied, "we have plenty of time."

The crowd made way for us as we turned from the mosque, and we walked on beyond it up through the bazaars. The men had begun to fight and wrangle amongst themselves, the narrow street was tightly packed, and the crowd surged up behind us as we walked on.

We were in the covered part of the bazaars; the usual bright-coloured keffiyehs hung outside: gaudy cotton coats of Eastern make lay on the top of bales of Manchester prints and flannelettes; there was the leather stall, with gorgeous beaded bridles and handsomely embroidered native saddles; and next it was the boot bazaar, with none of our blackness about it, but a mass of red and yellow sandals. We had seen it all, just the same in a score of similar villages, but I took it all in this time as I had never taken it in before.

"What a funny baby's garment that is," said X.

The crowd behind were beginning to push.

"Yes," I said, "I wonder how it gets outside the baby."

An angry buzz arose just behind us; were they going to stick us in the back? We both disdained to turn our heads to see.

"I hope Hassan will think of getting some spinach," I said, "there was some in the vegetable bazaar."

"He knows you like it," X answered, "he is sure to get it."

We had come to the end of the row of stalls; we slowly turned and faced the mob.

"This is the obvious moment for annihilation," I thought to myself, "I wonder why I'm not afraid."

I was waiting in momentary expectation of death, but at the same time I could not realise that we were going to be killed. I did not seem to be able to take in what being killed was – I felt very indifferent, and noticed that I had lost a button off my coat. But the crowd made way for us and we sauntered back. Further down we met Hassan.

"What is all this crowd about?" he said.

X told him; he made no answer and we walked on together.

We got outside the gates of the town but were still a few minutes' walk from the river.

"I'm tired," said X; "let's rest here a minute," and she lay down on the ground.

I looked round. There was still a noisy crowd at the gates of the town, and we were being followed by some of the rowdier members. I had a vague idea that it would have been more comfortable to lie down on the raft, but there was no accounting for tastes, and it was all in the day's work. I sat down beside X. There was a white stone a few yards away, larger than the others which lay about; I picked up a handful of the smaller stones.

"Best out of ten," I said to myself; "if I hit we get, if I don't hit we are done for. There is no current about this, it's all chance," and I started lazily throwing at the large stone. Hassan stood by smoking. I missed the first, and the second, and the third. Ali Chous looked uneasily at the crowd beginning to straggle out towards us. The fourth hit, and the fifth; the sixth missed. Two more misses and we should be done for. Ali Chous begged us to come on. The seventh and the eighth hit, the ninth missed. The next throw would settle the question.

Two men had come up and stood looking at us.

"Let's come on now," said X, sitting up.

"One minute," I said, and I carefully picked out a nice round pebble. It hit.

"What a baby you are!" said X.

We boarded the raft and pushed off. It was a lovely calm evening. The current was straight enough for us to glide quietly along with no assistance from the oars; the last traces of the setting sun slowly disappeared, and gradually the stars reflected twinkling points of silver in the black water, dancing brightly in the moving current. A silence as of death reigned over everything; the blackness of death peered out of the deep waters; the slow but surely moving current was drifting us on relentlessly towards an uncertainty suggesting death. And with it there was a tremendous sense of stillness and peace.

I was sitting very near the edge looking into the dark waters.

"I don't want to die yet," I said.

"You are such a time taking things in," said X, "that you would not be aware that you were dead until so long after the event that it would hardly matter to you. You weren't afraid, were you?"

"No," I answered. We were silent for a while, then Hassan spoke.

"If you had crossed the chain," he said, "there would have been no more Pashas for me to travel with. Inside is the tomb of the last Imam of the race of Ali, and no Christian may look upon it and live." I looked again into the deep waters and began to take it all in, what I had seen in the men's faces and how they would have done it. Hassan put a rug over me; I had shivered. I wasn't cold. It was all over, we were safe; but I was knowing what it was to be afraid.

CHAPTER 18

THE END OF THE RAFT

We were now only sixty-five miles from Baghdad, and with luck we should reach it next day. We travelled on all night, and on waking up next morning found ourselves floating past cultivated banks and creaking waterwheels, and sighted in the distance dark patches of palm-groves.

But, in spite of Ali's prayers to the "God of the favouring breeze," our enemy the wind rose up once more and compelled us to put to shore. From this point it was only a few hours by land to Baghdad. We could faintly see the town itself on the distant horizon line to the east, separated from us by a great expanse of sandy desert. We were told, however, that the river wound in and out so much that it was still a day's journey off by water.

We kicked our heels disconsolately on shore – a sandy shore this time; little sandy hillocks alternated with patches of struggling tufts of grass. We sat there all day. The sand blew into our faces, and the river rolled on past us – and just behind me a rat put its head occasionally out of a hole to see if we were still there. Arten also at intervals put his head out of the hut and held up his hand in the hurricane to feel if the wind was blowing.

"There is still much wind," he would say, and as no one paid any attention to his original remark he retired again into the hut, and the rat looked out of his hole. I always mixed up Arten with rats after that day.

By and by a goufa appeared on the scene. A goufa is a native boat made of pomegranate branches laced together with ropes and covered inside and out with bitumen. It is like a circular coracle, eight to ten feet across and about four feet deep, and is propelled with a single paddle.

The crew disembarked just above us. First came half a dozen Arabs, then a veiled woman, then a donkey, then a buffalo, then another woman, then three more men.   One donkey still remained inside with two men. He refused to be jumped over the side like his predecessors. All the people on shore yelled at him and the men in the boat hit him. Hits and cries were of no avail; he sneered at the yellers and kicked at the hitters. The donkey on land gazed mournfully at his companion and brayed.

Finally the offender put his two fore feet on the edge of the boat and the men behind seized his hind legs and heaved him overboard. He rolled over in the water, shook himself unconcernedly, and started to browse the withered grass. Then everybody disappeared behind sandy hillocks, the goufa floated past us, and we were once more left alone with the wind and the rat.

Towards sunset we made a start again, and floated on most of the night. Small mud villages and plantations of palms and orange-trees were scattered thickly on each side of the rive. We seemed to be quite close to Baghdad; gilded domes and minarets stood up on the sky-line above confused masses of flat-topped houses and groups of palm-trees. But al the morning we wound slowly round and round endless loops of the river and hardly seemed to get any nearer to our destination. The banks now teemed with life; goufas shot across past us from one bank to another with mixed consignments of men and animals; mules plodded up and down drawing skins of water over windlasses; groups of Arabs lay about on the sunny banks and shouted inquiries at the kalekjis as we passed. The houses, which had been mud hovels higher up the river, now looked more substantial, and were each surrounded by high walls enclosing shady orange gardens. Finally we hove in sight of the bridge of boats which guards the entrance to the town, and ran into the shore just above it. The bridge, we learnt, had to be broken down before the raft could pass through, and as this seemed likely to take some hours we landed and drove up to the Consulate. H. M. Vice-Consul was away, and so we proceeded to the Babylon Hotel.

Baghdad can be reached in a normal way up the Persian Gulf to Busra and from thence by the weekly mail steamer; it contains, therefore, certain concessions to the ideas of occasional European agents and commercial travellers. The Babylon Hotel is one of these concessions. There was a dining-room hung all round with the framed self-assertions of various wine and spirit merchants whose names, strangely familiar, mocked us from the wall as a first greeting from the borders of civilisation. Hassan stood in the middle of the room and gazed at them open-mouthed. These were to him English works of art, decorations of great English houses, in keeping with the gaudily covered chairs and meaningless glass ornaments. Each one had unmistakable pictorial aspects of the bottle. He pointed at first one and then another.

"Ingilhiz," he said in a tone of congratulation. He was always pleased when we met with anything which would seem to remind us of our native land. We were irresponsive; he studied them further.

"Raki?" (Whisky) he added, the note of inquiry tinged with apologetic scorn.

The hotel was built, like all the better modern houses, along the banks of the river, with overhanging balconies. I escaped from the further evidences of Western vulgarity, and, leaning over the rail of the balcony, let the passing river wash them away from the disturbed crevices of my brain.

Just beneath, on one side, the narrow street which led to the hotel was continued past it down to the shore; and here came an incessant stream of natives; women with waterskins to fill and men with mules carrying baskets of town refuse to empty; the same spot served admirably for both purposes. The Eastern has an overwhelming love for "taze su" (fresh water); he drinks it, he sings to it, he worships it, he makes an emblem of it, and yet – with his extraordinarily consistent inconsistency – he makes the town midden and the town watering-place one and the same spot.

A nearly naked child sprawled about amongst the dirt and rubbish, unearthing hidden treasures in the form of bright tin lids. The mules strayed about at the water's muddy edge, putting in a drink on their own account whilst their masters, having emptied the loads, filled waterskins for the return journey.

A big, lumbering sailing boat was being unloaded just below me; the men swung themselves to and fro together as they pitched heavy bales overboard.

"Allah, Allah, Allah," they sang out as they swung. Round their heads circled and swooped white gulls talking of the sea.

And now, through the distant broken bridge, clumsily floating down the current, came our raft, square and stubborn amongst the twirling, swiftly paddled goufas. Like a great, uncertain, bewildered animal, turning now this way and now that, guided by the unwieldy poplar poles, it lurched up the watering-place and stuck on the midden.

From every corner of the narrow, winding street sprang out half-clothed, jabbering Arab forms; gesticulating, fighting, jostling, they proffered their services in the task of unloading.

In a few moments all our belongings were removed; the cooking-pots, the rugs, the beds, all the personal requirements which had made it into our home for so many weeks. Stripped and deserted, looking almost ashamed of itself, it lay there in all its naked clumsiness. By to-morrow even this vestige of our journey will have disappeared for ever from the realms of historic evidence. The felt strips, the walls which have sheltered us through so many stormy nights, will be sold to the highest bidder; they will serve henceforth as carpets in some native hovel, on which the Mahomedan will kneel to say his prayers or squat to smoke his pipe. The poles and oars will go as firewood; and the skins, deflated, will return to the country we have left. Nothing will remain but the memory of it to a few human minds. We are glad that it is to be so; as it has been exclusively ours in the past, so will it remain ours only in the future. We made it what it was, and without us it will cease to be.

The waters gave it a farewell lap as they passed on. We had stopped; but they went hurrying on, taking with them all those mixed memories of peace and danger, of contemplation and exertion, of idleness and hurry which they, and they only, had shared with us. They had borne us from the wilds and fastnesses of the unconquered East to the gateway of the Western invasion; through the dreariness and desolation of desert lands, through the magnificent isolation of gorgeous mountain scenery, past the ruined evidences of ancient Western civilisations still mocked by the persistence of squalid tribal huts; and now, having deposited us to draw our own conclusions in this decayed city of the Khalifs, they hurried on, lapping scornfully in their course at the rocking pleasure-boat of Messrs. Sassoon's representatives and the white steam launch of H. M. British Vice-Consulate.

Impartially, as they had borne us up, so down here they bore up alike the brass trinkets shipped in their thousands from Manchester, the emissary of the British and Foreign Bible Society, the golf clubs and society papers for the English Club; and with an indescribable roar, as of grim laughter, rushed headlong into the salt blue waters of the Persian Gulf, where, surrendering irretrievably their own bounded individuality, they merged themselves in the larger life of the untrammelled Eastern seas.

A Goupa.

"Drawing Skins of Water."

"I read on a porch of a palace bold,
In a purple table letters cast –
'A house though a million years old,
A house of earth comes down at last;
Then quarry thy stones from the crystal All,
And build the dome that shall not fall.'"

"We Follow and Follow the Journeying Sun."

PART III

BAGHDAD TO DAMASCUS

CHAPTER 19

BABYLON

The eastern gate of heaven was unbarred; Shamas, the Sun-god of Babylonia, flamed forth and stepped upon the Mount of Sunrise at the edge of the world. As he had poured the light of heaven upon the luxuriant gardens and fertile cornlands of the Babylonians, so was he pouring it upon the same spot, now an arid and deserted wilderness.

We were crossing it on our way to visit Babylon. It was pitch dark when we had left Baghdad in the procession of covered arabas which conveyed pilgrims to Kerbela and merchants to Hillah. We had been roused at 2 a.m., and had threaded our way silently through the sleeping streets by the light of a dim lantern. Huddled human forms lay about in angles and on doorsteps; and at every moment we stumbled over the outstretched limbs of a yellow dog. We crossed the Tigris in one of the round native boats, and landed within a few minutes' walk of the khan from where the arabas started.

We had an araba to ourselves; an oblong wooden box on four wheels, with a light canvas top and canvas sides that could be rolled up or let down at leisure; a narrow wooden plank, with a singularly sharp edge and an uncomfortably hard face, ran down each side, and was called a seat. We were going to sit on it for twelve hours. We were drawn by four mules harnessed abreast. Our driver had knotted the reins and hooked them on to his seat; his hands were rolled inside his cloak, and he sat huddled up on the box in the freezing air of sunrise. The mules galloped ahead at their own discretion; the araba lurched over ruts; sudden jerks shot us against one another, or threw us in the air, from whence we descended with some emphasis in the vacuum between the two sharp edges.

Now the horizon on the left blazed orange and red, and the desert sands were pink. Stunted tufts of grey-green grass tried to assert themselves in the barren soil; mounds, marking the site of ancient villages, occurred at random; walls of sand, indicating the course of old irrigating canals, broke the level plain; they could almost be taken for the work of Nature, for the hand of Time had obliterated the marks of man.

Every twenty minutes the arabas came to a sudden stop to give the mules breathing time; there is a general dismounting of the passengers; the plain is suddenly dotted with bending, praying forms, groups of excited talking Arabs, isolated, contemplative, smoking individuals, fussy superior Turkish officers flicking the specks of travel off their smart uniforms; veiled women peep from behind the curtain of a closely packed conveyance; a small Arab child plants himself with outstretched legs in front of us, and sucks his thumb in complete absorption as he gazes upon us like a little wild animal.

Then the whole scene dissolves itself into a sudden rush for the carriages, as of so many rabbits bolting into a warren at the sound of an alarm, and off goes the whole train at a gallop; belated loiterers hang perilously on the step of any conveyance they can catch, and try to snatch the lash of the whip with which the driver good-humouredly flicks them.

Finally, we approach a collection of mud huts; we dash through them, scattering hens and children, and draw up in a long line opposite a large khan in the centre of the village. This is one of the regular halting places for caravans, and we have a short wait while the mules are being changed. A stall close by is already closely besieged by our fellow-travellers clamouring for tea, which is sold in small glasses after the Persian custom. We buy a little blue dish of thick cream from an Arab girl in a blue smock, and make a sumptuous breakfast off it and dates.

With a fresh set of mules we start off again; the party is more lively. We dash up the sides of an embankment, catch a glimpse of a silted-up canal as we waver for a moment on the top; then a fearful double lurch throws us about as the two front wheels go downwards whilst the two back ones are still going upwards. A short, sharp descent follows, then comes a level stretch; the driver boys shout and race one another, we overtake and are overtaken, we jeer and are jeered at.

And the Sun-god pursues his journey in silence and unconcern across the dome of heaven.

We pass bands of Persian pilgrims on their way to the sacred Tomb of Hosein, son of Ali and grandson of the Prophet. Many of them trudge along on foot, grasping only the stout staff which one's mind associates with pilgrims; these give a true feeling of sackcloth and ashes. Some ride mules and carry a few worldly goods in saddle-bags. There is a Pasha mounted on a fine Arab horse and followed by servants; large pack trunks on mules in his train make one doubt the existence of his hair shirts. The women sit in covered wicker cradles suspended on each side of mules; donkeys bear rude coffins strapped crossways over their backs, for the ambition of the true believer is not only to make the pilgrimage during life, but that after death his bones may rest in peace in the holy ground of Hosein's martyrdom.

At Mushayhib we halt again to get a fresh relay of mules. Here the roads branch and we part company with the rest of the party, who are going to Kerbela. We jerk along over the ridged and rutty ground. I find myself wondering whether cushions in the chariots were amongst the luxuries of wicked Babylon, and if so, whether it was part of the punishment of the fourth generation that we should be deprived of them.

We come to a marshy tract with water standing in pools; the driver thrashes the mules vigorously and shouts, the animals plunge forward, and the boy bends his body to and fro with them as they plunge. We go headlong into the marsh and stick; the boy uses his whip unsparingly; the light, energetic members of our party dismount, the fat and heavy ones remain seated; we all shout in anger or encouragement, and by means of these strenuous endeavours are landed on the other side.

On the horizon in front we see a black line; it is formed, we are told, by the rows of palm-trees which border the Euphrates. We are now soberly trotting towards a great mound which, rising abruptly out of the level plain, appears in the distance like a sudden thought of Nature's, tired of the monotony of her own handiwork. But as we approach, its symmetrical sides and flat table-top proclaim it to be the work of man. Our native escort tell us, in subdued tones of awe, how Marut and Harut, the fallen angels, are suspended by their heels in the centre awaiting the Day of Judgment.

We leave it at some distance to the right. In front of us stretches a tract of land more desolate and naked even that that through which we have been driving; small heaps are scattered amongst a few larger mounds, and all are enveloped in a network of high-banked canals, now mostly silted up. There are marshy pools here and there, and rough tussocks of coarse grass catch the blown sand.

"And Babylon shall become heaps," said Jeremiah. It was the heaps of Babylon we were looking upon. Babylon, the "glory of nations," was laid out in front of us.

The Sun-god had reached the pinnacle of his height, and covered the spot with the brightness of heaven.

We made a detour round the edge to avoid the embankments and marshy places, and then struck to the right across the uneven ground, at a jolting foot's pace, towards a clump of palms on the banks of the river. The trees partially concealed the one stone house of the district, the home of three German professors who are superintending the work of excavation now going on. A mud wall separated it from a collection of mud huts; here live the natives employed in removing the sand which buries the architectural monuments of ancient times.

We were at the foot of one of the larger mounds; it is called the Kasr by travellers and Mujelibe (the overturned) by the Arabs, and represents the only part of Babylon which is not altogether buried. We climbed up the great square mass composed entirely of the débris of former habitations; the surface was strewn with broken bricks and tiles; in the centre stood the remains of solid blocks of masonry. Looking down into a large ravine at the further end we saw – half-blocked with rubbish – walls, courtyards, doorways, pilasters, and buttresses built of pale yellow-coloured bricks, each bearing the name of Nebuchadnezzar. Here and there architectural ornaments were built in with the walls; bits of bright coloured enamel and pieces of broken pottery lay about. We wandered among the huge ruin, balancing ourselves on the edges of low remaining walls and clambering from one courtyard to another.

A jackal darted from under our feet with a shrill bark; he was answered from behind distant walls by innumerable hidden companions. An owl flew out of a dark corner and perched, blinking, a little way off; a great black crow hovered uneasily overhead. The broad walls of Babylon were indeed utterly broken, and her houses were indeed full of doleful creatures. We sat down and listened to the wild beasts crying in her desolate houses; it was indeed "a dwelling-place for dragons, an astonishment, and an hissing without an inhabitant."

Shamash, the Sun-god, was nearing the western gate of heaven. The gate-bolts of the bright heavens were giving him greeting.

The Euphrates and its wooded banks lay between us and the horizon; above the river-line we saw a row of jet black palms in an orange setting, and below it a row of jet black palms standing on their heads in the rippled golden water. Shamash has reached the summit of the Mount of Sunset; he slowly descends; the orange changes to red, the general conflagration becomes streaked and barred; the waters of the river grow black, almost as black as the reflected palms, the streaks slowly die away. Shamash has entered into the Kirib Shame, the "innermost part of heaven, that mysterious realm beyond the heavenly ocean, where the great gods dwell apart from mankind."

> "Oh Shamash, thou art the judge of the world,
> Thou directest the decisions thereof…"

Thus prayed the dwellers of the city four thousand years ago. And with the same light with which you lit the pomp and splendour of the works of their time, you light the decay and ruin and hideous desolation of the present.

"Verily there is a God which judgeth the earth," say we, four thousand years later.

And as you smiled on those who worshipped you as the supreme God and Creator of all things, so you smile on us who look upon you, bound and fixed, with no will of your own, following the inevitable laws of Nature. Will you, four thousand years hence, light with the same light sojourners in this land, and will they wonder at our conception of your nature and function, as we wonder at the faith that your ancient worshippers had in you? Or will you, before then, have run your allotted course and consumed the whole world, whether in the fiery furnace of your wrath or in the uncontrolled madness of your broken bonds?

The next morning we visited Babel, the mound we had passed the day before. We walked for more than a mile through the palm-groves by the river. Under the shade of the trees were numerous huts made of mud, covered and enclosed with piles of fine brushwood. There were various signs of human occupation. Two cows were toiling peacefully up and down an entrenchment, drawing water in skins over a rough windlass; the skins emptied themselves into a channel, and the water wandered about in vaguely directed irrigation. On the bank beside them lolled an Arab with a long pole, who prodded the sleepy beasts in the moments when he was more awake than they were. A large mass of brushwood was moving in front of us; it looked like one of the huts endowed with a pair of very thin brown legs. As we overtook it the mass half turned towards us, and a woman's form, doubled in two, looked small in the middle of it.

At the doors of the enclosures naked children sprawled about, all with gleaming white teeth and closely shaven heads, save for the one lock of hair, with which they are to be pulled up to heaven; women with tattooed faces and dangling ornaments pounded barley in primitive stone mortars, and baked thin cakes of bread on flat stones.

Leaving the river-side we struck out to the right for half a mile across the bare, parched ground, where tufts of rough grass were trying to get a footing in the white, barren soil. We climbed up the mound, passing bands of workmen tunnelling in the sides and removing the bricks which lay about in tumbled heaps or in bits of standing walls.

From the top of Babel we could look right over the tract of land once enclosed by the walls of Babylon. The descriptions of Herodotus enable the traveller to call up some sort of idea of the scene in his time. We learn from him that the city was built in the form of a square, surrounded by walls of enormous strength; each side of the square was fourteen miles long, each side had twenty-five gates of solid brass and was defended by square towers built above the wall; twenty-five streets went straight across the city each way from gate to gate. The city was thus cut into squares.

The houses, three or four stories high, faced the street and were built at a little distance apart from each other; between them were gardens and plantations. A branch of the river ran through the city; its banks were one long quay. The larger buildings stood in the centre of the square, each apparently fortified and surrounded by walls of its own. It is of these smaller walls only that any trace can be detected.

From the foot of Babel, where we stood, remains of earthern ramparts could be traced for two or three miles southwards; they then turned at right angles towards the river and extended as far as its eastern bank. The mounds they enclosed were presumably the site of the more important buildings. Babel itself is supposed to represent the temple of Belus. The Mujelibe, or Kasr, lying to the south of us, is identified with the Palace of Nebuchadnezzar and the hanging gardens; further south still was a lesser mound, Amram. We knew that Birs Nimroud, the great ruin which is looked upon as the Tower of Babel, lay beyond this again, although we could not see it from where we stood.

The whole gleamed white in the strong sunshine. On our right the Euphrates rolled along, as unconcerned in his course as the Sun-god overhead. We could trace the direction of the river southwards to the horizon, marked by the palms along its banks. They made a thin, dark line across a wide, light plain – an alluvial tract which is only waiting to yield its hidden gifts on the day when Man joins hands with Nature and distributes the waters of the river. But not so the actual soil of Babylon; that soil, consisting as it does of building dust and débris, is of a nature which destroys vegetation. "The Lord of Hosts hath swept it with the besom of destruction," and it is doomed perpetually to be a "dry land, a wilderness, a land wherein no man dwelleth."

As we looked upon the great plain which stretched away all round until it carried the eye on into the sky above, we could almost believe with the ancients that the edge of the earth joined the dome of heaven and that both were supported by the waters of Apsn – the deep.

A great wave of silence rolled out of the desert and broke over us. It seemed natural to be immersed in silence; could anything else be expected from a land which had never been alive with the stir of humanity even in far-off ages, of which one might now feel the hush while listening for the echo? The desert had always been silent and would be silent for ever more – a dead, unconscious silence, with no significance save of absence of life.

But when we looked at the site of Babylon stretched just beneath us, we became vividly conscious of a real, living silence; we were listening to the "hum of mighty workings;" voices of souls long since dead, the dust of whose bodies lay at our feet, were "wakening the slumbering ages." Had not Nebuchadnezzar entered into the House of the Dead in the great cavern Araltu, the Land of No Return? The dead had been stirred up, even the chief ones of earth, to greet him as he entered hell: "Art thou also become weak as we? Art thou become like unto us? Thy pomp is brought down to the grave, and the noise of thy viols: the worm is spread under thee, and the worms cover thee, ..." and they looked at him narrowly saying, "Is this the man that made the earth to tremble?"

And yet still for us "the wind uttered" and "the spirit heard" his vainglorious cry: "Is not this the great Babylon that I have built for the house of the kingdom by the might of my power and for the honour of my majesty?"

The silent answer to it lay at our feet. And, listening, we heard the solemn warnings of Daniel, the sorrowful forebodings of Jeremiah, and, above all, the ironical voice of Isaiah: –

> "Let them stand up and save thee,
>   Mappers of heavens, Planet observers, Tellers of new moons,
>   From what must befall thee."

As we listened again we heard the noise "like as of a great people; a tumultuous noise of the kingdoms of nations gathered together ...

"A sound of battle is in the land and of great destruction ...

"A sound of a cry cometh from Babylon and great destruction from the land of the Chaldeans ...

"One post ran to meet another post, and one messenger to meet another to shew the king of Babylon that his city is taken."

Then we heard a sound of much feasting and revelling; we heard a solemn hush when there came forth fingers of a man's hand and wrote upon the wall. Even as we listened to the hush it seemed to grow into the great hush of ages, and we remembered that we stood alone in the living silence of these great dead, surrounded by the deal silence of an uninhabited land.

Overhead the Sun-god silently vaunted his eternal existence; at our feet the Euphrates rolled fresh waters of oblivion from an eternal source to an eternal sea.

Changing Mules

"A large mass of brushwood was moving in front of us."

CHAPTER 20

THE SOUND OF THE DESERT

The Syrian desert between Baghdad and Damascus; two white tents, a prowling jackal, and a starry sky.

* * * * * *

There was a sense of stir in camp; a rattle of tins and a neighing of animals; a faint odour of lighted charcoal was wafted in at the tent door. I opened one eye; X still slumbered peacefully at the opposite side of the tent. Arten appeared at the door with a jug of water and a light. "One o'clock," he said laconically as he placed them on the ground and retired. The stars were still shining, my bed was very warm. True, it was one o'clock in Turkish time only, but no Christian ought to be roused at that hour. X fell out of bed with a determined thump.

"It's late," she said.

I made no response, but, knowing from experience that X was always right, tried to reconstruct my ideas about time and reconcile the fact that it was late with its being one o'clock in the morning. Besides, if X ordained that it was late, in another half-hour the tent ropes would be loosened regardless of the stage our toilet had reached, and a falling tent, when one has just got one's back hair into shape, is exasperating if not damaging.

I got up, and just managed to hurl myself through the door, mostly clothed, as the tent collapsed on the ground. X was already seated cross-legged on a rug outside, holding one blue hand over a few charcoal embers while she munched a piece of dry bread held in the other.

"You need not think I have eaten all the butter," she said, "because there wasn't any." Satisfied with the explanation, I munched my bread in silence and swallowed a cup of thick tea; we had been carrying water for three days and it was getting opaque.

The stillness of the night with reigned outside as being invaded by the cries and movements of men; dark forms flitted about as they watered the animals and adjusted the nose-bags for the morning's feed. A horse, impatient of his tether, had broken loose and was galloping defiantly round the camp, inspired to further mischief by the methods of his pursuers, whose idea of reassuming their authority over him was to rush in his direction flourishing whips and uttering piercing cries. He was finally brought to bay entangled in some tent ropes, and a sudden lull fell on the disturbed atmosphere. The Oriental can work himself into a pitch of excitement which would keep a European in hysterics for several hours, and then suddenly drop the matter and become instantly silent and unconcerned. There seems to be no half-way stage between excessive noise and an indifferent silence.

Somewhat awakened by this incident, the men set to work to pack up the camp; the mules were unloosed and stood about with looks of resignation as the loads were adjusted on the creaking pack-saddles and secured with ropes. There was a subdued din and confusion without any sense of hurry. "Allah! Allah!" the native cries when he exerts himself in any way. "Aha, aha!" he cries with equal ardour, mingled with satisfaction, when his task is accomplished.

And now the last knot has been tied, the last cloak laid across the saddle; the last ember of the dying charcoal fire has been carefully raked out to light the cigarette, and we straggle slowly out into the gloom, leaving one charred spot and a sardine tin in the sandy waste.

There had been a suggestion of redness in the gathering light for the last few moments; streaks of silver and bars of gold lined the dusky sky. It is disconcerting to be travelling westwards when one wishes to be aware of a rising sun. I twisted myself round in the saddle and, leaving my horse to pick his way, advanced backwards. The whole scene was soon a vast glow of colour, the yellow sand of the desert holding and reflecting the brilliant reds and yellows; and now the sun appeared on the horizon line and slowly rose, until the whole disc of fire stood out in glowing magnificence and then gradually grew paler as he shared his substance with the surrounding sky. The long straggling line of our caravan, which had looked like a black serpent twisting through a sea of fire, became less black in the growing light, and men and animals assumed individual shapes.

In another half-hour the broad light of day showed the surroundings in their common aspect. I twisted round again in the saddle, and, having turned my back on poetry and romance, became only conscious of the temperature of my extremities. The cold was intense; X and the soldiers were far ahead; the caravan lagged behind; I was alone with cold hands and feet. Poets and philosophers have talked of being alone with the sun and the earth: if ever conditions were favourable for enjoying the sole companionship of these two elements, it might seem to be under the present circumstances.

But in the desert one can be more alone even than this, for in some frames of mind the sky and the earth give one no sense of companionship. Cold and implacable the grim silent desert stretched away in front beyond the realms of space; the hard blue sky overhead stared into the abyss of Time, offering no link between Nature and Man. There was nothing one could take hold of; no cloud in the sky of which to ask the question "Whither?"; no shadow on the earth to which one could say, "Whence?" You were thrown back on yourself, were only conscious of your beating heart and a void. The words of a great lover of nature rose up in my mind: "There is nothing human in nature. The earth, though loved so dearly, would let you perish on the ground and neither bring forth food nor water. Burning in the sky the great sun, of whose company I have been so fond, would merely burn on and make no motion to assist me."

You felt keenly alive in the middle of this cold dead space, and you knew there was something alive in you which demanded something of it; had you no place in the economy of this great silent Universe, was there no way of making yourself heard or felt? Is it that the soul of man must be there to make things alive, and you were now crossing earth where no soul of man had crossed before, and all things were dead?

From sheer agony I cried out; no answering echo followed; the sound fell flat and dead. The cold heavens stared placidly on, the surface of the earth was unruffled. I drew rein and listened intently: I heard the roar of London's streets; the cry of the newsboy, the milkman's call, the tramp of a million hurrying feet; I heard the rush of trains and the screech of engines; I heard a thousand discordant voices in divers tongues where men were struggling and rushing after material ends.

And dominating all this, infinitely louder and more distinct, making itself heard supreme and all powerful, filling the great space in which one had seemed eternally lost, I heard – the Silence of the desert. Why wish to make one's self heard? – better be still and listen to the voice of silence; let its words sink into you and become part of you, and so take some of its quiet and peace back with you into those crowded cities of men.

If there is a link between anything in you and this grim stretch of barren sand and impassive depth of distant sky, it is the response of its silence to the silence in you. It is the material aspect of silence in its crudest form appealing to and recognising in you the unspeakable realms of silence which exist in the region you are dimly conscious of beyond your senses. As we pray to the sea for its depth and calm, to the wind for its freedom, to the sun for its light, so we pray to the desert for its silence. Let your nature expand to the width of this horizon, to the height and depth of this sky, and fill it all with the eternity of this silence.

Ask of the sun why it shines, and if there is light in you it will answer; ask of the wind why it blows, and to fettered and free alike it gives its answer; ask of the desert why it is silent, and if there is silence in you you need no answer.

Is there any calm for you in the sea until you put it there? Do you feel any freedom in the wind until you have created it? But can you, in any mood or under any circumstance, evade the silence of the desert? Its influence extends alike to those who receive it and those who resent it.

The men who have no region of silence in themselves are under the power of its physical aspect; to them it is oppressive, wearying, and deadening; there is an absence of life, a presence of monotony from which there is no escape. But once we recognise its silence as being of the nature of what we possess in ourselves, the shadow of monotony and oppressiveness is lifted. Can its effect be better described than it is in that fundamental doctrine of Islam, where it almost coincides with the teachings of Christianity in its endeavour to give expression to the truth.

"Islam," that is the resignation of our own will to that of one great power, the effacement of self, the futility of putting our own will or mind against that of the great, silent, all powerful, inevitable laws of Nature – the Moslem idea of Fate and Power – the Christian's blending of his own will with the Divine will – the scientist's recognition of Law – you may put it how you will; are they not but different interpretations of the unseen power, which, silent in itself and only understood in silence, holds supreme sway in moments of silence, and, when expressed in its physical aspect in these barren regions of the earth, appeals through our eyes and ears to the regions in us, beyond these senses, where it exists in its essential condition?

I rode on; the sun had warmed my left side through and the right was beginning to thaw. My shadow, which had been keeping pace with the horse on the right, now began to creep in front as the sun rose higher. By the time its burning rays poured straight down overhead the foreshortened shadow seemed to be leading the way along the desert track.

In time the heat became almost unbearable, and, suddenly awakening to the stern realities of physical discomfort, I brought my whip down on the horse's flank; he leaped, startled, in the air, and then flew after his shadow in a settled gallop. Air, of which one had become unconscious, rushed past one's face, and the muffled thud of his hoofs on the sand seemed to measure time and space.

I dashed up to X and stopped dead beside her. She looked round inquiringly.

"Let's eat," I said. She looked at her watch.

"We have been riding four hours," she said; "we might stop at the next good place."

I looked ahead significantly.

"One place looks much the same as another," I said.

"I think there is a dip in the ground further on," she answered, "where we might get a little shelter."

There did seem to be a slight wave in the flat expanse and we rode on to it, but, like all dips in this country, when we arrived at it, it did not seem to be there. We had had so much experience in riding after delusive dips that we decided to stop here, and slid off our horses. The cook unpacked the lunch from his saddle-bags and placed hard-boiled eggs, biscuits, and dates beside us. He carefully filled a cup with a thick, brown liquid from the bottom of his waterskin.

"Bitdi," he said, by which expression he conveyed that the fresh water was now finished.

Then he and the men retired a few yards and ate their lunch. Nothing was heard but the steady munch of human jaws. Then they stretched themselves on the sand and absolute silence reigned, broken by occasional snore. We too lay back, each concealed from the other under two huge umbrellas, which seemed rather to focus the sun's rays than shade them from us.

When one was alone the desert had seemed full of unqualified silence; in company with others the silence seemed even greater, for the slight sounds which there were made one more conscious of the sound which was not. The clank of the horses' bits, the quiet breathing of one's companions, the stir of a foot, made one realise the intensity of the silence of the whole vast expanse.

The far-off tinkling of the mule bells in the approaching caravan gave one a sense of distance in a way one would hardly experience by simply gazing at an unapproachable horizon. The heat and the slight fatigue added a feeling of drowsiness which would make even the solid things around one seem shadowy and distant. It was a waking sleep; one's senses were numb because of the absence of anything to call them into play, though one might "see, hear, feel, outside the senses." In the same way that one is alone in a London street one can live in a whirl in the desert; the throb of humanity ——— X's umbrella shut with a bang.

"Wake up, the caravan is coming."

A cloud of dust, a stamping of animals, a shouting of men, and we were off once more. It was our habit to keep pace with the camp in the latter half of the day, and for the next three hours we dawdled along at caravan pace.

It was a motley crew. The muleteers trudge along behind the laden animals, taking turns on the back of a patient, sorrowful donkey, on which they ride sideways with dangling legs, pricking its side with a long needle, the secondary object of which is the repairing of broken straps. The pack mules go doggedly on in front, jostling one another with their unwieldy loads. Occasionally one gets off the track and wanders aside, only to be urged back into line with yells and blows. Another stops dead, feeling its load slip round sideways. The men rush at it with shouts of "Allāh! Allāh!" the load is shoved up and the ropes tightened. There is a general din of shouting and swearing and jangling of bells; and above it all the disdainful camel moves deliberately on with measured step and arched neck, unmindful of the petty skirmishes so far below it; its owner, infected by its spirit, rocking on the top, surveys the whole scene with a dejected, uninterested air. Bringing up the rear, motionless and erect on small donkeys, ride one or two older Arabs, wrapped in long sheepskin cloaks, their faces entirely concealed in the folds of a keffiyeh, save where two stern and solemn eyes gaze unceasingly at you with expressionless imperturbability. Wild sons of the desert, product of this eternal silence, are you so much a part of it that you are unconscious of its power?

The only gay and careless element is introduced by the Turkish soldiers. Mounted on splendid Arab mares they ride in front, sometimes dashing ahead at a wild gallop, holding out their rifles at arm's length, wheeling suddenly round and coming to a dead stop in front of an imaginary enemy, upright in their stirrups;   in their more subdued moments breaking into song with the mournful Eastern refrains.

And so, forming one small world of our own, we "follow and follow the journeying sun," and as it sinks lower on the horizon and its fierce rays cease to beat pitilessly down on the parched ground and thirsty animals, a silence falls on the moving band.   The spirit of the desert again holds sway.   The men cease quarrelling, the animals' heads sink lower, the donkey looks more resigned, the mule more dogged, the camel more superior, the silent Arab more stern and forbidding;   the soldier hums where he sang before.   Then at last the walls of a solitary guard-house heave in sight.   The men hail it with joyful cries, the soldiers dash ahead, the pack animals prick their ears and quicken their steps to an amble.

There is a general rush and tumble, culminating in a dead halt on the ground which has formed the place for caravans since caravans crossed the desert.   All is noise and confusion.   The loads are unloosed and fall in promiscuous heaps amongst the medley of animals, who, released of their burdens, roll over on their backs, kicking up the dust.   A line of men draw water from the well, pulling at a squeaky chain and invoking the aid of Allah in chorus as they pull.

A fight is going on in one corner;   men are knocking one another down, encouraged by a circle of yelling spectators.   The din of excited quarrelling voices, the hammering of tent pegs, dominates everything, broken at times by the sudden neigh of a horse bitten by its neighbour or the harsh, imperious cry of the camel for its supper.   And in the middle of it all the Turkish soldier spreads his cloak upon the ground, turns his face to Mecca, and offers up his murmured prayer to Allah, the one restful form in this scene of chaos.

"Allah Akbar" (God is great), prays this son of Islam, and with his hands upon his knees, he bows his head; "Subhana 'llah" (I praise God), and he falls upon his knees;   "Allah Akbar" (God is great), and he bows his head to touch the earth;   "Subhana 'llah, subhana 'llah, subhana 'llah," and he sits upon his heels;   "Allah Akbar," and he again prostrates himself; "Allah Akbar, subhana 'llah."

And on this scene the sun casts his final rays of gold and red.   As the shades of night draw in, quiet reigns once more;   the men collect round the blazing camp fire, and it its light we see the outline of their dark forms seated cross-legged, as they eat out of the common bowl or take turns at the bubbling nargheli;   to one side the mules are tethered in two lines forming half a square: a muleteer is grooming them, and one hears the rattle of his scraper and the ever tinkling bell.

The cook is stirring our evening meal in a pot on the fire outside our tent. Hassan fetches our rugs and spreads them on the ground; we lie down and he covers us over with his sheepskin cloak. "Rahat" (Rest), he says, and lifts his hands over us as if pronouncing a blessing. Then he sits down beside us and lights a cigarette.

"Bourda ehe," he goes on, describing the universe with a sweep of his hand. "Kimse yok" (It is well here – there is no one).

"Is Allah here?" asks X.

"Allah is here," he answers with simple reverence, "Allah is everywhere;" and we all lie motionless under the stars unwilling to probe the silence by the sound of uttered thoughts. The murmur of the men's voices gradually dies away as, one by one, they doze off; a jackal cries in the distance; a star falls down to earth. The day is over, and in this land of the Oriental there is no thought of the morrow.

The passive silence of sleep; the active silence of communing souls; the silence of night – all fitful expressions of the one great Silence brooding over all, be one asleep or awake, by night and by day, in desert places and in busy haunts of men.

Our muleteers. Syrian desert.

Water wheel on the Euphrates.

The Takht-er Van entering Ana.

Watering pack mules at Ana.

CHAPTER 21

PALMYRA

It burst upon us all at once, Palmyra in the desert – a chaos of golden pillars in the glow of the setting sun. We had been riding all day towards an indefinite shape on the horizon; slowly it had resolved itself into a barrier of yellow rock with dark lines becoming distinguishable against it. We had passed through the patches of rising corn, making green holes in the brown desert; we had wound through the gardens of pomegranate and plantations of palm trees and turned the corner of the ugly konak which barred the ruins from our view; and there it lay, the desert-girt city, in the unutterable lonely magnificence of its reckless confusion.

We drew rein under the Triumphal Arch; from here the eye is led on down the great colonnade from column to column, now upright, now fallen, to where a mile away a castle crowns a peak of the range under which Palmyra crouches – an old-time harbour for the sand sea beyond.

Behind us the present village of Tadmor was concealed inside the walls of the great Temple of the Sun; its mud hovels lie rotting behind the gigantic columns of the inner court in the dirt which chokes the massive archways. Here it is that the present life of Palmyra, such as it is, is slowly obliterating the remaining evidences of her past; while on the opposite side of the ruins, where the hills cleave to form a lonely valley, the dead of Palmyra, buried in a line of square tomb-towers, still keep alive the memory of her ancient greatness.

* * * * * *

Was it the sun only, with its light on the yellow columns, that made one think of Palmyra purely as a city of gold? Or were one's thoughts unconsciously influenced by the fact that its traditions all rest on the getting of gold; its power was built up on trade; its great men were the successful traffickers of the desert; its statues and columns were raised to the memory of those who brought the caravans of goods from India and Persia unharmed through the dangers of the desert; its temples were dedicated to the Sun God by those whose lives were speared in their getting of great wealth, or to the memory of those who perished in the attempt.

Those were the days when it was a man's boast that the blood of a merchant ran in his veins – when a youth could aspire to no higher goal that that of being a merchant prince of his proud city.

Her prosperity had been her ruin; the gold had led to her undoing; and now the Sun, to whom the temples had been raised at the time of her pride, mocked her ruins by giving them the semblance of scattered gold.

*   *   *   *   *   *

This is the best way to realise Palmyra – to make it the culmination of a long and tedious journey through the desert. The first sight of it under any conditions must indeed be wonderful, but coming in from Damascus, which is the natural approach for visitors to the ruins, one could never feel about it in quite the same way. Civilisation is only five days behind you; the country you pass through, moreover, although desert enough in a way, does not give you the same sense of being utterly cut off from everything in limitless space; there are chains of mountains to be seen in the distance, and cultivated patches stretching round villages are more frequent. Then when you arrive at Palmyra you ride first through the valley of tombs – it is the dead that give you the first greeting; you get glimpses through the opening ahead of the highest columns, and are slowly prepared for what is coming, until, emerging finally through the gap, the whole scene is laid out before you, with the gleaming desert beyond.

*   *   *   *   *   *

But approach it from the desert side, and all the meaning and force of its one time existence is borne in upon you with an overwhelming realisation. For three weeks you have been following the old trade route from the Persian Gulf. You have made one of a caravan amongst the doggedly jogging mules and the slow stepping camels, both heavily laden with the clumsy pack-saddles holding bales of merchandise; the sound of their jangling bells is the only sound you hear through the long, monotonous ride under the blazing sun; you have spent night after night in the circle round the camp-fire, with the men crouched under the bales of goods piled up on the ground to form a rude shelter; the places where you stop have been the regular halting places for caravans for all time – now they are oases big enough to support a village, now it is merely a well and a guard-house.

As you ride through the immeasurable expanse every dark object on the horizon line forms a subject for speculation. Its appearance is a signal for the hasty consolidation of the straggling line of men and animals, arms are looked to, you all close up and ride on, apparently unconcerned, but equally prepared for a sudden onslaught or a friendly greeting. For it is not only the difficulties and dangers due to Nature's barrenness that have to be guarded against. What must it have been in the days when the countless hordes of wealth of a huge caravan were at stake, and when the whole desert was beset with marauding tribes specially on the look-out for such prey?

What must have been the feelings of those responsible for its safe conduct when they once more saw the first dim outline of the Palmyra hills in the distance? The goal would be reached that day; the troubles, the anxieties, the sleeplessness of the watching nights would be over; proud and triumphant they would ride down the long colonnade, the pack animals jostling one another in the unaccustomed crush of the bounded way, and the noise of shouting drivers and jangling bells sounding strangely loud and near in the confining space. Down on them from the columns above would look the statues put up to honour those who had achieved the same feat which they themselves had just accomplished. Their names too would now be written up and handed down from generation to generation in remembrance of the service they had rendered their State. For such deeds as these had built up the great city, and their fellow-citizens honoured them in this way.

At first it would seem that Tadmore was merely an Arab encampment, a stopping place amongst others for the passing caravans. The abundance of its water and its position on the meeting point of two great trade routes would gradually cause it to become an important centre. Dues were levied on all goods passing in and out, and even the privilege of using the wells was heavily taxed.

Slowly it became the market-place of the East and the West; its inhabitants were the carriers between the Persian Gulf and the Mediterranean Sea. As the foundations of the city were built up on trade, so commerce was a pursuit for its aristocracy, involved as it was with all the elements of warfare and danger. Its merchants would be pure Arabs of good blood, welcomed as equals by the sheikhs of the desert tribes through whose territory their goods had to pass.

Palmyra had thus gradually built up her own existence as an independent State. Political evens then added to her power. The wars of Rome with Persia made her an important military post; recognised by Rome more as a partner State than a dependency, she was able to pursue her own policy with such effect that she tried to assert her entire independence and cut herself adrift from the Western power. Taking advantage of the temporary ascendance of Persia over the Roman arms, the desert Queen, Zenobia, fulfilled her ambition as sole Queen of the East.

After her defeat by Aurelian the town was partially destroyed; a change in the political factors which had contributed to her importance now hastened her downfall by lessening the significance of her geographical position; safer trade routes further south led to the decay of her commercial prosperity. Bit by bit she loses her place in historical records, and at the present day Palmyra stands a lonely ruin on a deserted trade route, inhabited by a score of Arab families.

In one sense Time has dealt gently with her; there is no decay from the growth of vegetation in this dry climate. Neither moss nor ivy has softened the aspect of destruction; the overturned columns show as true and sharp a face now as the day they were set up, and the ornate carving stands out in the same relief. One thinks of the place as built entirely of columns; they lie in rank profusion everywhere, like a great forest of trunks overturned by a gale.

The great central avenue runs from the Temple of the Sun in a north-westerly direction to the castle on the range of hills which bounds the city to the north. It has been calculated that it alone contains 1,500 columns. Much of this still remains standing, but the gaps become more frequent, until at the castle end the whole thing has collapsed, forming a perfect sea of broken columns and fragments of carved pilasters. It is evident that the minor streets also were lined with pillars in the same way; short rows of them stand up here and there in various directions. Groups of twos and threes suggest also their attachment to some public building or temple. The statues were placed on brackets projecting from the upper part of the pillars, and the inscriptions below, which have escaped destruction, give the names and dates of those whom they were intended to honour.

* * * * * *

As we had entered Palmyra with a vivid conception of its life, so we left it with an equally vivid conception of its death.

Standing guard like a row of sentinels at the base of the hills are the square tomb-towers in which Palmyra buried its dead. The proud merchants seem to have been imbued with two main ideas: the erection of columns in their lifetime and of resting places for their families in death. Many of the towers are over a hundred feet high and consist of five and six storeys. The bodies were arranged in tiers in the recesses on either side of a central chamber. Some of these buildings are still nearly perfect, others are practically heaps of ruins. The bones of the proud merchants are mingled with the bones of the wild beasts who have sought refuge there through the long ages.

We turn our backs on the city and ride away through the gap in the hills. The city is hidden from view, but the tomb-towers still stand in silent rows down the valley on either side.

We forget the golden pillars and all the ruined magnificence: we can think of nothing but these ghostly towers seeing us out, as it were, from this city of the dead.

High up on the hill above, in the still morning air, a shepherd boy pipes merrily at them, and flocks of goats and sheep browse unconcernedly at their feet.

A climb to the Saracenic Castle at Palmyra.

Palmyra. Triumphal arch.

Temple of the King's Mother.

Chapter 22

An Armenian and a Turk

I. Arten

Arten was an Armenian;   he was quick, thin, methodical, dirty, intelligent, and untruthful;   he was also the cook.   I say *the* cook advisedly, for *a* cook he was not.   No doubt he would have made an excellent cook if he had known anything about the art;   but it was not till after we had engaged him in this capacity that we discovered that he had not thought this qualification necessary.   At any rate, he knew, being a hungry man himself, that we were in need of food of some sort at stated intervals.   In this he was a decided improvement on the Greek cook we had just dismissed;   this man had a habit of coming to us, after we had been waiting hours in momentary expectation of a meal, and saying with a languid air, "Do you wish to eat?"   He was a good cook, but always seemed overcome with astonishment when we expected him to cook.

Arten was a dirty man, and he looked dirtier than he was owing to his dark complexion and hairy hands;   besides this, his unbrushed and greasy black European clothes showed off to disadvantage amongst the simpler Eastern garments of his companions.

"Arten is not a clean cook," Hassan would say, and Arten would smile sadly.   He must have been slightly conscious of this defect, for he never handed me a plate or spoon without saying "Temiz" (clean) as a forestalling measure before I had even looked at it.   He spent a good deal of time rubbing smeary plates with a blackish cloth, murmuring "Temiz, temiz."

He had a sincere desire to please us;   but he always imagined this object was attained by the vigorous assertion of any fact that seemed necessary for our pleasure.   "Taze" (fresh) he would say every time he handed me an egg;   and, when I cut off the top and an explosion followed, "Taze" he would say again.

"Eat it yourself then," I would suggest, handing it back to him;   after putting his great nose right into it, "Taze" he would say.   But he never ate it;   he kept it for omelettes.

His nose was his chief feature. One saw the nose first and then the man behind it. On cold days, when we all wrapped our heads and faces entirely in keffiyehs, Arten would always be distinguishable from the others by this protrusion. He had a jet black drooping moustache which he was always wiping furtively with a jet black pocket-handkerchief, for Arten was a greedy man and the only person who loved the taste of his own cookery.

"I like to see him getting fat," X would say; "he looked half starved when he came to us."

But Hassan and I were not so charitable.

"Look," Hassan would say, "the door of the tent is shut; that pig Arten is stealing the food," and he would go and kick at the tent until Arten looked out, guiltily wiping his moustache.

"You are cold, I suppose," says Hassan with lofty sarcasm. Arten mops his perspiring brow – he was always perspiring.

"How cold?" he answers with well feigned surprise.

"Because you shut the tent door," answers Hassan.

"Amān," rejoins Arten, "what am I to do? If the muleteers see me cooking, they come and ask for food; they are such greedy men, the muleteers."

Hassan returns to us snorting.

"Arten says the muleteers are greedy men. Mashallah! Greedy men! We know who is the greedy man!" And he slaps his thigh vehemently.

Arten's notions of cookery were, as I have said, limited. His staple dish was a mixture of mutton, potatoes, onions and rice, which were all cooked up together in the same pot, each ingredient being thrown in according to the length of time it took to cook. It certainly tasted very good, and I would suggest the method to those in England who dislike washing many saucepans.

His other idea of cooking mutton was less satisfactory in results, though simpler in method, and I have no hesitation in not recommending it to English housewives, though I append the recipe as a matter of interest from its originality.

Take a piece of sheep, and with an axe cut it into chunks, regardless of bones or gristle; take a chunk and throw it on to red-hot charcoal in a brazier; when there is a distinct smell of burning and the hissing has nearly ceased, turn it over on the other side. When it resembles a piece of burnt charcoal, remove it and serve at once; swallow whole, as if you try to bite it your teeth will remind you of it for a considerable time, and in any case you will be conscious of its resting-place for the remainder of the day.

When staying at a consulate in the middle of our tour, the consul's wife, horrified at our fare, offered to let her cook teach Arten a few simple dishes which would considerably add to our comfort. Arten acquiesced with very good grace, and was inducted, amongst other things, in the art of making cutlets. On our departure our kind hostess, moreover, provided us with a piece of meat suitable for cutlets.

The first evening there was an undercurrent of excitement in the air; there were to be cutlets for dinner. Arten had an important, self-conscious bustle about him and looked mysterious; the Zaptiehs seemed awed and asked questions under their breath; the greedy muleteers were distinctly interested; we pretended to be unmoved.

Finally, with a modest air, through which bumptiousness glared furiously, Arten announced that supper was ready. There was a covered dish keeping warm under the brazier; Arten very deliberately placed it before us and with a dramatic flourish removed the cover. We were only conscious of a yellow-looking crumby paste.

"Where are the cutlets?" we asked, keeping up our courage nobly.

"That is cutlets, Pasha."

We tasted it: it appeared to consist of fried eggs and breadcrumbs. We felt justified in contradicting him, but he still persisted that it was cutlets.

"But we want the cutlets like those the Effendi's cook showed you how to make."

"Yes, that is it Pasha; that is what the Effendi's cook showed me."

"But cutlets are meat," we persisted.

"Yes, Pasha; but that is cutlets without the meat."

This reasoning was incontrovertible. We tried to fill up with dates and rice and went to bed crestfallen and hungry. The next day we returned to the charge. I undertook to show Arten how to cook cutlets, though I had not the smallest idea myself how it ought to be done. I had an inkling, however, that egg and breadcrumbs were in it somehow.

"Arten," I said, "cut the meat as the Effendi's cook did for cutlets." Arten obeyed.

"Make egg and breadcrumb," I said. He did this also.

"Now do with it what the Effendi's cook did," I said. Arten smeared the meat with it. I began to see light and breathed more freely, but I had still one venture to make.

"Now cook the meat as the Effendi's cook did," I said.

I held my breath; for all I knew they might now have to be boiled in a saucepan or toasted on a fork. But Arten appeared to know what he was doing. He took a frying pan and fried them in fat. A glow of satisfaction crept all over me as I watched them beginning to resemble the finished appearance I was acquainted with. When they were actually on a dish, I said loftily: –

"Please remember for the future that when we say we want cutlets, this is what we mean."

"As you please," he answered affably; "I call them frisolen. I knew how to cook them before the Effendi's cook showed me," he went on.

"Why did you never let us have them, then?" I said severely.

"How could I know you would like them?" he answered with injured innocence.

"How did you know we liked tough chunks burnt on a brazier?" was my icy retort.

Arten shrugged his shoulders; there never has been any accounting for the whims of women.

Small differences of opinion such as these were continually cropping up between us; and I would tell him in calm and measured tones, though in forcible English, what I thought of him. As the language was unintelligible to him, this method had the advantage of relieving my feelings without hurting his.

But there were secret bonds of sympathy between us. We both suffered intensely from the cold, and Arten would carefully wrap things round me so that the apertures and crevices were not on the windward side. There is a good deal of art in this, and he did it very scientifically.

"Little things feel the cold," he would say compassionately, and in such a kindly spirit that, for the moment, I forgave him his greed and forgot to feel undignified.

We were also on common ground when I tried to cook dishes which I did not know how to cook. Currents of great sympathy ran between us when things did not seem to be turning out right and Arten would tentatively suggest various ways and means. But he never did what a foolish or disagreeable person would have done: he never expressed in his looks that I was not better than himself, which obviously would not have been true, since I did not pretend to be a cook, while Arten did.

And then when the critical moments of our existence arrived and we placed the dish before X, we both watched with the same intensity for the expression of her face after the first mouthful.   X was singularly appreciative, and, when she kept assuring us how excellent it was, Arten would glance at me encouragingly and appear to share the delight I experienced at my own prowess. X thought Arten's cookery good, too, but then she never knew what she was eating, and, if you do not know the name of the dish, how can you judge whether or not it is cooked as it ought to be?

"What is this?" X would ask one day.

"Mutton," Arten would answer.

"What is this?" she would say the next day, when the identical substance was handed to her.

"Chicken," Arten would answer. And X was perfectly satisfied.

The next day it would be "tinned meat," and it was all the same to her – and to me; but then I knew what a liar Arten was.

His kindness of heart and his desire to please us made it all the more difficult not to be irritated with him when circumstances did not draw out the better side of his nature. It is uncomfortable to despise people in a qualified manner, and I found it impossible to despise Arten unreservedly and therefore happily. There was no doubt that he was a horrible coward. If he had said, "I am a coward – I am afraid," he would have enlisted my sympathy for what it was worth, because I was a coward myself and admired sincerity. If he had even preserved a decent silence on the subject I should have been unable altogether to despise him, for the was the course I pursued myself. But when any real or imaginary danger was past he would come out with assumed and aggressive hilarity, and make tales about it and his prowess, which latter he had already made conspicuous enough by its absence.

Yet his position was no doubt complicated: he knew that the Turks in our train despised not only him but his race, there was no one to suggest his courage if he did not do it himself, and, as he was unable to exhibit it in deeds, I have no doubt he saw no other course to pursue but that of publishing it by word of mouth.

Moreover, he had suffered personally from bad treatment; the tale was a piteous one. Near his native town of Adana he had a small mill where he ground corn through the season. On one occasion he had done well and was on his way back to his wife and children in the town, carrying his earnings, which were to keep them through the winter. Half way home he was attacked by a band of robbers, who relieved him not only of his gold but of all his clothes. He had to remain in hiding by the roadside until some one passed from whom he could borrow a garment in which to return starved and penniless to his expectant family. Small wonder that the poor man shuddered at the word "Khursus" (brigand) which we laughingly joked about.

"What is it to you?" he said one day; "you have rich relations, kind friends, and a just Government. If you are robbed, justice is done to you. But what can I expect but more abuse and ill-treatment? – and I have a wife and small children into the bargain!"

When he was not posing as a hero, he was posing as a feature in the landscape. This was particularly exasperating, for no amount of pity for his condition would turn him into a picturesque martyr, even in the foreground of ancient ruins. No sooner was my camera produced than Arten produced himself. The only occasion on which I knew him keep out of sight was when I was trying to get a snap-shot of the band of Kurds who held us up on the Tigris. He seemed to have no desire to show himself, although I was considerate enough to invite him to occupy a prominent position for once.

His appearance as not calculated to enhance the effect of any picture. He was like a starved black scarecrow dressed up in tight and clerical garments, with a fez on the top – and then there was the nose. He would have made any warm desert scene look cold, as it would not be obvious that he was perspiring, and in any group of picturesque natives he would look ludicrous.

I recall, as I write, isolated moments of exasperation – when, for instance, he sat, singing a hymn, kicking up the dust with his heels, when we were trying to inflate ourselves with worthy feelings on the contemplation of Babylon, awed by the silence and desolation of the scene around us. Or again, how in a fit of nervousness he hurled the whole of our dinner in agitation on the floor, while we, after an unusually long fast, could have cried for food.

But reviewing him calmly at a distance, one remembers a man that one alternately laughed at and pitied; who annoyed one by his transparent faults, but who commanded one's sympathy by his tragic condition, and one's admiration by his cheerful willingness in trying circumstances. A man who was meant by nature to be light-hearted and happy, kind to his fellows, energetic and interested in his work, ambitious for his children; but who fate dictated was to have his spirit quenched, his nature hardened, and mean and cowardly qualities developed owing to the fear, injustice and poverty in which, like the rest of his countrymen, he was condemned to live.

II. HASSAN

Hassan was an Albanian Turk; he belonged to one of the old Turkish families and looked every inch the gentleman that he was. Introduced to us by a common friend, he accompanied us during our seven months' wandering through Asiatic Turkey in a semi-professional capacity, but what that capacity was it would be difficult to define by any particular name.

A dragoman he was not, though he called himself our "tergeman." "Tergeman," literally translated, being "interpreter," he could claim nothing entitling him to this function, for he spoke no European language, and it as not till we learnt Turkish that we could hold any spoken communication with him.

Briefly, he acted as a sort of amateur dragoman without any of the qualifications usually expected of these gentlemen – and possessing a great many of the virtues in which, as a rule, they are sadly lacking.

Essentially he was our Figure-head, and a splendid one he made, six foot six in stature and broad in proportion, as straight as a die and as supple as a willow, with a handsome head set well back on strong shoulders and keen, kindly eyes which looked out very straight from under shaggy eyebrows. When he walked he put into his great stride a grace and dignity which soon earned for him the nickname of "the Prince."

His chief characteristics were that gentleness which comes of great strength under perfect command; the courtesy which arises from a sense of other people's worth measured by a sense of his own; and an imperturbability which could be as irritating as it was admirable. "Ne faidet?" (what is the use?), was a favourite expression of his, and "ne faidet" he looked all over.

In scenes of human quarrel, excitement, or danger, one was chiefly conscious of his calm indifference of mind and manner as he silently surveyed his companions in fear of brigands or in joy over a piece of meat. Yet he was a man full of the passions of his race, capable of an iron self-control when he thought fit to make use of it, but occasionally roused into a state of temper bordering on madness. On these occasions he would afterwards say his "jan" had had him by the throat, and he did not know what he was doing.

A great man with a great imprisoned soul, as free and light-hearted as a careless boy when roaming in the great forests or on the bare mountain side of his native home, fettered and fretful when the bonds of artificial civilisation held him.

"What a Kallabalak! What is the use of this Kallabalak?" he would say with a wave of disgust when he got into the middle of a noisy crowd. "This is good, this is keyf," was his comment, with great gasps of enjoyment, when we three sat on the ground together in some lonely spot of a lonely desert. One felt he was breathing freely again.

A silent man by nature, he could not bear loquacious people. "Burra, burra, burra," he would say, pointing his thumb at them; "burra, burra, burra, what is the use of all this talking?" If the remarks were addressed to him, they were always answered with stern courtesy. A talkative young Armenian rode with us one day and tried to draw him into conversation. "Is not that mirage in front of us? What a wonderful sight – trees and water and mountains! Do you not think it must be mirage, Effendi?"

"With the eyes that Allah has given me, it does seem to be so, young man," was Hassan's grim answer, and he rode on without turning his head to right or left.

Yet on occasion he enjoyed a refined "Kallabalak." One night in Cairo, when we had done for the time with camping and were seated in cleanliness and finery in the hotel garden, a confetti feast was going on. Serious young men and maidens, larky old men and festive matrons, were diverting themselves in the essentially hilarious proceeding of scattering confetti on one another. The garden was hung with Chinese lanterns; fireworks hissed and spluttered, shooting flames of colour. Hassan sat in convulsed enjoyment of the gay scene. It was a revelation to him of the lighter side of life. And when a charming young lady, bolder than the many who cast coy and curious glances at the handsome Turk, came and administered a dose of confetti down the back of his neck, he was overcome with glee and merriment. Afterwards, on subsequent wanderings in wilds and deserts, he would turn to us after hours of silence, and, bursting into a deep roar of laughter, would say, "Do you remember the paper and the foolish men and women?"

His function, as I have said, was first and foremost that of Figurehead; he escorted us on our visits to Turkish officials and dignitaries, and, with grave dignity and courtly manner, unembarrassed by his own unshaven chin or the stains and dust of travel on our weather-worn and unwashed garments, he would make the most of anything entitling us to belong to "the great ones of England." He cast a general air of respectability over us, and we always felt it was largely due to him that we were shown so much consideration in a land where all travellers are treated with suspicion, and where women are not regarded in a particularly chivalrous light.

But beside this, he was general caretaker of our personal comforts: he put up our camp beds and arranged our tent; he always sat beside us at meals, which we took seated cross-legged on the ground, either outside by the camp-fire, or in bad weather on the floor of the tent. His first self-constituted duty was to peel the oranges with which we generally finished a meal; he removed the peel to form two cups, in which he neatly piled the sections and placed them beside us, carefully counting the pieces to make sure that he had treated us alike.

"Shimdi" (now) he would say when we had finished the first course and we would ask for dates. "Shimdi" he would say again when the last of these were demolished. "Shimdi Kahiveh," and coffee would come in its turn "Shimdi."

"Nothing more."

"Nothing," he would exclaim; "nothing?"

"We will smoke now."

"Tütün (tobacco), aha, Shimdi tütün," and he would light us each a cigarette.

Then, when this too was finished, "Shimdi" – "Shimdi Rahat" (now rest), we answer – and he makes pillows for us with our saddle-bags and cover us over with rugs.

This process was repeated every day until it became a stock joke. His jokes were all of this kind; there were certain standing ones which had to be gone through periodically.

My Turkish was limited to about fifty words, so that conversation between us did not flow, but X, who had learned to speak more fluently, would ride with him for hours together, holding endless conversations on Turkish religion, habits, and ideas. When X and he fell out he would come and joke with me: one day I teased him about being a better friend to her than to me.

"How can that be?" he said gravely.

"Because," I answered, "you quarrel with the Vali Pasha" (X was the Vali Pasha and I was the Padishah), "and then you make it up and are great friends again. But you are never cross with me. If I too were your friend you would quarrel with me, too. But I am glad I am not your friend, or you would get angry with me."

This idea seemed to tickle him immensely, and every day after this conversation there would be a moment when he would ride alongside of me, and, feigning an air of great disgust, would shrug his shoulders and say, "Istemen, istemen" (I do not want you). It was his singularly primitive way of acting a quarrel with me, and thereby showing that he and I were also friends.

X would also attack him on the subject.

"Why don't you go and scold the Padishah?" she said on one occasion; "she htinks the same as I do about these things, only she cannot talk Turkish, so she does not say them."

"The Padishah is but a child," he answered; "it would hurt her. It would be a shame to hurt a child."

As a matter of fact I was older than X in months, but her bodily proportions were larger than mine, and everything goes by size in the East.

As time went on, however, we too had our little rubs, and his methods of making friends again were what one would expect from his schoolboy nature. If I was in the tent, he would throw stones at it until I looked out smiling; this was taken as a sign that the quarrel was over; he would roll up an extra large cigarette for me, and we would sit on the ground and have a smoke of peace together.

Our friendship was of a silent nature. I made my fifty words express everything I had to say, and to simplify matters only used the verbs in the infinitive and nouns in the nominative. Long custom had established a certain meaning to various sentences between us which would have been unintelligible to any other Turk.

"What Turkish, amān, what Turkish she speaks!" he used to say to X, holding up his hands in amused dismay.

We taught him a few English sentences, of which he was very proud.

"Pull it up," he invariably said when he held out his hand to help us off the ground.

"Pull it down," was his formula when he arranged our habit skirts after he had helped us mount.

"Pull it off," when he helped us off with our coats.

When he was in a temper I made him say, "I am a silly man," which he pronounced:

"I am ———

"A Silliman."

Although he did not know the meaning of the words, he connected them with his own misdemeanours.

"Silliman yok (not), sillman yok," he used to say fiercely when he was beginning to repent and get ashamed of himself. He always said "Good-bight" for "Goodbye," confusing it with "Good-night."

Great was his pleasure whenever in the course of our travels we came across a European, or any one who could speak a language which I understood.

"See now," he would explain at the unwonted sight of me talking with any one, "she has found a friend!" And then, when we parted and I relapsed into silence: "See now, how sad she looks! She is thinking of her friend."

And he would ride up to me compassionately.

"Where is your friend now, Padishah?"

"Where indeed?" I answer. "I have no friend; you must buy me one in the bazaars next time we get to a town."

"And how much money must I give for him, Padisha?"

"You must not give much, because I am poor, but you must get a very good one."

"Amān, amān, see now what she says: I must get a good one, and yet not give much money. Do you hear, Vali Pasha?"

And when he came back from the bazaars:

"I have bought the friend, Padishah."

"Where is he? I don't see him."

"He is here, in my bag."

"How much did you give for him?"

"Ten piastres."

"He cannot be a good one if he is as cheap as that, and so small that he will go in your bag."

"Oh yes, he is a good friend," and he produces a roll of tobacco; "a good friend and little money. That was what you said, wasn't it, Padishah?"

And I reflect that there is many a true word spoken in jest.

"Has she no friend in England," he asked X one day, "or does she never speak in England either?"

"Yes," said X, "she has a friend in England, and she does not speak because she is thinking of him."

"And you, Vali Pasha, have you also a friend in England?"

"Yes," I answered for X; "she has twenty-nine friends in England, and you are only the thirtieth."

And Hassan would ride on in silence, pondering over the strange ways of English ladies.

Amongst his other duties he had to purchase the food, pay the muleteers and soldiers, and give tips; and it fell to my lot to do up the accounts with him periodically. The unusual mental exertion required by this he found very trying. His imperturbability would forsake him completely. On the first occasion he broke down altogether.

"What can I do with figures," he said, the tears rolling down his cheeks; "let me go back to my hills and forests; I am only a poor hunter. She brings out her little book and I shall not know how the piastres have gone, and she will think I have taken her piastres," and he laid his head on his knees and groaned aloud.

When we became better acquainted, however, "hisab" (accounts) became a joke, though they always caused him to perspire profusely.

At first my entire ignorance of the language made our intercourse over the account-book somewhat difficult. We would sit on the ground opposite one another, and Hassan would fumble in the folds of his belt until he had found his spectacles and his account-book.

"Are you ready?"

"Yes."

"Peki (very good), Effendim; yimurta (eggs) 2 piastres." I would write it down.

"Yasdin me?"

"Ne yasdin me?" (what is "yasdin me?").

"Yasdin me? Yasdin me? Yasdin me?"

I have not the smallest idea what "yasdin me" means, but I pretend to write it down and then say:

"How many piastres was it?"

Hassan makes a gesture of despair.

"Yasdin me? Yasdin me? Yasdin me?" he repeats again.

"X," I shout across the tent, "what does 'yasdin me' mean? I suppose it's some sort of food, only he won't tell me how many piastres it costs."

"It means 'Have you written it?'" said X calmly.

"Yasdin me?" repeats Hassan agin.

"Yes," I answer meekly.

"Aha, now she know," says Hassan, and he mops his forehead vigorously. "I say 'Yasdin me' and she says, 'How many piastres?' Amān, amān!"

"Peki, Effendim" (very good), he goes on.   "Etmek (bread), 3 piastres. Have you written it?"

"Yes."

"Peki, Effendim. Et (meat), 12 piastres. Have you written it?"

"Yes."

"Peki, Effendim. Pilij (chicken), 3 piastres."

"Ne Pilij?" (what is pilij?).

"Pilij, *pilij*, PILIJ."

"Yes, but what is it?"

"Pilij, pilij – she doesn't know pilij, and she learns it every day."

He begins to crow like a cock.

"Oh yes, I know."

"Ah, ah, now she knows. Peki: pilij 3 piastres. Have you written it?"

"Yes."

"Peki, Effendim."

And so we go on through all the items, and finally add up the total in our respective languages. By means of holding up our ten fingers a large number of times, we ascertain whether the results tally, for in those early days I could only count in Turkish up to twenty-nine, and knew the words for a hundred and a thousand. Then Hassan would give a great sigh, close his book, fold his spectacles, take off his fez, and wipe his head all over, and finally forget his troubles under the soothing influence of tobacco.

And so the days slipped away. At the end of six months we landed out of the Syrian desert into Damascus. An immense change came over Hassan when he was released from the anxieties of piloting us through impossible places and rumoured dangers. He became more boyish and cheerful and amused at everything. His first care on arriving at the end of our journey was, after spending several hours in a public bath, to go a clean and happy man to the Mosque, to return thanks to Allah for having brought us safely through.

We had been to call at the consulate, and, as we drove up to the hotel on our return, I caught sight of Hassan in the street with a crowd round him; he was strutting up and down in his shirt-sleeves, with his head even more thrown back than usual and a wild look in his eye.

"Good heavens," I said to X, "the Prince must have got into one of his tempers and killed a few people in the street," and I anxiously looked round for signs of gore. The Prince took no notice of us, but stalked up and down, the crowd making way for him with looks of awe.

"What are we to do?" I said; "he looks as if he has gone off his head and would knock down any one who comes near him."

"He does look like a prize-fighter," said X; "I have never seen him look like that before."

Our cook was standing on the steps.

"What is the matter with Hassan?" I said to him.

The man stared.

"Nothing," he said, "it's only his new shirt."

We went inside, telling him to fetch Hassan to us.

The Prince stalked into the room with the same air with which he had been stalking the streets, and stood in front of us with an excited and expectant expression.

"The cook is right," said X; "it is his new shirt. He is overcome with pride and conceit; he is on parade, that's all."

He certainly had something to be conceited about. The shirt was of fine silk in gorgeous yellow and red stripes; round his waist was a wide, bright-coloured cummerbund, round his head a new keffiyeh flashed all the colours of the rainbow. Clean and shaven, his tight-fitting shirt showing up the strong outline of his muscular frame, he exhibited, to say the least of it, a striking spectacle.

We were evidently expected to be overcome at the magnificence of his appearance, and certainly we did not disappoint him in this respect.

"You are grand," said X to him in his own language; "you quite surprise us."

Hassan put his hands into his trouser pockets and strutted up and down the room, speechless with delight.

"Who would have thought you could be such a turkey-cock, you old gander!" I said in English.

"What is she saying?" said Hassan to X.

"She says you are just like a very magnificent bird we have in England," answered X.

Hassan beamed triumphantly.

"You have fine clothes," he said; "I must not disgrace you."

"Is he always going about in his shirt-sleeves, I wonder?" I inquired. X asked him.

"It is quite usual in my country not to wear a coat in hot weather," he said; "my coat is old and dirty and my shirt is new and clean: why should I wear my coat?"

And he rarely put it on again.

He loved to see us in nice clothes, and took great delight in wandering about the bazaars with us buying presents for the "twenty-nine friends" in England. But we used to sigh over the good old camping days.

"Hebsi bitdi" (all is over), he would say dolefully, when anything particularly brought them back to our thoughts.

We rode down Palestine and took him over to Egypt with us. Evading with difficulty the importunities of Cook, and the rush of tourists on the beaten track, we tried to steal days which brought back a sense of our old free-and-easy times.

But there came a day when there was an end to it all, and end to the long silent rides, an end to the quiet smokes in desert places, an end to the little daily jokes, an end to the serious talks and the foolish quarrels, an end to the Kallabalaks and the Keyfs.

We stood on the steamer which was to take Hassan back to his old life in the forests of the Turkmendagh.

"You will soon be going on a long journey with some one else," said X cheeringly.

Hassan shook his head.

"No, indeed," he said; "I should take care not to go with two ladies again, and I shall not go with a man, for no man would be so much of a fool as to wish to go on such a mad journey."

The steamer gave vent to its first hideous whistle. We put our fingers in our ears.

"Good-bight, little Padishah," he said, as we clasped hands for the last time; "good-bight. Go home to your friend in England; he will be glad to see you looking so fat."

"Silly man," I said with a lump in my throat.

"Sillyman yok," he answered.

The whistle blew again, we turned and went our different ways. If there had been a stone he would have thrown it after me; as it was, when I turned he made a face and shouted, "Istemen, istemen!"

And now, looking back on those days, there rises invariably before us the memory of this companion in our many adventures – the memory of a simple-minded, honourable man, a trusted friend, a pleasant companion and a devoted servant, who, whether he was sharing the discomforts and dangers of winter travel in a wild, lawless country, or experiencing the joyous freedom of the roaming desert life we loved so well, or enduring the terrors of critical and carping civilisation, invariably put us in the foremost place, and, without swerving an inch from the traditions of his race, never offended the susceptibilities of ours.

Khan at Deir-el Zor.

The Vali Pasha.

Hassan.

CHAPTER 23

RETROSPECTIVE

Last night we were dirty, isolated, and free; to-night we are clean, sociable, and trammelled. Last night the setting sun's final message written in flaming signs of gold was burnt into us, and the starry heights carried our thoughts heavenward and made them free as themselves. To-night the sunset passed all unheeded and we gaze, as we retire from the busy rush of the trivial day, at a never-ending, twisting, twirling pattern on the four walls that imprison us, oppressed by the confining ceiling of our room in the Damascus Palace Hotel.

We are no longer princesses whose hands and feet are kissed, whose word is law, sharing the simple hospitality of proud and dignified wayfarers in desert kingdoms. Our word is law according to the depth of our purses, our hands and feet are kissed according to the height of our floor in the hotel. We are no longer in a land where men and women are judged by their capacities for being men and women: the cost of our raiment apportions our rank.

We are now no longer amongst people to whom we say what we mean and are silent when we have nothing to say. We are in surroundings where to say what you mean is an offence, where silence is not understood and looked upon askance as an uncanny visitor. The less we have to say, the more we make an effort to say it; and the more we have to say, the greater the effort to suppress it.

Everything seems unreal or unnecessary, everything is dressed up.

All these people moving about, sitting still, in a hurry, catching trains, eating long dinners, dressing themselves, looking at each other dressed – what does it all mean? Was all this going on when we were in that other world which we have just left, that great silent world where everything was itself and big, and not confused by accessories? Was all this din and bustle going on? It is strange that we should have had no inkling of it, for it seems of so much importance to all these people, idle with a great restlessness; it seems essential to them.

It is hard, too, to realise that that other world still exists out there in the distance, and that it would be quite possible to reach it by merely riding out on a camel. Can it indeed be true that the same sun which lights all these moving streets, these buyers and sellers, these catchers of trains, is lighting the desert out there as imperturbably as it lit us, journeying on after it day after day in the silent places; did it see all these people from its inaccessible height, and, sharing its gifts equally with them and with us, give us no hint of what it was looking down upon? It showed then no more favour to us than to these dwellers in towns, and yet was it not more to us? Were we not more conscious of its innumerable gifts; and did we not receive more from it as a result of our greater appreciation? No bars of windows, no roofy outlines, no sleepy oblivion hid the glory of its first appearance for us. As far as its rays could range, so far, and further, could we see. Not a pale silver thread or wiry line of gold, or faint reflection of its glowing colours on the opposite horizon, was lost to our vision; and, as we rode through the chilly morning air, were we not conscious of every separate ray of warmth as it grew and grew until we were bathed in its delicious heat, and all day it served as our sole guide, indicating direction in boundless space and hour in limitless time. No finger-posts, no winding up of clocks; only this sun with its fixed and unalterable decrees.

The sun, then, we share, although apparently in divers degrees. But was not the moon more for us alone? For they can shut it out from their lives altogether. It, too, looked down upon this city, but not on the noise and chaos of it. As far as it was concerned all the bustlers were dead, buried away in their roofed houses behind their shuttered windows. The silence of night is the moon's heritage, and it exercises its autocratic sway to the full; it admits no disturbing rush or unseemly hurry beneath its gaze. What do they know of you, who pull down blinds and light up the gas and dwell in curtained rooms? Accident may cause a benighted traveller to look at you with a passing sense of rest, a casual tossing sleeper may be half conscious of your charm, the weary toiler at the end of a long day may momentarily bless your soothing light, and in so far as they take hold of you they make themselves akin with us out there.

But you are not a part of them, as you are a part of us; you do not enter into the very heart of their existence and carry their minds up, night after night, to the realms where you live serene and calm, making us forget the saddle rubs, the parching thirst, the driven sand, the fire that would not light, the kettle that would not boil – all the little near things, the things which matter so much in the day, and which you remind us do not matter at night.

But here they matter so much more at night, all shut up with us inside these confining walls – inside these muslin curtains. The darkness and the enclosed space make them assume exaggerated dimensions; all the little trivialities in the room accentuate their importance. We see them cropping up again and again in that blue flower on the wall paper, or running round and run the red coils on the dado. We raise our eyes to heaven and encounter the fixed, inane smile of a painted lady with a wand, seated in a wreath of flowers. We shut our eyes, determined to forget her, but a terrible fascination makes us peep again and again, and always that same inane smile; and when at last the kindly shades of night hide it altogether in darkness, we are still conscious of her only, smiling away there, looking at us while we cannot see her. And all the time outside the steadfast moon and the stars eternally twinkling are telling the same tale that they told out in that other world, but we have shut them out and will not listen to their silent teaching.

In vain the Prophet of the Desert has said:

"And we have adorned the lower heaven with lamps and set them to pelt the devils with . . . we touched the heavens, and found them filled with a mighty guard and shooting stars, and we did sit in certain seats thereof to listen; but who so of us listens now finds a shooting star for him on guard."

Emblems of all the great abiding truths have been set up on high, where, one would have thought, every poor, striving mortal could not fail to see them; vastness and distance is displayed as a rest to those wearied with the smallness and nearness of things; solidity and eternity are there to comfort the grievers over passing men and disappointed hopes; the kindly darkness which hides us intermittently from our fellows is pierced with points of guiding light.

And yet we do not habitually, and as a matter of course, accept these gifts for which no price is asked; we go blundering on, intensifying the grim blackness of night by shutting ourselves up with it, surrounded with all the small things of earth, and this when we might forget them by reason of their very smallness in the vast distances of the vaulted heavens. It almost seems as though we would deliberately wish to hide from ourselves and each other the few simple sufficient laws of existence, for in this as in other things we not only avoid the truth but appear ashamed of it, and dress it up in every possibly accessory of human invention.

We dress everything up – our bodies, our minds, our food. I look down this long *table d'hôte*, and what do I see? I see a crowd of people dressed up, exchanging dressed up commonplaces, eating dressed-up food.

I feel that nothing is real.

But this unreality is so real that I ask:

"Have, then, the unrealities, the non-essentials of existence become the realities, and have we, emerging from a world where only the essentials of existence concerned us, given them an undue importance? Coming out of a state of primitive civilisation, are we unable to appreciate the true meaning of our surroundings? These people wear the burdens of fashion so lightly, they talk these complicated nothings so simply, they toil so contentedly discontented through these endless disguised dishes: what is it behind it all that our minds cannot grasp?"

I look again: I talk to them and they answer me; I eat another dressed-up dish. Here I feel a weary heart, there I touch a bored mind; now one gets a flash of intellect, now a gleam of soul, all alike so carefully wrapped up, and yet with a longing to be out. Why this unnatural dread of truth and simplicity? I am getting positively affected by it. I sit here amongst these smart people in my travelling clothes, and I confess to a new strange sense of discomfort in consequence. I feel ashamed of my old clothes.

Opposite to me is a lady with a kindly face and a comfortable look about her; her mauve dress gives a pleasing sense of colour, but as she moves two beaded flaps keep jumping about, which detracts from the sense of repose suggested by her comfortable look; when she leans back an array of stitched beads catches on the carved projection of the chair, and she has to be disengaged by the waiter. Her sleeves drooping gracefully from the elbow require elaborate gymnastics to prevent them dipping into her plate as she eats, and twice they caught in the pepper-pot and overturned its contents on the floor. But she bore it all with a pleasant apologetic smile which called out my admiration for such a display of schooled temper under these trying circumstances.

Then, with an unconscious transition of thought, I found myself comparing her to the Arab woman who brought the bowl of youart off which we supped last night. I recalled how I envied her the dignified carriage of her free unfettered form, the natural grace of her untrammelled manners. I recalled the simple graceful folds of her clinging single garment, so much a part of herself that she was quite unconscious of it, and I compare this lady trying to adapt herself to the elaborate creation in which she is enthralled. Long custom prevents her from realising how her form and movements are rendered artificial and ungraceful. As the Chinese lady, unconscious of her deformity in feet, would resent or wonder at our pity for her enslaved by the idea of a barbarous custom, so would my neighbour resent or wonder should I feel pity for her at this moment, equally a slave to a Western idea.

I glanced at my battered old coat and was pervaded with a sense of remorse at having been ashamed of it.

Here, in the middle of this bewildering appearance of unreality, it was telling me of so many solid facts. How often had it not covered the aching pangs of hunger, and the satisfied sense of that hunger appeased; it had felt the thumping of my heart stirred by danger, or hastened by exhilarating motion; it had known the long-drawn breaths of quiet enjoyment at a peaceful scene.

That tear was made on the rocks the day we climbed to the "written stone" at the top of the Boulghar Mountains, and I mended it one long quiet evening by the Euphrates.

I lost this button the night we scrambled up to the castle at Palmyra, my little friend Maydi pulled me up to a rock by it and it broke.

That burn mark was made by Mahmet, who dropped the live charcoal with which I was lighting my cigarette in the sheikh's hut at Harran.

All this and more is what my coat says to me . . . I am no longer ashamed of it. I feel sure if the kind lady opposite realised all this she would not regard me as an outcast, for there is something very honest about the coat.

But I had got no further away from the feeling of unreality. I tried to recall what it had felt like to live in civilisation, but all I could remember was how difficult it had been to disentangle ourselves from it. While we were still in it, we had not known what we should want outside it. But, once outside, all these difficulties had disappeared: everything at once seemed to happen naturally; we missed nothing of the things we had left behind.

And as it had been difficult while we were still in it to get disentangled from it, so now we were experiencing a difficulty in entering it again – a difficulty in once more taking up and using the things we had discarded for a time. It was as if we had never used them, so strange did they seem, and so little did we understand their meaning. Entering it differed, moreover, in this way from our entrance into the new life outside it; once in it nothing seemed to happen naturally. This was the more disconcerting since civilisation was not altogether a new world to us, in the sense that the other had been. We had spent many long years in it, and yet on returning we found it all strange and incomprehensible.

*   *   *   *   *   *

We rose and left the table. Hassan joined us at the door, and we all sat down on a red plush settee. Waiters hurried past us with trays of coffee and stronger drinks; ladies in bright colours rustled about the passage, and in the corners men in evening dress lounged and smoked.

Hassan stroked the settee gingerly.

"It is very soft," he said, "but the sand was better."

Then he looked round and paused.

"What are all these people doing?" he asked irritably; "why can't they sit down and be quiet? There is no quiet here; the sand was better."

Earlier in the day he had been pleased with the bright colours and the sense of movement, but now they seemed to vex him.

"Why do they keep on looking at us?" he went on; "is it because you are great Pashas?"

"No," I answered, "they have no idea that we are great Pashas."

"My countrymen in the desert looked at you because you were strangers from another country and they had not seen women like you before; but these are your own countrymen: why do they stare at you?"

"It is because we are not dressed like them," I said; "we have not got our beautiful clothes yet; when these come they will no longer look at us."

"But can they not see that you are travelling?" he said. "The people of my country, the Valis and the Kaimakams who prepared feasts for us, knew that you also had beautiful clothes in your own country."

"Yes, but our travelling clothes are not quite the same as those worn by our countrymen here," I explained, "so they do not understand us."

"But why," persisted Hassan, "should that cause them not to understand you?"

"We all do alike in our country," I explained; "if one person wears no pockets and big sleeves, then we all do the same."

"Who is this person then?" said Hassan; "he must be a very great Pasha."

"We none of us know who he is," I said; "in fact, he is not any one particular person; it is more like a sort of jinn who spreads about an unwritten law."

Hassan looked perplexed.

"And are there no written words," he said, "to tell you the meaning of this law?"

"Yes," I said; "the people in our land who have the most money write out the meaning of the law."

"And if you do not follow the law, what then?"

"Your fellow-creatures are rather afraid of you; they do not ask you to their feasts, neither do they give you places of command, however capable you may be."

"Is it this jinn that makes your men wear the hard black hats and the tight black clothes?"

I nodded assent.

"And it is not only our clothes," I added; "the jinn says we may not think differently from other people, or if we do, we must hide it."

"Is it a sin that your country has committed that it is thus condemned," he went on, "or is the jinn an evil spirit under whose curse it lies?"

"We do not know," I said. "There are some of the younger men who are trying to discover; they do not do as the jinn says, and so they do not live happily amongst others; many of them live apart, and we call them cranks and are afraid of them."

"Are they wicked men, then?"

"No, they are good men as a rule, but in our country we do not understand the people who do not do what others do."

"But if you all do the same," said Hassan, "how can you progress? We in the East have not changed our customs, so we do not progress. Do you never change then either, you in the West?"

"We change very slowly," I answered, "because we tend to the thought that if a thing has always been, then it is good."

"Amān, amān," said Hassan.

Appendix

Itinerary of Journey

Konia to Tarsus

Chumra
Kisilkeui
Karaman
Adeteppe
Buadjik
Eregli
Tchaym
Ulu Kishla
Boulghar Maden
Chiftekhan
Ak Kupru
Gulek Boghaz
A Khan
Tarsus

(These stages are from 5 to 8 hours.)

Adana to Diarbekr (18 stages)

	Hours	
Missis	4	Small village with khan.
Hamidieh	4½	Cotton-mills and town.
Kalakeui	5	Small Kurdish village.
Osmanieh	1½	Town.
Bagtsche	6	Village.
Shekasskeui	5	Village with khan.
Avjilar	5	Small Kurdish village. No khan.
Aintab	5	Town.
Urral	5	Village with khan.
Birejik	5	Town. Ferry across Euphrates.
Abermor	6	Kurdish huts.
Karekeui	6	Kurdish huts.
Urfa	3½	Town.

Sheksheligher	7	Khan.
Mismischen	7	Large khan.
Severek	6	Town.
Kaimach	7	Large khan.
Gergeli	6	Small Kurdish village.
Diarbekr	3½	

BAGHDAD TO DAMASCUS. (27 stages.)

....Hours

Menasseyeh	5	No village.
Fellujah	6	Village on Euphrates.
Rumadeyeh	6	Village on Euphrates.
Hit	10	Town on Euphrates.
Bagdadi	8	Ruined water-mill on Euphrates.
Hadittah	8	Village on Euphrates.
Fukaymeh	6½	Large khan on Euphrates.
Ana	7	Town on Euphrates.
Niteyah	8	Guard-house on Euphrates.
Gayyim	9½	Guard-house on Euphrates.
Abu Kalam	5	Village on Euphrates.
Salihiyyeh	7	Khan with a few Arab huts.
Micardin	9½	Village.
Deir-el-Zor	7	Town.
Pools of brackish water	2½	
Guard-house	8	Well of bad water.
Bir Jeddid	8	Well of bad water.
Suknak	9	Village with hot sulphur springs.
Erek	8½	Village.
Tadmor	6	= Palmyra.
Baytha	6	Khan with bad water.
Gusayr	16	

(Camping-place half-way, where water is found early in the year.)

Karietein	7	Village.
Nasariyeh	12	Village.
Kutayfah	5	Village.
Guard-house	2	
Damascus	4	

through the giant Swedish forests, and finally discover a passage around the treacherous Norwegian marshes.

Burnaby, Frederick; *A Ride to Khiva* – Burnaby fills every page with a memorable cast of characters, including hard-riding Cossacks, nomadic Tartars, vodka-guzzling sleigh-drivers and a legion of peasant ruffians.

Burnaby, Frederick, *On Horseback through Asia Minor* – Armed with a rifle, a small stock of medicines, and a single faithful servant, the equestrian traveler rode through a hotbed of intrigue and high adventure in wild inhospitable country, encountering Kurds, Circassians, Armenians, and Persian pashas.

Carter, General William, *Horses, Saddles and Bridles* – This book covers a wide range of topics including basic training of the horse and care of its equipment. It also provides a fascinating look back into equestrian travel history.

Chase, J. Smeaton, *California Coast Trails* – This classic book describes the author's journey from Mexico to Oregon along the coast of California in the 1890s. Smeaton Chase treats us to a treasure trove of observations, commenting on subjects as diverse as the architecture of the Spanish Missions, the hospitality of the people, and the beauties of a fabled countryside.

Chase, J. Smeaton, *California Desert Trails* – Famous British naturalist J. Smeaton Chase mounted up and rode into the Mojave Desert to undertake the longest equestrian study of its kind in modern history.

Clark, Leonard, *The Marching Wind* – The panoramic story of a mounted exploration in the remote and savage heart of Asia, a place where adventure, danger, and intrigue were the daily backdrop to wild tribesman and equestrian exploits.

Cobbett, William, *Rural Rides, Volumes 1 and 2* – In the early 1820s Cobbett set out on horseback to make a series of personal tours through the English countryside. These books contain what many believe to be the best accounts of rural England ever written, and remain enduring classics.

Codman, John, *Winter Sketches from the Saddle* – This classic book was first published in 1888. It recommends riding for your health and describes the septuagenarian author's many equestrian journeys through New England during the winter of 1887 on his faithful mare, Fanny.

Daly, H.W., *Manual of Pack Transportation* – This book is the author's masterpiece. It contains a wealth of information on various pack saddles, ropes and equipment, how to secure every type of load imaginable and instructions on how to organize a pack train.

Dixie, Lady Florence, *Riding Across Patagonia* – When asked in 1879 why she wanted to travel to such an outlandish place as Patagonia, the author replied without hesitation that she was taking to the saddle in order to flee from the strict confines of polite Victorian society. This is the story of how the aristocrat successfully traded the perils of a London parlor for the wind-borne freedom of a wild Patagonian bronco.

Farson, Negley, *Caucasian Journey* – A thrilling account of a dangerous equestrian journey made in 1929, this is an amply illustrated adventure classic.

Fox, Ernest, *Travels in Afghanistan* – The thrilling tale of a 1937 journey through the mountains, valleys, and deserts of this forbidden realm, including visits to such fabled places as the medieval city of Heart, the towering Hindu Kush mountains, and the legendary Khyber Pass.

Galton, Francis, *The Art of Travel* – Originally published in 1855, this book became an instant classic and was used by a host of now-famous explorers, including Sir Richard Francis Burton of Mecca fame. Readers can learn how to ride horses, handle elephants, avoid cobras, pull teeth, find water in a desert, and construct a sleeping bag out of fur.

Glazier, Willard, *Ocean to Ocean on Horseback* – This book about the author's journey from New York to the Pacific in 1875 contains every kind of mounted adventure imaginable. Amply illustrated with pen and ink drawings of the time, the book remains a timeless equestrian adventure classic.

Goodwin, Joseph, *Through Mexico on Horseback* – The author and his companion, Robert Horiguichi, the sophisticated, multi-lingual son of an imperial Japanese diplomat, set out in 1931 to cross Mexico. They were totally unprepared for the deserts, quicksand and brigands they were to encounter during their adventure.

Hanbury-Tenison, Robin, *White Horses over France* – This enchanting book tells the story of a magical journey and how, in fulfilment of a personal dream, the first Camargue horses set foot on British soil in the late summer of 1984.

Hanbury-Tenison, Robin, *Chinese Adventure* – The story of a unique journey in which the explorer Robin Hanbury-Tenison and his wife Louella rode on horseback alongside the Great Wall of China in 1986.

Hanbury-Tenison, Robin, *Fragile Eden* – The wonderful story of Robin and Louella Hanbury-Tenison's exploration of New Zealand on horseback in 1988. They rode alone together through what they describe as 'some of the most dramatic and exciting country we have ever seen.'

Hanbury-Tenison, Robin, *Spanish Pilgrimage* – Robin and Louella Hanbury-Tenison went to Santiago de Compostela in a traditional way – riding on white horses over long-forgotten tracks. In the process they discovered more about the people and the country than any conventional traveller would learn. Their adventures are vividly and entertainingly recounted in this delightful and highly readable book.

Haslund, Henning, *Mongolian Adventure* – An epic tale inhabited by a cast of characters no longer present in this lackluster world, shamans who set themselves on fire, rebel leaders who sacked towns, and wild horsemen whose ancestors conquered the world.

Heath, Frank, *Forty Million Hoofbeats* – Heath set out in 1925 to follow his dream of riding to all 48 of the Continental United States. The journey lasted more than two years, during which time Heath and his mare, Gypsy Queen, became inseparable companions.

Holt, William, *Ride a White Horse* – After rescuing a cart horse, Trigger, from slaughter and nursing him back to health, the 67-year-old Holt and his horse set out in 1964 on an incredible 9,000 mile, non-stop journey through western Europe.

Hopkins, Frank T., *Hidalgo and Other Stories* – For the first time in history, here are the collected writings of Frank T. Hopkins, the counterfeit cowboy whose endurance racing claims and Old West fantasies have polarized the equestrian world.

James, Jeremy, *Saddletramp* – The classic story of Jeremy James' journey from Turkey to Wales, on an unplanned route with an inaccurate compass, unreadable map and the unfailing aid of villagers who seemed to have as little sense of direction as he had.

James, Jeremy, *Vagabond* – The wonderful tale of the author's journey from Bulgaria to Berlin offers a refreshing, witty and often surprising view of Eastern Europe and the collapse of communism.

Kluckhohn, Clyde, *To the Foot of the Rainbow* – This is not just a exciting true tale of equestrian adventure. It is a moving account of a young man's search for physical perfection in a desert world still untouched by the recently-born twentieth century.

Lambie, Thomas, *Boots and Saddles in Africa* – Lambie's story of his equestrian journeys is told with the grit and realism that marks a true classic.

Landor, Henry Savage, *In the Forbidden Land* – Illustrated with hundreds of photographs and drawings, this blood-chilling account of equestrian adventure makes for page-turning excitement.

Leigh, Margaret, *My Kingdom for a Horse* – In the autumn of 1939 the author rode from Cornwall to Scotland, resulting in one of the most delightful equestrian journeys of the early twentieth century. This book is full of keen observations of a rural England that no longer exists.

Maillart, Ella, *Turkestan Solo* – A vivid account of a 1930s journey through this wonderful, mysterious and dangerous portion of the world, complete with its Kirghiz eagle hunters, lurking Soviet secret police, and the timeless nomads that still inhabited the desolate steppes of Central Asia.

Marcy, Randolph, *The Prairie Traveler* – There were a lot of things you packed into your saddlebags or the wagon before setting off to cross the North American wilderness in the 1850s. A gun and an axe were obvious necessities. Yet many pioneers were just as adamant about placing a copy of Captain Randolph Marcy's classic book close at hand.

MacCann, William, *Viaje a Caballo* – Spanish-language edition of the British author's equestrian journey around Argentina in 1848.

Muir Watson, Sharon, *The Colour of Courage* – The remarkable true story of the epic horse trip made by the first people to travel Australia's then-unmarked Bicentennial National Trail. There are enough adventures here to satisfy even the most jaded reader.

O'Reilly, CuChullaine, *Khyber Knights* – Told with grit and realism by one of the world's foremost equestrian explorers, "Khyber Knights" has been penned the way lives are lived, not how books are written.

O'Reilly, CuChullaine, (Editor) *The Long Riders, Volume One* – The first of five unforgettable volumes of exhilarating travel tales.

Östrup, J, (*Swedish), Växlande Horisont* - The thrilling account of the author's journey to Central Asia from 1891 to 1893.

Pocock, Roger, *Following the Frontier* – Pocock was one of the nineteenth century's most influential equestrian travelers. Within the covers of this book is the detailed account of Pocock's horse ride along the infamous Outlaw Trail, a 3,000 mile solo journey that took the adventurer from Canada to Mexico City.

Pocock, Roger, *Horses* – Pocock set out to document the wisdom of the late 19th and early 20th Centuries into a book unique for its time. His concerns for attempting to preserve equestrian knowledge were based on cruel reality. More than 300,000 horses had been destroyed during the recent Boer War. Though Pocock enjoyed a reputation for dangerous living, his observations on horses were praised by the leading thinkers of his day.

Post, Charles Johnson, *Horse Packing* – Originally published in 1914, this book was an instant success, incorporating as it did the very essence of the science of packing horses and mules. It makes fascinating reading for students of the horse or history.

Ray, G. W., *Through Five Republics on Horseback* – In 1889 a British explorer - part-time missionary and full-time adventure junky – set out to find a lost tribe of sun-worshipping natives in the unexplored forests of Paraguay. The journey was so brutal that it defies belief.

Ross, Julian, *Travels in an Unknown Country* – A delightful book about modern horseback travel in an enchanting country, which once marked the eastern borders of the Roman Empire – Romania.

Ross, Martin and Somerville, E, *Beggars on Horseback* – The hilarious adventures of two aristocratic Irish cousins on an 1894 riding tour of Wales.

Ruxton, George, *Adventures in Mexico* – The story of a young British army officer who rode from Vera Cruz to Santa Fe, Mexico in 1847. At times the author exhibits a fearlessness which borders on insanity. He ignores dire warnings, rides through deadly deserts, and dares murderers to attack him. It is a delightful and invigorating tale of a time and place now long gone.

Schwarz, Hans *(German)*, *Vier Pferde, Ein Hund und Drei Soldaten* – In the early 1930s the author and his two companions rode through Liechtenstein, Austria, Romania, Albania, Yugoslavia, to Turkey, then rode back again!

This book is more than just a well-written adventure tale. Schwarz's trip, and the resulting book, inspired three generations of German-speaking Long Riders to take to the saddle.

Schwarz, Otto *(German)*, *Reisen mit dem Pferd* – the Swiss Long Rider with more miles in the saddle than anyone else tells his wonderful story, and a long appendix tells the reader how to follow in his footsteps.

Scott, Robert, *Scott's Last Expedition* – Many people are unaware that Scott recruited Siberian ponies for his doomed expedition to the South

Pole in 1909. Here is the remarkable story of men and horses who all paid the ultimate sacrifice.

Skrede, Wilfred, *Across the Roof of the World* – This epic equestrian travel tale of a wartime journey across Russia, China, Turkestan and India is laced with unforgettable excitement.

Steele, Nick, *Take a Horse to the Wilderness* – Part history book, part adventure story, part equestrian travel textbook and all round great read, this is a timeless classic written by the foremost equestrian expert of his time, famed mounted game ranger Nick Steele.

Stevens, Thomas, *Through Russia on a Mustang* – Mounted on his faithful horse, Texas, Stevens crossed the Steppes in search of adventure. Cantering across the pages of this classic tale is a cast of nineteenth century Russian misfits, peasants, aristocrats—and even famed Cossack Long Rider Dmitri Peshkov.

Stevenson, Robert L., *Travels with a Donkey* – In 1878, the author set out to explore the remote Cevennes mountains of France. He travelled alone, unless you count his stubborn and manipulative pack-donkey, Modestine. This book is a true classic.

Strong, Anna Louise, *Road to the Grey Pamir* – With Stalin's encouragement, Strong rode into the seldom-seen Pamir mountains of faraway Tadjikistan. The political renegade turned equestrian explorer soon discovered more adventure than she had anticipated.

Sykes, Ella, *Through Persia on a Sidesaddle* – Ella Sykes rode side-saddle 2,000 miles across Persia, a country few European woman had ever visited. Mind you, she traveled in style, accompanied by her Swiss maid and 50 camels loaded with china, crystal, linens and fine wine.

Trinkler, Emile, *Through the Heart of Afghanistan* – In the early 1920s the author made a legendary trip across a country now recalled only in legends.

Tschiffely, Aimé, *Bohemia Junction* – "Forty years of adventurous living condensed into one book."

Tschiffely, Aimé, *Bridle Paths* – a final poetic look at a now-vanished Britain.

Tschiffely, Aimé, *The Tale of Two Horses* – The story of Tschiffely's famous journey from Buenos Aires to Washington, DC, narrated by his two equine heroes, Mancha and Gato. Their unique point of view is guaranteed to delight children and adults alike.

Tschiffely, Aimé, *This Way Southward* – the most famous equestrian explorer of the twentieth century decides to make a perilous journey across the U-boat infested Atlantic.

Tschiffely, Aimé, *Tschiffely's Ride* – The true story of the most famous equestrian journey of the twentieth century – 10,000 miles with two Criollo geldings from Argentina to Washington, DC. A new edition is coming soon with a Foreword by his literary heir!

Warner, Charles Dudley, *On Horseback in Virginia* – A prolific author, and a great friend of Mark Twain, Warner made witty and perceptive contributions to the world of nineteenth century American literature. This book about the author's equestrian adventures is full of fascinating descriptions of nineteenth century America.

Weale, Magdalene, *Through the Highlands of Shropshire* – It was 1933 and Magdalene Weale was faced with a dilemma: how to best explore her beloved English countryside? By horse, of course! This enchanting book invokes a gentle, softer world inhabited by gracious country lairds, wise farmers, and jolly inn keepers.

Wentworth Day, J., *Wartime Ride* – In 1939 the author decided the time was right for an extended horseback ride through England! While parts of his country were being ravaged by war, Wentworth Day discovered an inland oasis of mellow harvest fields, moated Tudor farmhouses, peaceful country halls, and fishing villages.

Wilkins, Messanie, *Last of the Saddle Tramps* – Told she had little time left to live, the author decided to ride from her native Maine to the Pacific. Accompanied by her faithful horse, Tarzan, Wilkins suffered through any number of obstacles, including blistering deserts and freezing snow storms – and defied the doctors by living for another 20 years!.

Wilson, Andrew, *The Abode of Snow* – One of the best accounts of overland equestrian travel ever written about the wild lands that lie between Tibet and Afghanistan.

de Windt, Harry, *A Ride to India* – Part science, all adventure, this book takes the reader for a thrilling canter across the Persian Empire of the 1890s.

Winthrop, Theodore, *Saddle and Canoe* – This book paints a vibrant picture of 1850s life in the Pacific Northwest and covers the author's travels along the Straits of Juan De Fuca, on Vancouver Island, across the Naches Pass, and on to The Dalles, in Oregon Territory. This is truly an historic travel account.

Younghusband, George, *Eighteen Hundred Miles on a Burmese Pony* –
One of the funniest and most enchanting books about equestrian travel of
the nineteenth century, featuring "Joe" the naughty Burmese pony!

Our list of titles is constantly growing, so please check our website for
the latest information: **www.horsetravelbooks.com.**

Lightning Source UK Ltd.
Milton Keynes UK
UKOW051430060212

186753UK00002B/58/A